C
PROGRAMMING

C
PROGRAMMING

A Self-Teaching Introduction

By
RAJIV CHOPRA, PhD

MERCURY LEARNING AND INFORMATION
Dulles, Virginia
Boston, Massachusetts
New Delhi

Publisher: David Pallai

MERCURY LEARNING AND INFORMATION
22841 Quicksilver Drive
Dulles, VA 20166
info@merclearning.com
www.merclearning.com
1-800-232-0223

R. Chopra. *C Programming: A Self-Teaching Introduction.*
ISBN: 978-1-68392-090-8

Library of Congress Control Number: 2017934665

171819321 Printed in the USA on acid-free paper.

CONTENTS

Preface   *viii*

Acknowledgments   *x*

Chapter 1: C Overview   **1**
    1.0   Introduction   1
    1.1   The Concept of Algorithms and Pseudocodes   2
    1.2   Flowcharts   8
    1.3   Compiler Overview   15
    1.4   Assembler, Linker, and Loader   19
    1.5   Structure of a Simple "Hello World" Program in C   22
    1.6   Overview of the Compilation and Execution
          Process in an Integrated Development Environment
          (preferably CodeBlock)   30
          Summary   32
          Exercises   32

Chapter 2: Programming Using C   **35**
    2.0   Introduction   35
    2.1   Preprocessor Directives/Compiler Directives/C Preprocessor   35
    2.2   C Primitive Input-Output using getchar and putchar   40
    2.3   Simple Input/Output   42
    2.4   Function Calls from a Library   44
    2.5   Data Types in C   44
    2.6   Enumeration   47
    2.7   Operators   51
    2.8   Type Casting (or Coercion) in C   62

2.9	Conditional Executing Using If-Else	63
2.10	Switch and Break	68
2.11	The Concept of Loops—While Loop, Do-While Loop, For Loop, Nested Loops, Break Statement, Continue Statement	73
2.12	Storage Classes: Auto, Static, Extern, and Register	119
	Summary	135
	Exercises	135

Chapter 3: Arrays And Pointers — **141**

3.0	Introduction	141
3.1	1D, 2D, and 3D Arrays	142
3.2	The Concept of Subprogramming	212
3.3	Functions	213
3.4	Parameter Transmission Techniques—Call by Value and Call by Reference	228
3.5	Pointers	234
3.6	Relationship between Array and Pointer	239
3.7	Argument Passing Using Pointers	241
3.8	Array of Pointers	243
3.9	Passing Arrays as Arguments	244
	Summary	269
	Exercises	269

Chapter 4: Structures And Unions — **275**

4.0	Introduction	275
4.1	Structures versus Unions	296
4.2	Structures and Pointers	298
	Summary	312
	Exercise Questions	313

Chapter 5: File Handling In C — **317**

5.0	Introduction	317
5.1	File Pointers	317
5.2	Character Input / Output with Files	320
5.3	String I/O Functions	321
5.4	Integer I/O Functions	321
5.5	Formatted I/O Functions	322
5.6	Block (or Record) I/O Functions	323
	Summary	338
	Exercises	338

PREFACE

The right temperament required for research originates from the right exposure and environment that a student receives during study. And good books help in this direction.

Programming is an art. You have to learn this art, as only then will you learn how to write good programs.

This book is an outcome of lecture notes prepared during my long years of teaching Introduction to Programming (C), augmented by consulting a large number of books available on the subject. I thank my students, colleagues, and teachers, as well as all the authors who have helped in shaping my approach to this knowledge.

Appendices   341

A: C Programming Lab Projects   341

B: Keywords in C   343

C: Escape Sequences in C   344

D: Operator Precedence and Associativity   345

E: Standard Library String Functions   346

References   347

Index   349

ACKNOWLEDGMENTS

A dream is visualized by a pair of eyes; however, many pairs of hands join together and work hard toward its realization. This book has been a similar enterprise.

I next thank my college staff, director, and HOD for their contributions to this book on the C programming language.

I would also like to thank the entire staff of Mercury Learning for bringing the book to a new market.

Finally, I would like to thank my wife, Mrs. Shakti, my twin kids, Arjessh and Arshitha Chopra, as well as my parents who cooperated with me in all terms in order to write this book.

Dr. Rajiv Chopra

CHAPTER 1

C OVERVIEW

1.0 INTRODUCTION

The C programming language was developed by Dennis Ritchie at AT&T Bell Laboratories in the early 1970s. Soon after, Bell Laboratories developed a new operating system, called UNIX. About 90% of the code for the Unix operating system (OS) was exclusively in C. As C gained popularity, more and more vendors joined the race and developed their own compilers. This was necessary because until the late 1970s, only Bell Laboratories had a C compiler.

In the early 1980s, realizing the need to standardize the C language, the American Standards Institute (ANSI), an organization that handles such matters, began the task. In 1990, the first official ANSI standard definition of C was published. Soon C became omnipresent and thus there was a need of further standardization. The International Standards Organization (ISO) adopted a standard called ISO/IEC 9899:1990. After 1990, many additional changes were made in the C language. In 1993, an ANSI C committee (known as X3J11), was formed to standardize C. The most recent standard was adopted in 1999. It is known as ANSI C99 or ISO/IEC 9899:1999. Since then, ANSI C has been implemented on a wide variety of computers, including IBM-compatible personal computers (PCs), mainframes, minicomputers, and workstations.

C is a ***higher-level language*** that nevertheless allows the programmer to deal with hardware at a much lower level. **Please note that although C is a general-purpose programming language, it was designed with systems programming applications in mind.** So it provides a lot of power and flexibility.

This chapter discusses some basic terminology related to C and also explains the process of compiling a program written in the C language.

1.1 THE CONCEPT OF ALGORITHMS AND PSEUDOCODES

A computer is a dead piece of hardware if it is not loaded with software. It may be application software, system software, embedded software, or other types of software. **The basic operations of a computer system form the computer's instruction set.** Now in order to solve a problem using a computer, you will have to express the solution to the problem in terms of the instructions for the particular computer. So we define a computer program as a collection of instructions necessary to solve a specific problem. **The approach or method that is used to solve the problem is known as an algorithm. For example**, if you want to find the factorial of a number, then the set of statements that solves the problem becomes a **program**. You first express the solution to the problem in terms of an **algorithm** and then *develop a program that implements that algorithm*. A program may be written in any programming language of your choice, such as C/C++, JAVA2, Visual Basic 9, and so on.

An algorithm is a formal step-by-step method for solving problems. Let us now look at some of the characteristics of algorithms:

1. An algorithm consists of an **ordered sequence of instructions**.
2. Each step of the algorithm should be unambiguous—that is, it should not have many meanings.
3. It should have a **finite number of steps**.
4. It should **terminate/stop** after this finite number of steps.
5. It should have **some input** and may or may not produce any **output**.

Algorithms should be concise and compact to facilitate verification of their correctness. Verification involves observing the performance of an algorithm with a good quality set of test cases.

For example, we might want to write an algorithm to find the maximum from a set of n positive numbers. We assume that the numbers are stored in an array X.

Algorithm to Find the Maximum from an Array X

INPUT: An array X with n elements.

OUTPUT: Finding the largest element, MAX, from the array X.

Step 1: Set MAX=0/* Initial value of MAX */

Step 2: for j=1 to n do

Step 3: if(X[j] > MAX) then MAX = X[j]

end for

Step 4: Stop

As a problem-solving tool, programmers usually introduce at least one intermediate step between the English-like problem definition and C. This intermediate step is known as a **pseudocode (pseudo=false). Pseudocode is a restatement of the problem as a list of steps, in an English-like format, describing what must be done to solve it**. Using the pseudocode, a programmer then writes the actual program. In a nutshell we can say that **pseudocode consists of statements which are a combination of English and C, in which pseudocode is not quite C code but can be easily translated**. It can be refined and gradually made more precise. The practicality of this approach is that the pseudocode used at one stage of the development process will often be a comment at the next stage.

For example, for the **preceding algorithm**, Max, we now write its **pseudocode** as follows:

Initialize a variable, MAX, to 0.

Check through the entire set of elements.

If any element from the set is greater than the Max then max is that element.

Print the MAX number.

Before further discussion, let us solve some examples.

Example 1: **Write an algorithm to find the greatest of three numbers and then validate your algorithm by giving it dry runs.**

Solution 1: The algorithm to find the greatest of three numbers (a, b, and c) is as follows:

```
Step 1: Input three numbers from the user: a, b, c.
Step 2: Check,
```

```
                        if (a > b)
Step 3:         do if (a > c)
Step 4:            then Print 'a' and go to step-12.
Step 5:          else
Step 6:                    Print 'c' and go to step-12.
Step 7:        else
Step 8:                do if (b > c)
Step 9:                    then Print 'b' and go to step-12.
Step 10:                   else
Step 11:                  Print 'c' and go to step-12.
Step 12: Stop
```

Now let us validate this algorithm.

Dry Run 1:

Input: a = 10
        b = 20
        c = 30

Expected Output: 30

Process: Is (a > b) ?
        Is (10 > 20) → false
        Is (b > c) ?
        Is (20 > 30) → false

Observed Output: 30

Dry Run 2:

Input: a = 10
        b = 20
        c = 30

Expected Output: 30

Process: Is (a > b) ?
            Is (10 > -20)→ true
        Is (a > c) ?
            Is (10 > 30) → false

Observed Output: 30

Example 2: **Write an algorithm to read a, b, and c as the coefficients of a quadratic equation and to find its roots; then validate your algorithm by giving it dry runs.**

Solution 2: The algorithm to find the roots of a given quadratic equation is as follows:

Quad_equation (a, b, c)

Step 1: Input three numbers: a, b, c.
Step 2: if (a= =0)
Step 3: Then Print 'Not a quadratic equation' and go to step-12
Step 4: else
Step 5:   put D = b2 – 4 a c
Step 6: check if (D > 0 or D < 0)
Step 7:   then ROOTS = (–b + sqrt (b2 – 4ac)) / 2a
Step 8:   and Print 'ROOTS' and go to step 12.
Step 9:   else do ROOTS = –b/2a
Step 10:   and Print 'ROOTS' and go to step 12.
Step 11: Stop.

Now let us validate this algorithm.

Dry Run 1:

Input: a = 1
        b = 2
        c = 3

Expected output: ROOTS = -1 + sqrt(2) / 1

Process:

```
        Is  a= =0 ?
          Is  1 = = 0 → false
                D = b2 – 4ac
                D = –8
        Is D > 0 or D < 0 ?
                D < 0 → true
                ROOTS = (–b ± sqrt(b2 – 4ac)) /2a
```

Observed Output:

        –1 ± sqrt(2) / 1

Dry Run 2:

Input: a = 4
        b = 2
        c = 1

Expected output: ROOTS = -1 ± sqrt(3) / 4

Process:

```
             Is a= =0 ?
     Is 4 = = 0 → false
                     D = b2 - 4ac
                     D = -12
        Is D > 0 or D < 0 ?
                     D < 0 → true
                     ROOTS = (-b + sqrt(b² - 4ac)) /2a
```

Observed Output:

```
       -1 ± sqrt(3) / 4
```

Dry Run 3:

Input: a = 0
       b = 2
       c = 1

Expected output: Not a quadratic equation.

Process:

```
        Is a= =0 ?
        Is 0 = = 0 → true
```

Observed Output:

        Not a quadratic equation.

NOTE *In all of the preceding dry runs, the expected output equals the observed output.*

Example 3: **Write an algorithm to read x, y, and z as the three sides of a triangle and to check the type of triangle formed; then validate your algorithm by giving it dry runs.**

Solution 3: The algorithm to check for the triangle type is as follows:

Triangle_type (x, y, z)

Step 1:   Input three sides of triangle: x, y, z.

Step 2:   check if (x + y > z) && (y + z > x) && (x + z >y)

Step 3:   then do if (x= y && y = z)

Step 4:   then Print: 'Equilateral triangle' and go to step 17.

Step 5: else

Step 6: do if $(x = y$ && $y! = z)$ || $(x = z$ && $z! = y)$ || $(y = z$ && $x! = z)$

Step 7: then do if $(x = \text{sqrt}(z^2/2))$ || $(x = \text{sqrt}(y^2/2))$ || $(y = \text{sqrt}(x^2/2))$

Step 8: Print: 'Right Angled Isosceles Triangle' and go to step 17.

Step 9: else

Step 10: Print: 'Isosceles Triangle' and go to step 17.

Step 11: else

Step 12: do if $(x = \text{sqrt}(z^2 + y^2))$ || $(y = \text{sqrt}(z^2 + x^2))$ || $(x = \text{sqrt}(x^2 + y^2))$

Step 13: then Print: 'Right Angled Scalene Triangle' and go to step 17.

Step 14: else Print: 'Scalene Triangle' and go to step 17.

Step 15: else

Step 16: Print: 'Not a triangle' and go to step 17.

Step 17: Stop.

Let us validate this algorithm now.

Dry Run 1:

Input: x = 1
        y = 1
        z = 2

Expected output: Not a triangle

Process:

```
Is (x + y > z) ?
Is (1 + 1 > 2) → false
```

Observed Output: Not a triangle

Dry Run 2:

Input: x = 3
        y = 4
        z = 5

Expected output: Right Angled Scalene Triangle

Process:

```
Is (x + y > z) && (y + z > x) && (x + z > y)?
True
Is x = y && y = z?
        False
Is (x =y && y!=z) || (x=z && z!=y) ||(y=z && z!=x)?
        True
        Is (3² + 4² = 5²) → True
```

Observed Output: Right Angled Scalene Triangle

Dry Run 3:

Input: x = 6
        y = 6
        z = 6

Expected output: Equilateral Triangle

Process:

```
Is (6 + 6 > 6) ? → True
Is (6 = 6 = 6) → True
```

Observed Output: Equilateral Triangle

<hr>

NOTE *In all of the preceding dry runs, it is seen that the expected output equals the observed output.*

1.2 FLOWCHARTS

A flowchart is defined as a pictorial representation of an algorithm. It serves as a means of recording, analyzing, and communicating problem information. Programmers often use a flowchart before writing a program, although this is not always mandatory. **Practically speaking, sometimes drawing of the flowchart and writing of the code in a high-level language go side by side.** Flowcharts are of two types.

(a) Program flowchart

(b) System flowchart

A program flowchart (or simply a flowchart) shows the detailed processing steps within one computer program and the sequence in which those steps must be executed. Different notations are used in a flowchart to denote the different operations that take place in a program.

On the other hand, **system flowcharts show the procedures involved in converting data on input media to data in output form.** Here, the focus is on the data flow into or out of a program, the forms of input, and the forms of the output. **Please understand that a system flowchart makes no attempt to depict the function-oriented processing steps within a program.** A system flowchart may be constructed by the system analyst as part of problem definition. **Note that algorithms in data structures are always expressed in the form of flowcharts.**

This difference is clear from Figures 1.1a and 1.1b.

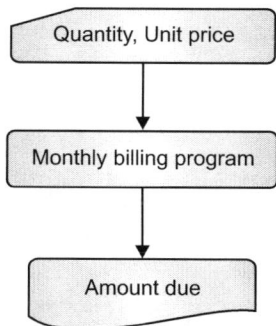

Figure 1.1a A System Flowchart Example

Contrast this with a program flowchart.

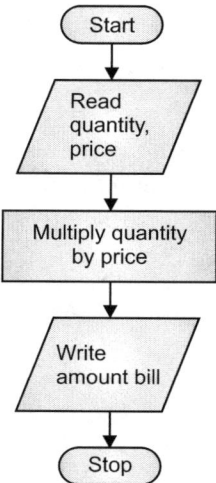

Figure 1.1b A Program Flowchart Example

A flowchart is a tool to show the logic flow of a program. Programmers use flowcharts to design a complete program. The primary purpose of a flowchart is to show the design of an algorithm. The flowchart frees a programmer from the syntax and details of a programming language while allowing focus on the details of the problem to be solved.

A flowchart is a combination of symbols. Symbols enhance the readability of the flowchart. They do not directly show instructions (or commands). They show the start and stop points, the order and sequence of actions, and how one part of a flowchart is connected to another.

Golden Rule

1. Each algorithm should have only one entry point and one exit point.

2. A null statement is shown by a flow line; there is no symbol for null.

Some of the notations used are shown in Figure 1.2.

An **oval** shows the beginning or ending of an algorithm.

Flow lines show the order or sequence of actions in a program.

A **connector** is used when we reach the end of a page. It is also used when we need to show the logic details that do not fit in the flow.

Assignment statements are shown using a **rectangle**, as in the following:

$$\text{Variable} \leftarrow \text{Expression}$$

A **parallelogram** shows any input read or output produced. A rectangle with two vertical bars inside represents a module call.

Selection statements (Decisions) may be two-way or multi-way selections. In both cases, the statement ends with a connector where the true and false flows join. In this case, the connector has nothing in it. This is applicable to switch statements or even for, while, and do-while loops of C (to be discussed later).

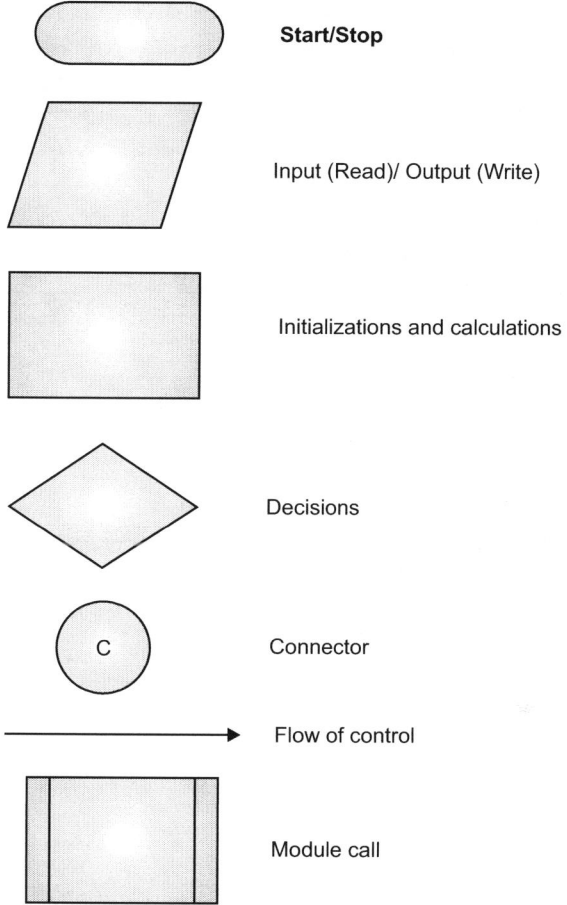

Figure 1.2 Flow Chart Notations

Both flowcharts and algorithms are isomorphic—that is, one can be converted to another form without the loss of data (although there are some differences).

Let us now distinguish between a flowchart and an algorithm.

Flowchart	Algorithm
1. The graphical or pictorial representation of the logic of the problem in hand	1. Step-by-step finite procedure of solving the problem in hand
2. Use of different shapes that are joined by flow lines	2. Written step by step
3. Use of flow lines	3. Flow control moves from top to bottom
4. The task to be performed written within boxes in English	4. All instructions written in English
5. Easily converted into algorithm or program in high-level language	5. Easily converted into flowchart or program in high-level language
6. Drawn after writing algorithm.	6. Normally written before flowchart

We are in a position to solve some examples now.

Example **1: Draw a flowchart to find the greatest of three numbers.**

Solution 1: The flowchart is as follows:

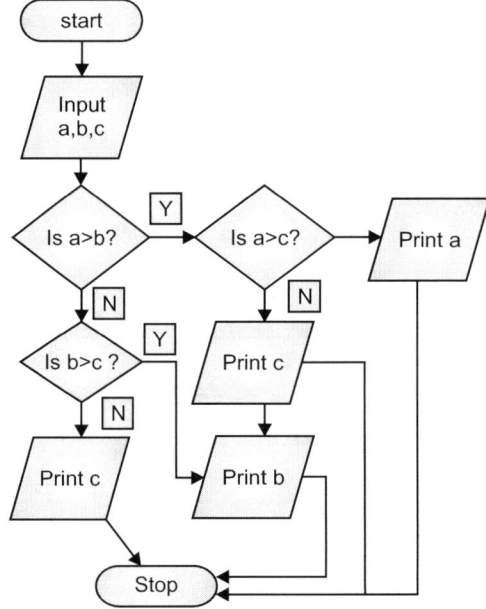

Example 2: **Draw a flowchart that finds the roots of a given quadratic equation, using a, b, and c as its coefficients.**

Solution 2: The flowchart is drawn as follows:

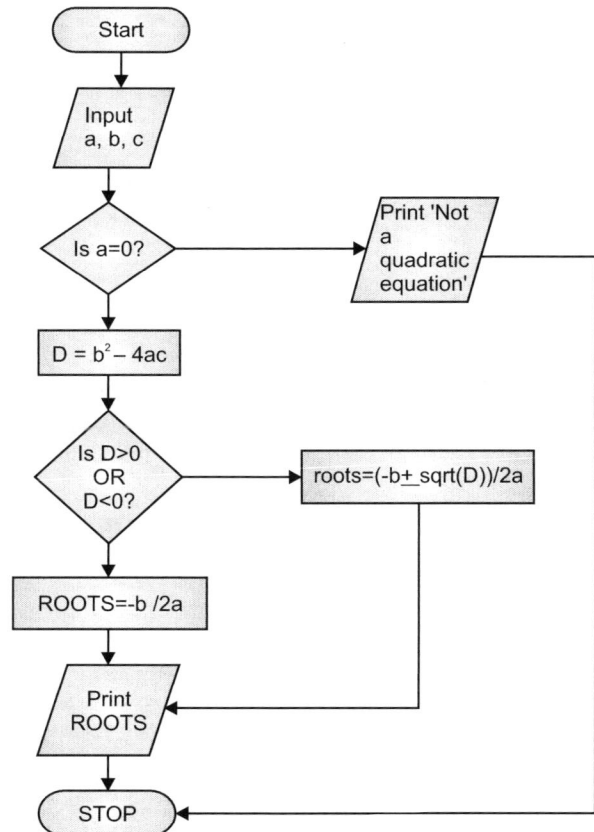

Example 3: **What is the difference between a flowchart and a dataflow diagram?**

Example 4: **Define flowchart. Write are the advantages of and the symbols used in a flowchart. Draw a flowchart to find the smallest of three numbers.**

Example 5: **(a) What is the difference between a flowchart and an algorithm?**

(b) Differentiate between a linker and a loader.

Example **6: It is desired to add n numbers. Write the following for this problem:**

(a) **Plain English**

(b) **Structured English**

(c) **Pseudocode**

(d) **C code**

Hint: (a) Plain English: First, read n numbers to be added. Initialize a resultant value to 0. Then add these numbers to this resultant value one by one. When all the numbers have been added, display the result.

(b) **Structured English:**

Step 1: Start

Step 2: Initialize sum and number of elements to add to 0.

Step 3: Read the number of elements to add—that is, read n.

Step 4: Read a number to be added and let it be a.

Step 5: s=s+a and i=i+1

Step 6: If i<n, go to step 4, else go to step 7.

Step 7: Display (output) the value of sum.

Step 8: Stop.

(c) **Pseudocode:**

```
Algo_ add(a, n)
    {
            s:= 0.0;
            for i:=1 to n do
            s:= s + a [i]; S + a [i];
            return s;
    }
```

(d) **C Code:**

```
int add(int a[ ] , int n)
    {
            int i, s=0;
            for(i=0; i <n ; i++)
            s=s + a[i];
            return s;
    }
```

1.3 COMPILER OVERVIEW

A compiler is a software program that analyzes a program developed in a particular computer language and then translates it into a form that is suitable for execution on your particular computer system. The GNU C compiler gcc is the best compiler available for the C language. In fact, it is a suite of compilers, as the package contains g++ (a compiler for C++) and facilitates compiling other languages like Objective-C and Objective-C++, Fortran in both fixed form and free form, ADA, and JAVA2. It can handle different dialects of C. It is also able to generate executable code for CPU families like ARC, AVR, ARM, Darwin, DEC Alpha, HPPA, i386 and x86-64, IA-64, MIPS, PDP-11, POWERPC, SPARC, and so on. When you invoke gcc, it normally does preprocessing, compilation, assembly, and linking. The **overall options** allow one to stop this process at an intermediate stage. For example,

-c Compile or assemble the source files but do not link. The linking stage is not done. The output is in the form of an object file for each source file.

-S Stop after the stage of compilation proper; do not assemble. The output is in the form of an assembler code file for each nonassembler input file specified.

-E Stop after the preprocessing stage; do not run the compiler proper. The output is in the form of preprocessed source code, which is then sent to the standard output.

-o Place output in file *file*.

- wall A warning option—displays all possible warnings and is very useful during initial debugging of a code.

Actually, gcc has a large complement of options for warnings, debugging, optimization, preprocessor, linker, assembler, and the target machine or language—for example, a C compiler, a C++ compiler, etc.

The steps involved in entering, compiling, and executing a computer program developed in the C programming language are shown in Figure 1.3.

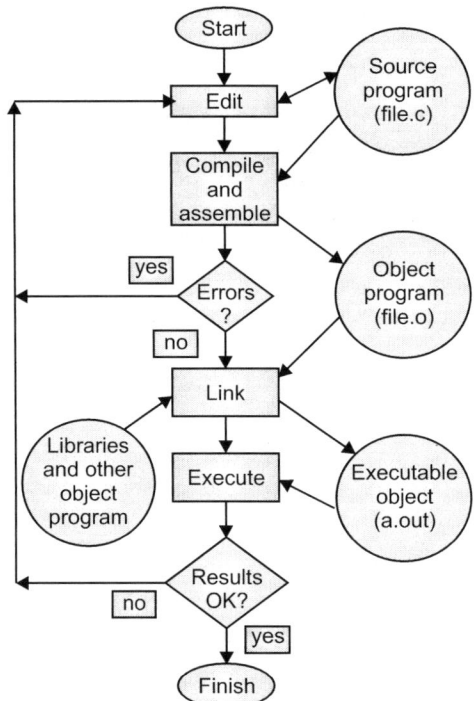

Figure 1.3 Basic Steps for Entering, Compiling, and Executing C Programs

Explanation: The program that is to be compiled is first typed and saved into a file. C programs are saved with a .c extension. Thus, program1.c might be a valid filename for a C program. **A C program is typed, saved, and edited in a text editor. For example, vi** is a popular text editor used on Unix systems. **The program that is entered into the file is known as the source program because it represents the original form of the program expressed in the C language.** After the source program is entered into a file, you can then proceed to have it compiled. The compilation process is initiated by typing a special command on the system. When this command is entered, the name of the file that contains the source program must also be specified. For example, on Unix systems, the command to initiate program compilation is called cc.

But please remember that if you are using the popular GNU C compiler, the command you use is gcc. So typing the line

gcc program1.c

has the effect of initiating the compilation process with the source program contained in program1.c.

In the first step of the compilation process, the compiler examines each of the program statements contained in the source program and checks to ensure that each conforms to the syntax and semantics (meaning) of the language. Practically speaking, the C compiler normally makes a prepass of the program looking for special statements. This is also known as a **preprocessing phase**. If any mistakes are discovered by the compiler during this phase, they are reported to the user and the compilation process ends right there. Then the errors have to be corrected in the source program using an editor and the compilation process must be restarted. Typical errors reported during this phase of compilation might be due to an expression that has unbalanced parentheses (syntax error) or due to the use of a variable that is not defined (i.e., semantic error).

When all the syntactic and semantic errors have been removed from the program, the compiler then proceeds to take each statement of the program and translate it into lower form. **This means that each statement is translated by the compiler into the equivalent statement or statements in assembly language needed to perform the task.**

After the program has been translated into an equivalent assembly language program, the next step in the compilation process is to translate the assembly language statements into actual machine instructions. This step might or might not involve the execution of a separate program known as an **assembler**. On most systems, the assembler is executed automatically as part of the compilation process. The assembler takes each assembly language statement and converts it into a binary format known as **object code which** is then written into another file on the system. This file typically has the same name as the source file under Unix, with the last letter as "o" (for object) instead of a "c". In Windows, the suffix letters "obj" typically replace the "c" in the filename.

After the program has been translated into object code, it is ready to be linked. This process is once again performed automatically whenever the cc or gcc command is issued under Unix. **Also understand that the purpose of the linking phase is to get the program into a final form for execution on the computer.** If the program uses other programs that were previously processed by the compiler, then during this phase the programs are linked together. Programs that are used from the system's program library are also searched and linked together with the object program during this phase. **The process of compiling and linking a program is known as building.** The final linked file, which is in an **executable object code format,** is stored in another file on the system, ready to be **run or executed.**

Under Unix, this file is called a.out (by default).

Under Windows, the executable file usually has the same name as the source file, with the c extension replaced by an exe extension.

The command **a.out** is used to execute the program. This command will load the program called a.out into the computer's memory and initiate its execution. When the program is executed, each of the statements of the program is sequentially executed in turn. If the program requests any data from the user (called input), the program temporarily suspends its execution so that the input can be entered. Or the program might simply wait for an **event,** such as a mouse being clicked, to occur. Results that are displayed by the program (called outputs) appear in a window (also called console). Or the output might be directly written to a file on the system.

If the program works correctly, there is no problem, but this does not often happen on the first attempt. If the program does not produce the desired results, it is necessary to go back and reanalyze the program's logic. **This is known as the debugging phase,** during which an attempt is made to remove all known problems or **bugs** from the program. Doing this requires making changes to the original source program. **Please note that in such a case, the entire process of compiling, linking, and executing the program must be repeated until the desired results are obtained. Also note that in general, gcc follows the following processing steps:**

Step 1: Preprocessing (invokes cpp)

Step 2: Compilation

Step 3: Assembly (invoke as)

Step 4: Linking (invokes ld).

This can also be shown graphically, as in Figures 1.4 and 1.5.

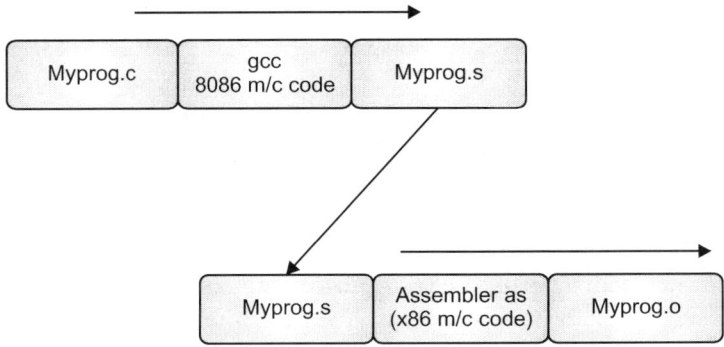

Figure 1.4 gcc Converting from C to obj Using Assembler

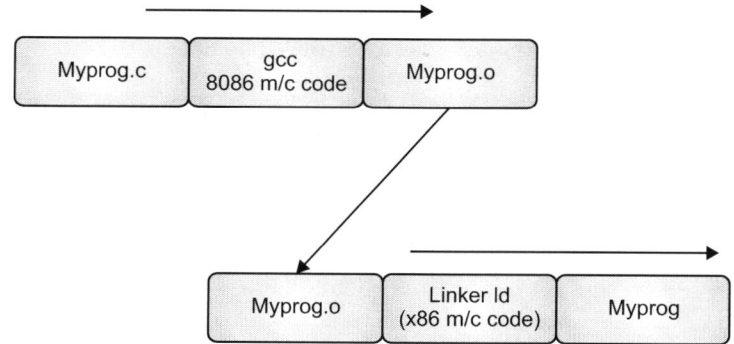

Figure 1.5 gcc: The Linker Converts an obj File to an Executable

In gcc, the level of attempted optimization is controlled by -0 and other switches but one has to be very careful for embedded and device driver codes.

1.4 ASSEMBLER, LINKER, AND LOADER

If we look at the history of programming languages we find the following:

(a) In the 1940s, machine languages were used.

(b) In the 1950s, symbolic languages were used.

(c) In the 1960s, high-level languages were used.

Each computer has its own machine language that is made of streams of 0s and 1s. This is so because computers are made up of switches, transistors, and other electronic devices that can be either in 1 (logic high) or 0 (logic low) states. These are also named as 0 (off state) and 1 (on state).

NOTE   *The only language understood by computer hardware is machine language.*

In the 1950s, Admiral Grace Hopper, a mathematician, developed the concept of a special computer program that would convert programs into machine language. It used symbols (also called mnemonics), which is why the languages used in these programs were known as **symbolic languages. Because a computer cannot understand this symbolic language, it must be translated** into machine language. **The program that translates symbolic code into machine language is known as an assembler.**

Then in the 1960s came the introduction of high-level languages that relieved the programmer of the tedious task of writing programs in assembly language. Both symbolic and higher-level languages share one thing in common—both must be converted into machine language. **And this process of converting them is known as compilation.**

For example, the first high-level language was FORTRAN (FORmula TRANslation). It was created by John Backus and an IBM team in 1957. C is also a high-level language used for developing system software and new applications.

Often a program is so large that it is convenient to break it down into smaller units. Each of these units is stored in a separate file. After these separate program files are compiled, they must somehow be linked together to form a single program. **This linking is usually accomplished by a program called a linkage editor, which is often run automatically when a program is compiled. This linker assembles all of the functions (both user-defined as well as system functions) into a final executable program.**

Once a program has been linked, it is ready for execution. To execute a program, we use an operating system command like the **run command.** This command will load the program into primary memory and execute it. **And getting the program into memory is the function of an operating system program known as the loader. It locates the executable program and reads it into memory. When everything is loaded, the program takes control and it begins execution.**

We are in a position to solve some examples now.

Example **1: Compare a compiler and an interpreter.**

Solution 1: The following chart compares a compiler and an interpreter:

Compiler	Interpreter
1. Converts the whole program into machine code and then executes the entire program.	1. Converts the program into machine code one step at a time and then runs only that step.
2. Lists all errors after compilation.	2. Immediately displays any error in any line of the program after the translation of that line.

3. Requires less execution time.	3. Requires more execution time.
4. Not especially efficient for debugging.	4. Efficient for debugging.
5. Creates only one .exe file (for example, C/C++ compilers, TC compiler, etc.).	5. Does not create .exe file (for example, V. B. 6.0 interpreter).

Example 2: **Compare a linker and linkage editor in a tabular form.**

Solution 2: The comparison is shown in the following chart:

Linker	Linkage Editor
1. Linking of object modules and necessary libraries are done and immediately loaded into main memory.	1. Linking of object modules and necessary libraries are done and stored in a file or library called a **linked program**.
2. Used only once.	2. Can be used many times.
3. A library search and the resolution of external reference is done each time.	3. Library search and resolution of external reference must be done only once.
4. Not suitable for a program which is executed repeatedly.	4. Suitable for a program which is executed repeatedly.

Example 3: **Compare machine language, assembly language, and high-level languages in tabular form.**

Solution 3: The comparison is shown in the following chart:

Machine Language	Assembly Language	High-Level Language
1. Programs written in machine language are difficult to write, debug, and understand.	1. Programs in assembly language are less difficult than machine language.	1. Programs in high-level language are easy to write, debug, and understand.
2. Programs are not portable.	2. Programs are not portable.	2. Programs are portable.

3. Programmer has to keep track of memory addresses.	3. Programmer has to keep track of memory addresses.	3. No need to keep track of memory addresses.
4. No translator is required to convert into machine code.	4. No translator is required to convert into machine code.	4. Compiler or interpreter is required.
5. The execution of programs is very fast.	5. The execution of programs is slower than machine language programs.	5. The execution of programs is slower than assembly language programs.

Example 4: **Name some commonly used assemblers.**

Solution 4:

       (a) Intel 8086 macro assembler (ASM 86)

       (b) Borland Turbo Assembler (TASM)

       (c) IBM Macro Assembler (MASM)

Example 5: **Explain briefly the compilation and execution process of a C program.**

1.5 STRUCTURE OF A SIMPLE "HELLO WORLD" PROGRAM IN C

In general, any C program comprises one or more preprocessor commands, a global declaration section, and one or more functions. That is,

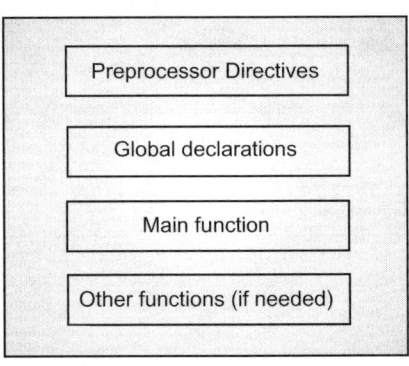

Every C program starts with some preprocessor directives or commands. These are special instructions to the preprocessor that tell it how to prepare a program for compilation. In every C program, we use a preprocessor directive named **include. This include command tells the preprocessor that we need information from selected libraries known as header files. By the time we type our C program (in some editors), all the preprocessor allocations will have taken place automatically.** *This means that the preprocessor actually analyzes these statements before the analysis of the C program itself takes place.*

Preprocessor statements are identified by the presence of a pound sign, #, which must be the first nonspace character on the line.

In C, a programmer inserts a directive **#include<stdio.h> that tells the preprocessor to include the header file stdio.h at this point in the program.**

Then a programmer can give **global declarations** (if any). Global declarations are those that are visible to all parts of the program. We shall study these a bit later.

Then comes the **main** where the actual execution of the program starts. We know that the actual work of the program is carried out by its functions, which are blocks of code that accomplish tasks within a program. **Only one function can be a main function in any program.** All functions in a program (also the main) are subdivided into two sections—**the declaration section and the statement section.**

The declaration section is at the beginning of the function. It specifies the data that you will be using in the function. *Declarations in a function are known as local declarations because they are visible only to the function that contains them.*

The statement section follows the declaration section. This section contains some instructions that cause something to be performed, such as dividing two numbers.

Let us consider the simplest C program that explains its structure.

```
   /* My first C program */
1. #include<stdio.h>
2. int main (void)
3. {
4. printf("Hello World! \n");
5. return 0;
6. }
```

This program has only one preprocessor directive. There are no global declarations and no local definitions. It simply displays "Hello World!" on the screen. Then there are two statements, one to print the message and the other to stop the program.

Let us learn about these parts now.

I. Preprocessor Directive/Command

As discussed earlier, a preprocessor is a part of the C compilation process that recognizes special statements that might be interspread throughout a C program. It actually analyzes these statements before analysis of the C program starts. The preprocessor is a section of the compiler which looks over the C program before it is compiled.

Working of Preprocessor

When you issue the command to compile a C program, the program is run automatically through the preprocessor. The preprocessor is a program that modifies the C source program according to the directives supplied in the program. An original source program is usually stored in a file. The preprocessor does not modify this program file but creates a new file that contains the processed version of the program. This new file is then submitted to the compiler.

When we compile this program, the compiler shows the number of lines compiled to be greater than 6. This is because during the preprocessing stage, the **include** preprocessor directive (line 1) searches the file **stdio.h** in the prescribed list of directories and if the header file is found, the include directive is replaced by the entire content of the header file. If the included header file contains another include directive, it will also be processed. **This processing is carried out recursively till either no include directive remains or till the maximum translation limit is achieved (ISO specifies a maximum of 15 nested levels of include files).** Thus, one line of source code gets replaced by multiple lines of the header file. During the compilation stage, these added lines will also be compiled. Thus, the compiler shows the number of lines to be greater than 6.

NOTE   *Some compilers enable the programmer to run only the preprocessor on the source program and to view the results of the preprocessor stage.*

Please remember the following points regarding preprocessor directives:

1.   They are placed at the **beginning of the program.**

2.   They start with a **pound/hash (#) sign**. This is its syntax (rule).

3.   There is no semicolon at the end of these directives.

4.   They can **start in any column but usually they start in column number 1.**

5.   They tell the compiler **to include the standard input/output library file in the** program. This library file prints a message on to the screen. Actually, printing is one of the input/output processes identified in this library.

6.   The syntax of this command as shown in line 1 must be **exact**.

7.   There is no space between the pound/hash sign and the reserved keyword **include**.

8.   **It tells the preprocessor that you want the library file in the angular brackets (< >) to be included in your program. The name of this header file is *stdio.h*.** It stands for *"Standard input/output header file"*.

9.   **The angular brackets tell the** preprocessor to search for the file in one or more standard directories. These directories contain header files that are provided by the system and those commonly used by several programmers (if the computer is a multiple-user machine).

10.   Sometimes the brackets are replaced with double quotation marks as in the following:

#include "stdio.h"

In this case the preprocessor will first look in the programmer's own directory or the same one that contains the program file. If it is NOT found there, then the standard directories are searched.

11.   The preprocessor can also add or delete C program statements.

12.   A preprocessor symbol is never replaced if it occurs within single or double quotation marks.

13. Header files also provide consistency among several program files. Often a program is large and thus it is possible to break it into smaller units, each of which is stored in a separate file. After these separate program files are compiled, they must somehow be linked together to form a single program. This linking is usually done by a program called the **linkage editor** (which is run automatically when a program is compiled).

14. A header file can contain other #include directives. **Please note that it cannot include itself because this would result in an infinite recursion. Also note that it cannot include another file that includes the first file as this would also result in an infinite recursion.**

15. Header files can contain any text at all. They may also contain C code to define structure templates, global variables, or function definitions. However, header files usually do not contain function definitions, as it is more efficient to store these in the function libraries set up by the user. But global variables are sometimes included.

16. If **stdio.h** is included in the program, the macro versions (to be discussed later) are used. On the other hand, if the programmer wishes to use the function versions they can be undefined after the **#include<stdio.h>** directive.

17. A preprocessor directive is terminated by the end of the line it occupies but if necessary it can be continued onto one or more lines by ending all but the last line with backslashes.

II. Main Function

Here starts the executable portion of your program (i.e., the code for which object and .exe files are generated). Main is a special C function. *The program execution starts from main and there can be only one main in every program.* The **int** preceding this keyword main says that the function main (here) will return an integer value to the operating system. The keyword void shows that the function main has no parameters (i.e., the parameter list is void). Following the main are two braces that show that main is a function. **Please note here that there is no punctuation after the function header.**

NOTE

If there are no parentheses following the main, it is not a function but is instead a variable. For example, sum is a variable but sum( ) is a function. This function may or may not return a value. We shall study this a bit later.

After identifying the main( ) to the system, we must now specify what this routine must do. And this is done by enclosing all program statements of the routine within a pair of curly braces (line 3). **Also note that all program statements included between the braces are taken as part of the main routine by the system.** In the Hello World! program, we have only two such statements. *The first statement tells that a routine named printf is to be invoked or called. The string of characters "hello world! \n" is the parameter or argument to be passed to the printf routine.*

Just remember that the printf routine is a function in the C library. It simply prints or displays its arguments on your screen in between double quotation marks. Also note that a blank space in a string counts as a character.

Also seen in line 4 are two special characters—the backslash (\) and the letter n—that are together known as the *newline character*. **This *newline character* tells the system to do precisely what its name implies—that is, go to a new line (next line).**

NOTE *Any characters to be printed after the newline character then appear on the next line of the display. This concept of newline character is similar to that of the carriage return key on a typewriter.*

Another **rule** in C may be stated as follows: **"All program statements in C must be terminated by a semicolon. That is why a semicolon appears immediately after the closing braces of the printf( ) statement. However, there are some exceptions; for example, after main( ) there are no semicolons!"**

Line 5 is the last statement (return 0); it tells the compiler to finish the execution of main and return to the system a status value of 0. **Please note that you can use any integer here. Also note that zero is used here by convention to show that the program completed successfully (i.e., without any errors).** Different numbers can be used to indicate different types of error conditions that occur, such as divide by zero, file not found, and so on.

NOTE *This exit status can be tested by other programs like the UNIX shell to see whether the program ran successfully.*

The end of the program is marked off by a closing brace. Remember the following programming tips:

1. **The number of opening braces and closing braces must be the same.**

2. These braces line up with the letter 'm' of the main( ).

3. This is not mandatory but will improve the program's readability.

4. The body of the function is indented within the braces. This also improves the program's **readability**.

5. **The function name like main is given parentheses—that is, ( ). On the other hand, the body starts and ends with two delimiters— that is, { and }. One cannot interchange them. They are design features of the C compiler.**

Now we are left with one more nonexecutable statement (see the "Hello World!" program again) called a **comment**. Comments are written within the code to make it more understandable and readable. These comments are **internal program documentations. C supports two types of comments:**

(a) Block comments

(b) Line comments

A block comment is used when the comment spans several lines of code. It uses an opening token (/*) and a closing token (*/). Anything that is enclosed within these is simply ignored by the compiler. *The tokens can start in any column and they do not have to be on the same line.* For example,

/* a block comment can go to

More than one line also */

On the other hand, **a line comment uses two slashes (//) to identify a comment.** There is no need for an end-of-line token here. This type of comment format is very much preferred by programmers as it is easier to write. It can also start anywhere on the line.

However, note another programming rule: "**Comments cannot be nested.**" We cannot have comments inside comments. This results in an error.

This is the complete anatomy of a C program.

Before further discussion, let us solve some questions now.

Q1. What delimiters are used to specify the start and end of a character string in C?

A1. Double quotation marks.

Q2. What is the character string in a printf statement called?

A2. The control string.

Q3. C is derived from which of the following languages:

(a) FORTRAN

(b) PASCAL

(c) C++

(d) B language

A3. (d) B language.

Q4. Give the output of the following statement:

printf("alpha\n\nbeta\n\ngamma\n");

A4. It prints three lines that are double spaced as follows:

alpha

beta

gamma

Q5. Give the errors in the following:

mane{ } /* this is a main …/*

(

print(' that's great. /n')

A5. The following errors are noticed in this program:

(a) The word **main** is not spelled correctly.

(b) Parentheses should be used instead of braces after the word *main*.

(c) The wrong slash symbol is used in the first comment symbol.

(d) The characters in the terminating comment symbol are reversed.

(e) The body of the program should commence with a left brace, not a left parenthesis.

(f) The function should be spelled as *printf* and not print.

(g) The literal should be delimited by double instead of single quotation marks.

(h) The newline character has an incorrect type of slash.

(i) The semicolon is missing from the printf statement.

(j) The final right brace is missing.

1.6 OVERVIEW OF THE COMPILATION AND EXECUTION PROCESS IN AN INTEGRATED DEVELOPMENT ENVIRONMENT (PREFERABLY CODEBLOCK)

IDE stands for Integrated Development Environment. An IDE is a window-based program that allows you to easily manage large software programs, edit files in windows, and compile, link, run, and debug your programs. **This process of editing, compiling, running, and debugging programs is managed by a single integrated application known as an IDE.**

For example,

(a) On the Mac OS, CodeWarrior and Xcode are two IDEs.

(b) Under Windows, MS Visual Studio is an IDE.

(c) Under Linux, Kylix is a popular IDE.

NOTE
All IDE applications greatly simplify the entire process of program development. CodeWarrior (by Metrowerks) can run on Linux, Solaris, and Windows, too. Kylix is sold by Borland.

All of the tools like text editor, preprocessor, compiler, and linker that are required for developing programs are integrated into one package known as an IDE.

Codeblocks is an open source, cross-platform IDE. A global variable or a function defined in one source file can be used in another source file in a multifile program. Let us see how.

Consider a program that consists of two source files, *t1.c and t2.c*. The source file t2.c contains the definition of a variable *var1* and a function *fun1*. These definitions are used in another source file t1.c of the program. Because the global variables and the function have external linkage, this usage is allowed. And this can be done with CodeBlock as follows:

Say, file t1.c has the following code:

```
#include<stdio.h>
          main( )
{
```

```
extern int var1;
printf("The value of var1 defined in other source file is
%d\n", var1);
                fun( );
                }
And t2.c has the following code:-
    int var1 = 95;
    fun( )
    {
printf("Function fun is defined in other source file");
                }
```

Then after running these files in CodeBlock we get the following output:

The value of var1 defined in the other source file is 95.

The function fun1 is defined in the other source file.

We are in a position to answer some questions now.

Q1. What are the advantages of writing an algorithm over the C program?

[**Hint:** a) It is simple, clear, and unambiguous and thus can be debugged by any programmer having no prior knowledge of any programming language.

(b) It is easier to understand the logic in an algorithm.]

Q2. Why don't we translate directly from the statement of the problem to C?

Q3. Which two lines will be used in all of our C programs?

Q4. "C is often described as a middle level language." Explain.

[**Hint:** C permits programs to be written in much the same style as that of most modern high-level languages like Fortran, Cobol, Basic, and Pascal. Where it differs is that C permits very close interaction with the inner workings of the computer. It is analogous to a car that has a luxury of automatic gears but at the option of the driver permits the manual shifting of gears. It is possible in C to deal with the machine at a fairly low level. Nevertheless, C is a general purpose structured programming language that has much in common with the best of the high-level languages. C is concise but at the same time it is a very powerful language, too.]

Q5. What is a preprocessor directive?

or

Q6. Distinguish between function and preprocessor directives.

[**Hint:** Preprocessor directives are the lines to be executed before the actual compilation of the code starts. And wherever in the program code the macros are called, the code of that macro is inserted. On the other hand, in a function call, the body of the function is executed at runtime. And wherever in a code the functions are called, the execution of the program jumps to the body of the function. Code is not copied as in the case of preprocessor directives.]

Q7. Name some popular C language IDEs.

[**Hint:** There are various IDEs on the market today targeted toward different operating systems. For example, Turbo C and Turbo C++ are popular compilers that work under MS-DOS, Visual Studio and Visual Studio Express Edition are compilers that work under Windows, whereas the gcc compiler works under Linux. Please note here that the Turbo C, Turbo C++, and gcc compilers can also be installed on machines running Windows. Both the Visual Studio Express Edition and gcc compilers are free of cost and can be downloaded easily.]

Summary

In this chapter, we have studied what an algorithm is. We have defined terms like flowcharts, pseudocode, and structured English. Also we have seen how a C program is compiled and run. The roles of assemblers, linkers, and loaders have also been examined. We have specifically focused on the gcc compiler. The chapter also shows the basic structure of any C program. It also discusses the IDEs that are used to compile and run C programs like CodeBlocks.

Exercises

Q1. What is a C preprocessor? Explain each of them.

Q2. How do you debug a C program? Discuss the purpose of preprocessor directive statements and macros as used in the C language?

Q3. What is an interactive debugger?

Q4. Distinguish between the following with examples:

(a) Syntactic errors and semantic errors

(b) Runtime errors and logical errors

(c) Debugging and testing

Q5. What is the scope of a preprocessor directive within a program file?

Q6. Draw a flowchart to find the sum of the following series:

Sum = 1+3+5+7+ ... up to 25 terms.

Q7. Write an algorithm to find the roots of a given quadratic equation $ax^2 + bx +c =0$, where 'a' is nonzero.

Q8. Draw a flowchart to determine whether a year entered through a keyboard is a leap year or not?

Q9. Explain the various stages in program development.

Q10. Describe in detail syntax errors, logic errors, and runtime errors.

Q11. Write an algorithm and draw flowcharts for the following:

(a) To generate the first n Fibonacci numbers

(b) To sum the first 80 even numbers

(c) To check whether a given number is prime or not

(d) To check whether a given number is even or odd

Q12. Define a bug and debugging.

Q13. What are the characteristics of a good algorithm?

Q14. What are the advantages of flowcharts?

[**Hint:** Better communication, effective analysis, proper documentation, efficient coding, proper debugging, and better program maintenance].

Q15. How will you test your program? What are dry runs?

Q16. What is top-down design? How is it done?

Q17. What is modular design? Should it be used or not?

Q18. Explain Wirth's equation:

Program = Algorithm + Data-Structure or Program-Algorithm = Data Structure

Q19. What is meant by program documentation? Explain.

Q20. Suppose you have a C program whose main function is in main.c and has other functions in the files input.c and output.c:

(a) What commands would you use on your system to compile and link this program?

(b) How would you modify the above commands to link a library called process1 stored in the standard system library directory?

(c) How would you modify the above commands to link a library called process2 stored in the home directory?

(d) Some header files need to be read and have been found in a header subdirectory of your home directory and also in the current working directory. How would you modify the compiler commands to account for this?

Q21. Suppose you have a C program composed of several separate files and they include one another as shown in the following chart:

File Name	Include Files
main.c	stdio.h, process1.h
input.c	stdio.h, list.h
output.c	stdio.h
process1.c	stdio.h, process1.h
process2.c	stdio.h, list.h

(a) Which files have to recompile after you make changes to process1.c?

(b) Which files have to recompile after you make changes to process1.h?

(c) Which files have to recompile after you make changes to list.h?

PROGRAMMING USING C

2.0 INTRODUCTION

C is a **general purpose, block-structured, procedural, case-sensitive, freeflow, portable, powerful high-level programming language.** This language is so powerful that an operating system like **UNIX is itself coded in C.** It is said that programming languages are *born, age, and eventually die but the C programming language has only matured* from the time it was born. It has the same relevance today as it had when it was developed by Dennis Ritchie at Bell Telephone Laboratories in 1972. The importance of the language can be easily fathomed from the fact that C is a prerequisite in any software industry today.

2.1 REVIEW OF PREPROCESSOR DIRECTIVES/ COMPILER DIRECTIVES/C PREPROCESSOR

As discussed earlier, a preprocessor is a part of the C compilation process that recognizes special statements that might be interspread throughout a C program. It actually analyzes these statements before analysis of the C program starts. The preprocessor is a section of the compiler which looks over the C program before it is compiled.

Working of the Preprocessor

When you issue the command to compile a C program, the program is run automatically through the preprocessor. The preprocessor is a program that modifies the C source program according to the directives supplied in the program. An original source program is usually stored in a file. The preprocessor does not modify this program file but creates a new file that contains the processed version of the program. This new file is then submitted to the compiler.

When we compile this program, the compiler shows the number of lines compiled to be greater than 6. This is because during the preprocessing stage, the **include** preprocessor directive searches the file **iostream.h** in the prescribed list of directories and if the header file is found, the include directive is replaced by the entire content of the header file. If the included header file contains another include directive, it will also be processed. **This processing is carried out recursively till either no include directive remains or till the maximum translation limit is achieved (ISO specifies a maximum of 15 nested levels of include files).** Thus, one line of source code gets replaced by multiple lines of the header file. During the compilation stage, these added lines will also be compiled. Thus, the compiler shows the number of lines to be greater than 6.

NOTE *Some compilers enable the programmer to run only the preprocessor on the source program and to view the results of the preprocessor stage.*

Please remember the following points regarding preprocessor directives:

1. They are placed at the **beginning of the program.**

2. They start with a **pound/hash (#) sign**. This is its syntax (rule).

3. There is no semicolon at the end of these directives.

4. They can **start in any column but usually start in column 1.**

5. They tell the compiler **to include the standard input/output library file** in the program. This library file prints a message onto the screen. Printing is one of the input/output processes identified in this library.

6. The syntax of this command must be **exact.**

7. There is no space between the pound/hash sign and the reserved keyword **include.**

8. **It tells the preprocessor that you want the library file in angular brackets (< >) to be included in your program. The name of this header file is *iostream.h*.** It stands for *"Standard input/output header stream file."*

9. **The angular brackets tell the** preprocessor to search for the file in one or more standard directories. These directories contain header files that are provided by the system and those commonly used by several programmers (if the computer is a multiple-user machine).

10. Sometimes the brackets are replaced with double quotation marks as in the following:

    #include "iostream.h"

    In this case the preprocessor will first look in the programmer's own directory or the same one that contains the program file. If it is NOT found there, then the standard directories are searched.

11. The preprocessor can also add or delete C program statements.

12. A preprocessor symbol is never replaced if it occurs within single or double quotation marks.

13. Header files also provide consistency among several program files. Often a program is large and thus it is possible to break it into smaller units, each of which is stored in a separate file. After these separate program files are compiled, they must somehow be linked together to form a single program. This linking is usually done by a program called the **linkage editor** (which is run automatically when a program is compiled).

14. A header file can contain other #include directives. **Please note that it cannot include itself because this would result in an infinite recursion. Also note that it cannot include another file that includes the first file as this would also result in an infinite recursion.**

15. Header files can contain any text at all. They may also contain C code to define structure templates, global variables, or function definitions. However, header files usually do not contain function definitions as it is more efficient to store these in the function libraries set up by the user. But global variables are sometimes included.

16. If *iostream.h* is included in the program, the macro versions (to be discussed later) are used. On the other hand, if the programmer wishes to use the function versions they can be undefined after the **#include<iostream.h> directive.**

17. A preprocessor directive is terminated by the end of the line it occupies but if necessary it can be continued onto one or more lines by ending all but the last line with backslashes.

Definition Section

In this section, we define a variable with some value in it. This is also known as a **special constant section.** Here, a define statement is used. The general syntax of a symbolic preprocessor or symbolic compiler directive can be defined using the following #define statement:

#define name value

For example,

#define PI 3.1417

This initializes a variable PI with a value of 3.1417. **But please remember the following points regarding a #define preprocessor directive:**

1. #define **cannot be placed anywhere** in a program.

2. The variables defined in these statements are symbolic constants and therefore must be written in **uppercase**, preferably.

3. There is **no semicolon** at the end of a #define statement.

4. **No spaces** are allowed between # and define.

5. *define* should be written as *define* only and not as *Define*.

6. If PI is a symbolic name, as in our example, then we cannot make it a variable also.

7. There is no equals (=) sign between PI and 3.1417.

8. Do not use special characters in these symbolic names.

9. You cannot concatenate these symbolic statements together (i.e., each symbolic name must be declared on a separate line).

For example,

> #define PI 3.1417 (is valid).

But   #define PI = 3.1417 (is invalid).

Similarly,   #define NAME "Rajiv" (is valid).

> #define R 'r' (is valid).

But   #Define PI 3.1417 (is invalid, as 'D' must be in lowercase).

> # define PI 3.1417 (is invalid, as no space is allowed between # and define).

> #define PI, R 3.14, 5 (is invalid, as multiple initializations are not allowed).

Global Declaration Section

Sometimes we need the same variables in both the functions and in the main program. In such cases, we use global variables. These variables are declared normally but are placed before the start of the main program. **Please understand here that if you want the data variables to be available in all parts of the program, then you have to either declare the variables as global or they must be passed as arguments** (to be studied a bit later). **Also understand that by using any of these methods the ultimate objective is that the data be available in all of the functions.**

NOTE   *Whenever there is a conflict between a global and a local variable, the local variable gets first priority.*

The main( ) Function

The main function is *where the compiler starts executing the program first.* If you don't have a main( ), your program will be compiled successfully but it will not run and the compiler will report an error that you have not defined a main( ) function. That is why a main( ) function is necessary. It is a special function that acts as a container for the entire C program. This section of our code contains input and output as well as the processing statements. It may or may not have a return type as follows:

    void main(void) //here everything is void as there is no value being returned by the main and that no

//arguments are being passed.

On the other hand, compare the following statement:

```
int main ( )
  {
    ......
    ......
    return (0); // is must
  }
```

Here the opening curly bracket "{" shows the starting of the main program while "}" shows its end. The variables declared after these braces are known as local variables—that is, they have a scope local to this main function. Then comes the portion where the user writes his or her program. This is known as the **user-defined section.**

A preprocessor directive is used to instruct the preprocessor to perform a specific action in the source program before its compilation. **A preprocessor is a program that manipulates the source program before this program is passed to the compiler.** *That is why these preprocessor directives are also known as preprocessor commands.* **The point to understand is that by the time you are typing your program, all preprocessor allocations will have taken place.** This software is always included in a C package along with the standard C library functions. As already explained, the C compiler automatically invokes the preprocessor in its first pass compilation whether you are using any preprocessor directives or not. But the programmer can also invoke the preprocessor to manipulate the source program without its compilation. *But it is not mandatory to know and use preprocessor directives, as programs also run without them. However, their usefulness lies in the fact that with their help we can easily change our source code even if we are working in different environments.* **Please remember that if we use any preprocessor directives, it means that the preprocessor has to perform specific actions like changing a lengthy string into a shorter one or ignoring some portion of the source program or inserting the contents of other files into the source file, and so on.**

2.2 C PRIMITIVE INPUT-OUTPUT USING GETCHAR AND PUTCHAR

We will now discuss the getchar( ) and putchar( ) functions of C.

I. The getchar Function: getchar( );

The getchar function reads a single character from standard input. It takes no parameters and it returns the input character. In general, a reference to the getchar function is written as:

variable = getchar( );

For example,

char c;

c = getchar( );

Please note here that the second line causes a single character to be entered from the keyboard and then assigned to c. If an end-of-file condition is encountered when reading a character with the getchar function, the value of the symbolic constant EOF will automatically be returned. Also note that this function can also be used to read multiple-character strings by reading one character at a time within a multipass loop.

II. The putchar Function: putchar(variable | constant);

The standard C function that prints or displays a single character by sending it to standard output is called **putchar.** This function takes one argument, which is the character to be displayed.

For example,

putchar('R'); will display the character 'R'.

Or

char var = '$';

putchar(var); displays the character $.

Let us provide an algorithm for this program:

Step 1: Read a character.

Step 2: If the entered character is nonblank, print it.

Step 3: Else print the first blank character and skip all consecutive blanks.

Step 4: Repeat steps 1 to 3 till the entered character is a newline character.

The following is the program:

```
#include<stdio.h>
#include<string.h>
```

```
void main( )
 {
    char c;
    printf("\nEnter the text:");
    c= getchar( );
    printf("The output text is: ");
    while (c!= '\n')
      {
          if (c = = " || c= = '\t')
            {
                c = ' ';
                putchar( c );
            }
      while(c = = ' ' | | c = = '\t')
        {
          c = getchar( );
        }
      putchar(c );
      c = getchar( );
      }
    printf("\n");
    }
```

OUTPUTS (after running)

Enter the text: DR. RAJIV CHOPRA

The output text is: DR. RAJIV CHOPRA

2.3 SIMPLE INPUT/OUTPUT

Certain functions are used for data input and data output. These functions are called **standard input-output functions.** In C, these functions are put under two categories:

(a) Formatted I/O functions

(b) Unformatted I/O functions

Let us discuss each of them.

I. Formatted I/O Functions

Formatted I/O functions are used to input data from a standard input device as well as to send output to a standard output device. Under this category, the **scanf( )** function is used to read values from the keyboard while the **printf( )** function is used to display values on the output terminal. **Both of these functions are defined in the <conio.h> header file.**

The **scanf( ) function** is used to accept input data from a standard device in a fixed format. Its syntax is as follows:

Syntax

scanf("format string", arguments);

where **format string** contains format specifiers which begin with the '%' character, listed as follows:

Format Specifier	Input Types	Data Type
%d or %i	Short signed integer	INTEGER
%u	Short unsigned integer	
%ld	Long signed integer	
%lu	Long unsigned integer	
%x	Unsigned hexadecimal integer	
%o	Unsigned octal integer	
%f	Single precision float	FLOAT
%lf	Double precision float	
%c	Signed character	CHARACTER
	Unsigned character	
%s	String	STRING

Arguments specify where the input data is to be stored while receiving it from a standard input device. There must be an argument for each input datum. Extra arguments are ignored; if there are too few arguments, the results become unpredictable. **The arguments to the scanf function are pointers. This is the reason why arguments are preceded by an ampersand (&) symbol (i.e., an address operator). The & operator assigns it a memory location. Also note that the order of these specifiers and their arguments must be the same or else an error is reported by the C compiler.**

Next let us discuss the printf( ) function. The **printf( ) function** is used to accept output data from a computer to a standard device in a fixed format. It is a formatted output function. Its syntax is as follows:

Syntax

> **printf("format string", arguments);**

For example,

```
printf("My name is Dr. Rajiv"); /* double quotes are
used */
```

For another example,

```
printf ("%d", a);
```

Also note that here the value of 'a' is inserted at the '%d' position and thus the value of 'a' gets printed.

2.4 FUNCTION CALLS FROM A LIBRARY

Functions like getchar( ), putchar( ), printf( ), and scanf( ) are defined in the stdio.h file. Functions like strlen( ), strcpy( ), strcat( ), strcmp( ), and strrev( ) are defined in a string.h header file. A function like exit(0) is defined in a process.h file. Similarly, functions like sin( ), cos( ), tan( ), and so on are included in a math.h header file. **Please note that all these functions that are included in one or the other header files are built into the C library. This means that the C compiler will automatically execute their code and give the desired result. Also note that we cannot modify these inbuilt functions.** If we want to modify any of these functions, we have to write our own functions, known as **user-defined functions.**

With every C compiler a large set of useful string handling library functions is provided. These functions are predefined in the compiler of the language and stored in a special library file.

2.5 DATA TYPES IN C

C has a concept of data types that are used to define a variable before its use. The definition of a variable will assign storage for the variable and define the type of data that will be held in the location. The value of a variable can be changed any time. In C, the following data types are given:

(a) int

(b) float

(c) double

(d) char

Please note that there is not a Boolean data type. C does not have the traditional view of logical comparison. Actually, data types in C are listed under three main categories:

(a) Primary data type

(b) Derived data type

(c) User-defined data type

Primary Data Types

All C compilers accept the following fundamental data types:

(a) Integer (i.e., int)

(b) Character (i.e., char)

(c) Floating point (i.e., float)

(d) Double precision floating point (i.e., double)

(e) Void (i.e., void)

The data type int is used to define integers (e.g., int count;). Integers are whole numbers with a machine-dependent range of values. **An integer takes 2 bytes in memory.** An int may be short int, int, or long int. All of these data types have signed and unsigned forms. A short int requires half the space of normal integer values. Unsigned numbers are always positive and consume all bits for the magnitude of the number. The long and unsigned integers are used to declare a longer range of values.

The char data type defines a character. **Each character occupies one byte in memory. The signed or unsigned qualifier can be explicitly applied to char. While unsigned characters have values between 0 and 255, signed characters have values from –128 to 127.**

Float is used to define floating point numbers, which are real numbers expressed to 6 digits of precision. When the accuracy of the floating point number is insufficient, we can use the double to define the number. **The double is the same as a float but with a greater precision. To extend precision further we can use a long double, which consumes 80 bits of memory space.**

For example, float a;

Void is used to specify the type of a function.

The size and range of each data type is shown in Table 2.1.

Table 2.1: Data Types, Sizes, and Ranges

Type	Size (bits)	Range
Char or signed char	8	–128 to 127
Unsigned char	8	0 to 255
Int or signed int	16	–32768 to 32767
Unsigned int	16	0 to 65535
Short int or signed short int	8	–128 to 127
Unsigned short int	8	0 to 255
Long int or signed long int	32	–2147483648 to 2147483647
Unsigned long int	32	0 to 4294967295
Float	32	3.4 e-38 to 3.4 e+38
Double	64	1.7 e-308 to 1.7e+308
Long double	80	3.4 e-4932 to 3.4 e+4932

Note that short, long, signed, and unsigned are modifiers. These modifiers define the amount of storage allocated to the variable. Also remember that as per ANSI **rules:**

short int <= int <= long int

float <= double <= long double

This means that a 'short int' should assign less than or the same amount of storage as an 'int' and the 'int' should require the same or fewer bytes than a 'long int'.

It is possible to find out how much storage is allocated to a data type by using the **sizeof operator.** These ranges are defined in the **limits.h** header file.

Variables

A variable is a named area of storage that can hold a single value (numeric or character). Every variable used in the program should be de-

clared to the compiler. This declaration tells us two things:

    1.   Tells the compiler the name of the variable

    2.   Tells the type of variable that it holds

Syntax

    variable-name1, variable-name1, ... variable-name-n;

For example,

int a;

float k;

double j;

Also, we can initialize these variables if needed:

int a= 10;

float k = 80.80;

double j = 90.89765;

When we have many variables to be declared, they are separated by commas and must end with a semicolon.

Rules for Forming Variable Names

1. A variable name must start with a letter.

2. A variable name is a combination of 1 to 8 letters, digits, or underscores. Some compilers allow it up to 40 characters.

3. A variable name must not have any commas or blank spaces.

4. A variable name must not have any special symbols other than underscores.

Invalid variable names: 2hb, we b, #west, $123se

Valid variable names: e_p_f, _wepp, ai

2.6 ENUMERATION

There are two types of user-defined type declarations in C. In the first, a user can define an identifier that represents an existing data type. The user-defined data type can later be used to declare variables. Its syntax is:

typedef type identifier;

Here, 'type' represents existing data type and 'identifier' refers to the name given to the data type.

For example,

> typedef int age;

> typedef float marks;

Here, 'age' is an integer type and 'marks' is a float type. Now they can be later used to declare variables as follows:

age a1, a2;

marks m1, m2;

So now a1 and a2 are indirectly declared to be of type age only and age is of type integer, so a1 and a2 are also of type integers only.

The second type of user-defined data type is enum (or enumeration). It is defined as follows:

enum identifier {value1, value2, …value n};

Its **syntax** is:

enum identifier v1, v2, v3, v4, … vn

where identifier is a user-defined enumerated data type, which can be used to declare variables that have one of the values enclosed within braces. The enumerated variables v1, v2, … vn can have only one of the values value1, value2, … value n.

For example,

enum day { Monday, Tuesday, … Sunday};

enum day week_st, week end;

week_st = Monday;

week_end = Friday;

if (wk_st = =Tuesday)

> week_en = Saturday;

Modifiers
Please note that one can alter the data storage of any data type by preceding it with certain modifiers. These are called data type modifiers.

They include short, long, unsigned, and signed. Not all combinations of types and modifiers are allowed in C. **Also note that *long and short* are modifiers** that make it possible for a data type to use either more or less memory.

Type Qualifiers

A type qualifier is used to refine the declaration of a variable, a function, and parameters by specifying whether the value of a variable can be changed or the value of a variable must always be read from memory rather than from a register. In C they are of two types:

1. const

2. volatile

Let us discuss them one by one.

I. const Qualifier

A const qualifier tells the C compiler that the value of a variable cannot be changed after its initialization. For example,

const float pi = 3.1417;

That is, now pi cannot be changed throughout the program.

Another way of doing this is using the #define preprocessor directive as follows:

#define PI 3.1417

But please remember that const and #define are different. #define constants are declared at the beginning of the program, even before main( ). On the other hand, const variables can be placed anywhere within the program. So const has finer control than #define. #define cannot be placed anywhere in the program. This gives an error.

II. Volatile Qualifier

The volatile qualifier declares a data type that can have its value changed in ways outside the control or detection of the compiler, like a variable updated by the system clock. This prevents the compiler from optimizing code referring to the object by storing the object's value in a register and rereading it from there rather than from memory, where it may have changed. **Please understand that the volatile modifier is a directive to the compiler's optimizer that operations involving this variable should not be optimized in certain ways.** A volatile modifier may be used in two cases:

Case 1: A memory-mapped hardware device may use it.

Case 2: Shared memory may use it.

Also understand that a system has a set of registers that can be accessed faster than its memory. This is because registers are faster than memory. A good compiler will perform some type of optimization called **redundant load and store removal.**

Volatile is a special type of modifier which informs the compiler that the value of the variable may be changed by external entities other than the program itself. This is necessary for certain programs compiled with optimizations—if a variable were not defined as volatile, then the compiler may assume that certain operations involving the variable are safe to optimize away when in fact they aren't. **Volatile** is particularly relevant when working with embedded systems (where a program may not have complete control of a variable) and multithreaded applications.

Concept of Local and Global Variables

In C, two types of variables are used:

(a) Local variables

(b) Global variables

Local variables are the variables whose scope is limited within the block in which they are defined or the function in which they are defined. They are always defined at the top of the block. When a local variable is defined, it is not initialized by the system; in fact, you must initialize it as a programmer. When the execution of a block or a function starts the variable is available and when the block ends the variable dies.

For example,

```
int x= 40;
main( )
  {
      int x = 20;
      printf("\n%d", x);
  }
```

The output of this program will be 20. Why? As we can see in the first line, we have initialized x to 40. This is known as a **global declaration of x and the variable is known as a global variable.** On the other hand, within main( )

again x is initialized to 20. Now, x is a local variable. And **the rule is that whenever there is a conflict between a local and a global variable, it is the local variable that gets first priority. Also note that since the global variable is available to the entire program, it need not be passed as a parameter.**

NOTE *There are two ways by which data can be made available to other parts of the program. Either declare them as global variables or pass them as parameters or arguments.*

Global variables are declared at the top of the program file. They are initialized automatically by the system when you define them.

2.7 OPERATORS

An operator is a symbol that causes the compiler to take action. In an expression like sum = a + b; we say that '+' is an operator while 'a' and 'b' are operands. C also supports certain operators that are discussed below.

Arithmetic Operators

C provides two unary and five binary arithmetic operators (see Table 2.2).

Table 2.2: Showing Arithmetic Operators in C

Symbol	Meaning
+	Unary plus
–	Unary minus
*	Multiplication
/	Division
%	Modulus (remainder operator)
+	Binary Addition
–	Binary Subtraction

In the statement ($u*v + w$), the multiplication operation is performed first and then addition is done. This is because * has higher priority than +. In general, multiplication, division, and modulus operators have higher precedence than the binary addition and subtraction operators.

Increment/Decrement Operators

In C, we have ++ (increment) and decrement (− −) operators that increment or decrement the variable's value by 1. This can be done in two ways:

(a) ++ count; and − − count; (called **pre-increment**)

(b) count + +; and count − −; (called **post-increment**)

Please note here that if we use these increment/decrement operators as count++; or count− −; they produce the same effect. However, also note that if you use these operators in an expression such as

count = count++;

or count =++count;

then these two expressions will not produce the same effect. This is because in the first expression, the value of count is assigned to count-variable (on the left-hand side) and the count's value will be incremented by one. On the other hand, **in the second expression, the count value increments first and then it is assigned to the variable −count on the left-hand side.**

We are in a position to solve an example now.

Example **1: Write a C program to show implement the concept of post- and pre-increment operators.**

Solution 1: The program is as follows:

```c
#include<stdio.h>
void main( )
  {
      int counter, precount, postcount;
      counter = 10;
      precount = ++counter;
      postcount= counter++;
      printf("%d %d\n",precount,postcount);
      counter=50;
      postcount = counter--;
      precount = --counter;
      printf("%d %d\n",postcount,precount);
  }
```

OUTPUT (after running):

11 11

50 48

Assignment Operators

We have already studied how the assignment operator assigns the value of the expression which is on its right to the left-side variable. Each assignment statement itself returns a value.

For example,

counter1=counter2 =1;

In this statement, the effect is to assign the value of 1 to both of the variables—counter1 and counter2. **Please note here that the assignment operator has right-to-left associativity;** that is, here counter2 is assigned a value of 1 first and then it is assigned to the variable counter1.

Arithmetic Assignment Operators°°

C provides arithmetic assignment operators that also shorten expressions.

For example,

counter = counter + 50;

Can also be written as counter += 50;

Table 2.3 shows the arithmetic assignment operators.

Table 2.3: Arithmetic Assignment Operators

Symbol	Meaning
+=	Addition Assignment
−=	Subtraction Assignment
*=	Multiplication Assignment
/=	Division Assignment
%=	Modulus Assignment

Relational Operators

Relational operators are used to compare two expressions. When two expressions are compared they return either a true or false value. C supports the relational operators shown in Table 2.4.

Table 2.4: Relational Operators

Symbol	Meaning
>	Greater than
<	Less than
= =	Equal to
!=	Not equal to
<=	Less than or equal to
>=	Greater than or equal to

Please note here that, in general, relational operators are used in conditional expressions that are responsible for program flow statements. These operators are used within the program control flow statement.

Logical Operators

In C, three types of logical operators are available (see Table 2.5).

Table 2.5: Showing Logical Operators

Symbol	Meaning
&&	Logical AND
||	Logical OR
!=	Logical NOT

Logical operators use true/false of expression to return a true or false value. The logical && operator returns a true value if both of its expressions are true. The logical || operator returns a true value if either of two expressions or both expressions are true. The logical ! operator works on a single expression. If the expression results in true then the NOT operator makes it false or vice versa.

Bitwise Operator

Bitwise operators perform operations on the bit level. **Please remember that you can use these operators with integer expressions only but not on floats or doubles. Also remember that with the help of these operators you can access and manipulate individual bits also.** The bitwise operators are shown in Table 2.6.

Table 2.6: Showing Bitwise Operators

Symbol	Meaning
&	Bitwise AND
|	Bitwise OR
^	Bitwise exclusive OR (XOR)
>>	Bitwise right shift
<<	Bitwise left shift
~	1s complement

NOTE *Logical operators work on expressions while bitwise operators work on bits.*

Let us now see how the bitwise AND Operator (&) works.

Bitwise AND Operator (&)

The bitwise AND operator works on two operands. It compares these two operands on a bit-by-bit basis. The truth table shown in Table 2.7 demonstrates how it works.

Table 2.7: Bitwise AND

A	B	A & B
0	0	0
0	1	0
1	0	0
1	1	1

For example, say one number is 12 and the other is 24. We know that an integer takes 2 bytes or 16 bits in memory, but for simplicity's sake, we will just take 8 bits and do the bitwise ANDing of these two numbers as follows:

That is, numb1 = 12 = 00001100

numb2 = 24 = 00011000

Now the expression numb1 & numb2 is interpreted as

00001100

& <u>00011000</u>

<u>00001000</u>

Note here that the result is in binary form only. Its equivalent decimal number is 8. Thus, the expression, numb1 & numb2 will return a decimal value of 8. **Please note here that the operation is being performed on individual bits and this operator of ANDing bits is completely independent of each other. Also note that this bitwise AND operator is used in general to check whether a particular bit of an operand is ON or OFF.** For example, say the bit pattern is 10010100 and you want to check whether a particular bit of an operand is ON or OFF (i.e., 0 or 1). To do so we will create a mask (i.e., we will keep the fourth bit of this mask as 1 and all others 0s) and then bitwise AND the two as follows:

10010100	(the given number)
<u>00010000</u>	(the 8-bit mask)
00010000	(result)

This means the result is 0001000 after ANDing and that is 16 in decimal. This further implies that the fourth bit is ON.

NOTE *Inside your system the bit pattern is numbered from 0 to 7 but from right to left rather than from left to right.*

Bitwise OR Operator (|)

Similarly, the bitwise OR operator works as shown in Table 2.8.

Table 2.8 Bitwise OR Operators

A	B	A|B
0	0	0
0	1	1
1	0	1
1	1	1

Please note here that the OR operation returns 1 when any of the two bits or both bits are 1. For example, for the above two numbers (12 and 24) numb1 | numb2 yields:

10010100	(the given first number)
<u>00011000</u>	(the second number)
00011100	(result)

This means the result is 0001110 after ORing, which is 28 in decimal. Thus, the expression numb1 | numb2 returns a decimal value of 28.

Also note that the bitwise OR operator is generally used to set a particular bit in a number ON. Thus, if you want to set the fifth bit of a number ON then you will OR this number with the bit pattern 00100000.

Bitwise exclusive OR (XOR) Operator (^)

The Bitwise XOR operator is used to perform an exclusive OR operation between two bit patterns. **Please note that the XOR operator returns 1 only if one of the two bits is 1.** Table 2.9 shows its truth table.

Table 2.9 Bitwise XOR Operator.

A	B	A ^ B
0	0	0
0	1	1
1	0	1
1	1	0

Also note that the XOR operator is used to toggle a bit ON or OFF.

For example,

If numb1 = 12

and numb2 = 24

then (numb1 ^ numb2) yields

00001100

`00011000

00001000 (result)

This yields 20 (decimal).

One (1s) Complement Operator

The bitwise 1s complement operator complements every bit of the bit pattern (i.e., 0s replaced by 1s and vice versa). Its truth table is shown in Table 2.10.

Table 2.10. One (1s) Complement Operator

A	~A
0	1
1	0

Right Shift Operator (>>)

The bitwise right shift operator shifts integer values right a specified number of bits. The right-hand side of the operator specifies the number of places the bits are shifted.

For example,

numb1 >> 4;

shifts all bits four places to the right. If numb1 = 154, numb1>>4 yields 5 in decimal value (00000101).

Please note that when the bits are shifted right, blanks are created on the left and these blanks are filled with zeros.

Left Shift Operator (<<)

The bitwise left shift operator shifts integer values left a specified number of bits. The right-hand side of the operator specifies the number of places the bits are shifted.

For example,

numb1 << 4;

shifts all bits four places to the left. If numb1 = 154, numb1<<4 yields 224 in decimal value (11100000).

Comma Operator

The comma operator (,) allows two different expressions to appear in one statement. *Each comma-separated expression is evaluated and the value returned from the group is the value of the rightmost expression.*

For example,

```
#include<stdio.h>
void main( )
 {
      int x, y, z;
      x=y=20;
```

```
    z = (x++, y--, x+y);
    printf("%d", z);
}
```

First, x++ is evaluated, then y– –, and finally x+y. Since x+y is the rightmost expression, the result of x+y is assigned to z. **Thus, the output is 40.**

The sizeof Operator

The sizeof operator returns the number of bytes the operand occupies in memory. It is *a unary operator*. Please remember the following points regarding the sizeof operator:

1. The sizeof operator has the same precedence as prefix increment/decrement operators.

2. The parentheses used with sizeof are required when the operand is a data type. With variables or constants, the parentheses are not necessary.

For example,

```
#include<stdio.h>
void main( )
  {
        printf("\n%d", sizeof(int));
        printf("\n%d", sizeof(long));
        printf("\n%d", sizeof(float));
        printf("\n%d", sizeof(double));
        printf("\n%d", sizeof(long double));
        printf("\n%d", sizeof(char));
  }
```

OUTPUT (after running):

2

4

4

8

10

1

Application: The sizeof operator is used, in general, to find out the length of secondary data types like arrays, structures, classes, and so on, when their sizes are unknown to the programmer.

Ternary Operator

C also provides a ternary operator that takes three operands (hence its name). Its syntax is:

expression1 ? expression2 : expression3;

That is, if expression1 is true, then expression2 is evaluated; else, expression3 is evaluated. **The ternary operators are also called conditional operators.**

For example,

```
#include<stdio.h>
void main( )
  {
        int u, v, w;
         u = 20;
         v= 30;
        w = (u > v ? u : v);
        printf("\n Greatest out of the two is %d", w);
  }
```

OUTPUT (after running):

Greater out of the two is 30

Precedence and Associativity

The priority in which operations are performed in an expression is called precedence and the order of evaluation, when they have equal priority, is called associativity. Table 2.11 shows precedence and associativity in C.

Table 2.11: Precedence and Associativity in C

Operators	Priority	Associativity
( ) [ ] . –	Highest	Left to right
- ~ ! * & ++ -- sizeof		Right to left
* / %		Left to right
+ –		Left to right
<< >>		Left to right
= = !=		Left to right
&		Left to right
		Left to right
|		Left to right
&&		Left to right

||			Left to right
?:			Left to right
= *= /= %= += -= <= &= |= ^=			Right to left
,		Lowest	Left to right

From the table, it is crystal clear that the comma operator has the lowest priority and the function expression operator has the highest priority. **Please note that the operations that have equal precedence are evaluated according to the associativity given in Table 2.11.**

For example, consider the following statement:

total = x * y/z;

The evaluation computes the value of x * y and then divides z into that value and assigns the resultant value to the variable 'total'. **Also note that to override this associativity, put parentheses around the expression as follows:**

total = x * (y/z);

This expression now computes (y/z) first, multiplies x by that value, and assigns the resultant value to 'total' (the variable). **Sometimes we do not need the default precedence to produce the desired result. For example,**

total = x + y * z;

Here, since the multiplication operator has a higher precedence over addition, the expression calculates y*z first and then adds this value to x. On the other hand, if you wish to compute x+y first and then multiply that result by z, use parentheses as follows:

total = (x + y) * z;

The rule can be stated as follows: "Parentheses are required whenever you want to override associativity as the default precedence. But within a pair of parentheses, the same hierarchy (as in Table 2.11) is operative. Also, if you have a nested set of parentheses, the operation within the innermost parentheses will be performed first, followed by the operation within the next innermost pair of parentheses, and so on."

2.8 TYPE CASTING (OR COERCION) IN C

C supports different data types like int, float, long, double, and so on. Each of these has a different range of values because of their size and their signed/unsigned properties. In practice, an expression can have an operation between two different data types (one can be an integer and another can be a float or vice versa). To handle such situations, C provides certain rules of type conversion in these cases. **Please understand that when a compiler encounters different types of operands in the same expression, the smaller type variable is promoted to a larger type variable.** The order of inbuilt data types is shown in Table 2.12.

Table 2.12: Inbuilt Data Types

Data Type	Number of Bytes	Order
long double	10	6 (largest)
double	8	5
float	4	4
long	4	3
int	2	2
char	1	1

Thus, if you assign a variable of a smaller type—say, an int—to a larger type—say, a float—then the (int) smaller value is promoted to a (float) larger value. On the other hand, if you assign a value of a larger type—say, a float—to a smaller type—say, an int—then the larger value is demoted and excess data can even be truncated or, in some cases, the compiler will warn you unless you implicitly type cast it.

This is done by the compiler automatically. But sometimes a programmer can also do type casting, which **is a technique by which you can convert one type to another type explicitly.** Typecasting/coercion in C is done as follows:

type(expression);

Here, 'type' is any valid data type in C to which conversion is to be performed.

2.9 CONDITIONAL EXECUTING USING IF-ELSE

The if statement is followed by a logical expression in which data is compared and a decision is made based on the result of comparison. Its syntax is:

```
if (testcondition)
{
    statement (s);
}
else
{
    statement (s);
}
```

Here, when the **testcondition** is true, the statements enclosed in the **if clause** are executed; otherwise, statements enclosed in the **else clause** are executed.

The **if statement** is used to create a decision structure which allows a program to have more than one path of execution. It can be represented by the flowchart in Figure 2.1.

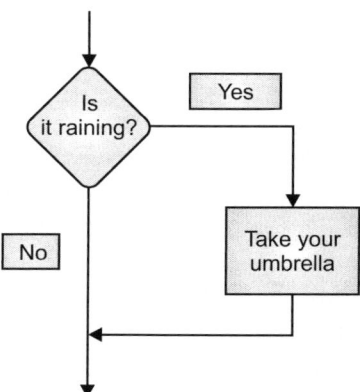

Figure 2.1: If-Else Decision Structure Logic Flowchart

Relational operators like >, <, >=, <=, = =, and != may be used. **But please remember that when you use the <= or >= operators, there is no space between them.**

Even though an **if statement** usually spans more than one line, it is really one long statement. For example, the following if statements are identical except for the style in which they are written:

if (salary > 100000)

printf("\n It is a good salary");

if (salary > 1000000) printf("\n It is a good salary");

Also note that in both of these examples, the compiler considers the if statement and the conditionally executed statement as one unit, with a semicolon properly placed at the end. Indentions and spacing are for human readers of a program, not the compiler.

Rules for Using if Statements

Rule 1: The conditionally executed statement should appear on the line after the *if statement*.

Rule 2: The conditionally executed statement should be indented one level from the *if statement*.

Recall that in most editors, when you press the tab key, you are indenting by one level. By indenting the conditionally executed statement, you are causing it to stand out visually. This is so you can tell at a glance what part of the program the *if statement* executes. This is the standard way of writing if statements.

NOTE

1. Don't put semicolons after the if(testcondition) portion, because the if statement is incomplete without its conditional part. But if you place a semicolon here, the compiler assumes that you have terminated the statement. No error will be displayed but the compiler will assume that you are placing a null statement there. Also note that the null statement (an empty statement that does nothing) will become the conditionally executed statement. The statement that you intended to be conditionally executed will be disconnected from the if statement and will always execute. For example,

int u=5, v=10;

if (u>v);

System.out.println("u is greater than v" + u);

The if statement in this code snippet is prematurely terminated with a semicolon. Because the println statement is not connected to the if statement, it will always execute.

2. Now consider another example,

```
if( salary > 200000)
  {
      tax = .30 * basic;
      bonus = 800;
  }
```

Herein, if the condition is true, then both of the statements in the braces will be executed in the order they appear. But if, say, the braces were left out or missed by mistake by the programmer, then the if statement conditionally executes only the very next statement—that is, say the braces are left out, as follows:

if(salary > 200000)

tax = .30 * basic;

bonus = 800;

In this case, only the statement tax = .30 * basic will be executed conditionally and the other one (bonus=800;) will always be executed.

Next let us see the working and the syntax of nested if-else.

When an if-else control appears as a statement in another if-else, it is known as a nested if-else construct. For example,

```
if (boolExpr1)
  if (boolExpr2)
     if (boolExpr3) {
       stml1;
       }
     else {
       Stml2;
       }
  else {
       Stml3;
       }
  }
```

This code is very confusing! **Please note that there is no else part for the first if construct.** The compiler associates the else part with the closest inner **if** construct which does not have an else part. Thus, each else part is associated with the respective **if.** To avoid this confusion, it is better to use braces appropriately for the association of each **else** part with its **if.** By using the braces, any **else** part may be associated with a particular **if** construct.

Let us now see the if-else-if control construct.

The else-if control construct follows the if control construct to allow multiple decision making.

Syntax

```
if (boolExpr1)
 {
      Stml1;
 }
 else
 if (boolExpr2)
     {
          Stml2;
     }
     else
      if (boolExpr3)
      {
          Stml3;
      }
   ............ .
          else if (boolExprN-1)
          {
              StmlN-1;
          }
          else {
              StmlN;
          }
```

Herein, if any **boolExpr** returns a true value, the **Stmt** associated with that **if** is executed and then the next statement to the whole **else-if** construct is executed. If no expression returns a true value, the last **else** part is executed. If there is no instruction needed for the last **else** part, then it can be omitted or it can be used for displaying the error messages due to invalid conditions.

We are in a position to write simple programs now.

Example 1: **Write a C program to read a number from the keyboard and to check whether it is a positive number.**

Solution 1: The following is the program:

```c
#include<stdio.h>
void main( )
 {
      int numb;
      printf("\n Enter your number: ");
      scanf("%d", &numb);
      if (numb > = 0)
            printf("\n It is a positive number.");
 }
```

OUTPUT (after running):

Enter your number: 80

It is a positive number.

Example **2: Write a C program to check whether the given year is a leap year. A leap year is a year which is divisible by 4 but not divisible by 100 (unless it is also divisible by 400).**

Solution 2:

```c
/* leap year program */
    #include<stdio.h>
    void main( )
     {
    int y;
    printf("\n Enter the year in four digits: ");
    scanf("%d", &y);
    if (( y % 4 ==0 && y%100 != 0) || (y %400==0 ))
     printf("\n\t It is a leap year");
    else
     printf("\n\t It is not a leap year");
     }
    }
```

OUTPUT (after running):

Enter the year in four digits: 2000

2000 is a leap year

2.10 SWITCH AND BREAK

C provides an extremely handy **switch-case construct** to facilitate selecting between multiple alternatives. Within the block of code controlled by a **switch statement,** the programmer can place **case statements** and (optionally) a **default statement. For example,**

```
switch (x) {
    case 0 : str = "none"; break;
    case 1 :
        str = "single" ; break;
    case 2 :
        str = "pair" ;
        break;
    default : str = "many" ;
}
```

Each case keyword is followed by an integer constant, followed by a colon. **Please note that the code block belonging to each *case* can immediately follow the colon on the same line or on separate lines.** If the value of x is not one of the values provided for in case statements, the **default statement** code is executed. **Also note that if there is no default statement and no exact match, execution resumes after the *switch* block of code.**

In the program example above, break statements are used that terminate the code for each *case* and cause execution to continue after the **switch code block. Please understand that if a break does not appear, execution falls-through to execute code in subsequent *cases*. For example,**

```
switch(x) {
  case 0 : printf("A, ");
  case 1: printf("B, "); break;
  default: printf("C");
}
```

Herein, a value of 0 for x would cause output of "A, B,".

Also understand that most of the errors that occur when we work with switch structures seem to be related to forgetting about fall-through. Therefore, we must always carefully check for the *break statements* whenever we write a program using a *switch statement.* The block of code associated with *each case* can be as simple as a single statement or it can be hundreds of lines of code. Moreover, this code block can have another **switch statement. But for better readability we should convert any com-**

plex code into a separate method and simply call that method from the case statement.

The following points may be made regarding switch statements:

1. The expression in a **switch statement** must evaluate to one of the 32-bit or smaller integer types: **byte, char, short, or int.** The compiler checks that the legal range of the integer type covers all of the constants used in the **case statements** in the **switch code block.**

2. The compiler throws an error if the legal range of the integer type in the switch statement does not cover all of the constants used in the **case statements.**

3. Each **case statement** must have a literal constant or a value the compiler can evaluate as a constant of a 32-bit or smaller integer type.

4. **It cannot have a float constant, a long constant, a variable, an expression, a string, or any other object.**

5. **The compiler checks that the constant is in the range of the integer type in the switch statement.**

6. **If you are using a byte variable in the switch statement, the compiler objects to it if it finds case statement constants outside the –128 through 127 range that a byte primitive can have.**

7. The code block associated with a case must be complete within the case. That is, we can't have an if-else or loop structure that spreads across multiple case statements.

8. Constants in case statements can be integer literals or they can be variables defined as **static and final.**

9. If a *continue label* is used instead of a break in a switch statement, then the next statement following it will not be executed; rather, it will resume the loop with the next value of the iterator.

10. The switch statement is an alternative to an if-else or if-else-if control construct.

11. The expressions and case labels are restricted to the following types: byte, short, char, int, and enum.

12. The expression is evaluated first and its value is then matched against the *case labels* that must be constant values. When a match is found, the statement following that case will be executed. If there is no match with any of the case labels, the statement following the default (if present) will be executed.

13. Different case statements in a switch-case statement may be arranged in any order.

14. The *CaseExpressions* of each *case* statement must be unique.

Switch versus If-Else (a Comparison)

The if-else statement can handle ranges, for instance as follows:

```
if(marks > 80 && marks <=100)
        //statements
else if(marks > 70 && marks <=90)
        //statements
```

But, unfortunately, the switch cannot handle these ranges. Each switch-case label must be a single value and that value must be an integer or a character. You cannot even use a floating case label. As far as the ranges or floating point numbers are concerned, you must use an if-else construct. On the other hand, if the case labels are integer constants or character constants, then the switch statement is more efficient, easier to write, and more readily understood.

We are in a position to write some programs using switch statements now.

Example 1: **Write a C program to check whether a supposed vowel read from the keyboard is a vowel. Use switch statements only. Now rewrite this program with mixed integer and character constants. Will the program compile?**

Solution 1: We write two separate programs—one with integer constants in case and the other with both integer and character constants.

//vowel program using switch with character constants only (in case)

```
#include<stdio.h>
void main( )
 {
   char ch;
   printf("\n Enter any vowel:");
```

```
    scanf("%c", ch);
    switch (ch)
      {
          case 'a':
                 printf("You entered a.");
                 break;
          case 'e':
                 printf("You entered e.");
                 break;
          case 'i':
                 printf("You entered i.");
                 break;
          case 'o':
                 printf("You entered o.");
                 break;
          case 'u':
                 printf("You entered u.");
                 break;
          default:
                 printf("You have not entered any vowel.");
      }
    }
```

OUTPUT (after running):

Enter any vowel: i

You entered i.

Enter any vowel: u

You entered u.

Enter any vowel: r

You have not entered any vowel.

//vowel program using switch with character constants and integer (in case), both.

```
#include<stdio.h>
void main( )
  {
    char ch;
    printf("\n Enter any vowel:");
    scanf("%c", ch);
    switch (ch)
```

```
        {
                case 'a':
                        printf("You entered a.");
                        break;
                case '101':
                        printf("You entered e.");
                        break;
                case 'i':
                        printf("You entered i.");
                        break;
                case '111':
                        printf("You entered o.");
                        break;
                case 'u':
                        printf("You entered u.");
                        break;
                default:
                        printf("You have not entered any vowel.");
        }
}
```

OUTPUT (after running):

Enter any vowel: i

You entered i.

Enter any vowel: u

You entered u.

Enter any vowel: r

You have not entered any vowel.

The output is therefore the same in both cases. Switches allow executing a set of statements for more than one case label. We have seen that whenever a switch statement finds a match, it executes all of the subsequent lines in the switch unless it encounters a break statement. **Also note here that if you don't use a default case and the switch statement does not find a match, then nothing gets executed within the switch statement and control is transferred to the next statement, if any, following the control structure.**

The goto Statement

A goto statement is an unconditional control statement. It directly takes the "control the program" statement wherever you want. Usually we don't recommend the use of a goto statement, as it is an unstructured way of programming. It makes programs nonreadable, unreliable, and difficult to debug.

For example,

start: **if (number < 0) {**

                    i++;

                        goto start;

                    }

Here we see that if a number < 0 then i++ is done and then an unconditional jump is made at the label 'start'. The label ends with a semicolon, after which the statements are placed.

It is generally recommended to use other control structures and loop statements whenever possible.

2.11 THE CONCEPT OF LOOPS—WHILE LOOP, DO-WHILE LOOP, FOR LOOP, NESTED LOOPS, BREAK STATEMENT, CONTINUE STATEMENT

A loop is a part of a program that repeats. **A loop is a control structure that causes a statement or group of statements to repeat.** C has three types of looping structures:

(a) while loop

(b) do-while loop

(c) for loop

Let us discuss these one by one now.

The while Loop

The while loop construct is used when a single statement or a group of statements is to be executed repeatedly as long as a given condition is satisfied. It consists of a *Boolean expression (boolExpr)* for modeling the condition and one or more statements *(Stmt)*. First the *boolExpr* is evaluated. If it returns true, the *Stmt* in the while loop is executed. The loop is terminated when the *boolExpr* yields a false value. The **boolExpr** is an expression that yields a Boolean literal. The **syntax of a while loop** is shown next, followed by its **working** (in Figure 2.2).

Syntax

```
while (boolExpr)
       {
        Stmt;
       }
```

Working of the while Loop

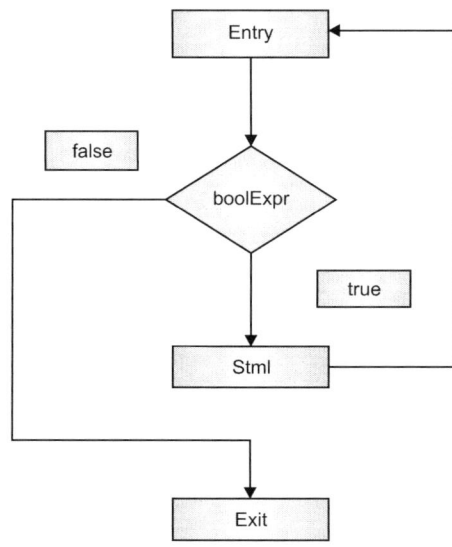

Figure 2.2: Syntax and Working of a while Loop

Explanation: The first line shown in the syntax is known as **a loop header.** The **Stmt part** is executed when the **boolExpr** returns a true value. When it returns a false value, the loop is terminated. It is possible to exit the while loop without executing the statement part in the loop if the **boolExpr** yields a false value the first time. **Thus, the minimum number of times the while loop is executed is zero. Please understand that since the condition is tested before entering the body of the loop, it is also known as pretested loop or a top-tested loop. Also understand that when the** *boolExpr* **always returns a true value, the loop becomes an infinite loop. For example,**

```
while (true) {
        Stmt;
    }
```

This is an **infinite loop.** Here, the Boolean literal true is used in place of a boolExpr. It may also be written as follows to form an infinite loop:

```
while (! false) {
        Stmt;
    }
```

Thus, if a loop does not have a way of stopping, it is called an infinite loop. **An infinite loop continues to repeat until the program is interrupted.** For example,

```
int numb =1;
while (numb <=5)
  {
        printf("Hello");
  }
```

This is an infinite loop because it does not contain a statement that changes the value of the numb variable. Each time the Boolean expression is tested, numb will contain the value 1.

Now, say, by mistake the programmer has put a semicolon at the end of the while loop as follows:

```
while(numb <=5);
```

Please note here that the semicolon at the end of the first line is assumed to be a null statement and disconnects the while statement from the block that comes after it. This while loop will forever execute the null statement, which does nothing.

Now, say, you forget to put the braces after the while header as follows:

```
int numb =1;
while(numb <=5)
        printf("Hello");
        numb++;
```

Here, the numb++ statement is not in the body of the loop. Because the braces are missing, the while statement only executes the statement that immediately follows it. **This loop will also execute infinitely because there is no code in its body that changes the numb variable.**

The rules that you must follow can be stated as follows:

Rule 1: If there is only one statement repeated by the loop, it should appear on the line after the while statement and be indented one additional level.

Rule 2: If the loop repeats a block, each line inside the braces should be indented.

There is no semicolon at the end of the loop header. Also note that this while loop works just like an if statement that executes over and over again as long as the expression in the parentheses is true. **Each repetition of a loop is known as an iteration. But the important feature of this loop is that it will never iterate if the Boolean expression is false to start with.**

Applications of a while Loop

1. **A while loop** can be used to create input routines that repeat until acceptable data is entered.

2. **This loop is useful for input validations also. We define input validation as the process of inspecting data given to a program by the user and finding out if it is valid.**

3. The read operation that takes place just before the loop starts is known as a **priming read.**

Before further discussion, let us solve some examples.

Q1. Give the general logic of performing input validation.

[**Hint:** The following steps are used for input validation:

1. Read the first input value.

2. Check whether the value is valid or invalid.

3. If it is invalid, then display the error message and read another value.

4. Else continue with the rest of the program.]

Q2. Give the output of the following code snippet:

```
int i =40;
while (i >=0) {
 if ( i%2 ==0)
     printf("d", i);
 i++;
 }
```

[**Hint:** It prints 40. Try to change i++ to i– – and find your result].

Q3. Write a C program to print the reverse of a number.

[**Hint:**

```
void main ( ) {
        int n;
        printf ("Enter a number:");
        scanf ("%d", &n);
        printf ("The reversed number is:");
        while (k !=0) {
        /*extract the individual digits by repeat-
        ed mod and division*/
                int m = n % 10;
                k=n/10;
                n=k;
                printf ("%d", m);   //print the digit
                }
        }
}
```

OUTPUT (after running):

Enter a number: 321

The reversed number is: 123].

Q4. Write a C program to find the GCD (greatest common divisor) of two positive numbers by different methods:

Method 1:

The GCD of 2 positive numbers is defined as the largest common divisor of both the integers. For instance, the GCD of 24 and 36 would be:

Divisors of 24 are 1, 2, 3, 4, 6, 8, 12, 24

Divisors of 36 are 1, 2, 3, 4, 6, 9, 12, 18, 36

Thus, the largest/greatest common divisor is 12. So the GCD of 24 and 36 is 12.

Method 2:

You can use **Euclid's algorithm** as follows to find the GCD of two numbers:

while m is greater than zero

do

if n is greater than m, swap m and n.

subtract n from m.

end

final n is the GCD.

Method 3:

Yet another algorithm may be followed:

1. Read 2 numbers a, b.

2. Repeat through step 5 while a is not equal to 0.

3. Set gcd =a

4. a = b % a

5. b = gcd

6. Print gcd

7. Exit

[**Hint:** Method 1:

```
void main( )
    {
    int n1, n2;
    printf("\n\t Enter two numbers:");
    scanf("%d %d", n1, n2);
    int greaterNumber = n2;
    int gcd =1;
    /* assign the greater value to the greaterNumber
    variable */
    if (n1 > n2)
        greaterNumber = n1;
    /* start finding GCD from the minimum gcd: 2 */
    int index =2;
    /* keep checking unless the index is larger than
    the greater value and */
    /*greater value is larger than 2 */
    while (index <= greaterNumber && greaterNumber
    > 2)
      {
        if ((n1 % index ==0) && (n2 % index ==0)) {
            gcd = index;
```

```
     }
     /* check the next value */
     index++
     }
     /*print the GCD */
      printf("\nGreatest Common Divisor (GCD) is %d",
      gcd);
      }
   }
```

OUTPUT (after running):

Enter two numbers

6

9

Greatest common divisor (GCD) = 3

Method 2

```
int gcd(int m1, int n1) {
      int m = m1;
      int n = n1;
      int temp;
      while (m >0) {
       if(n > m) {temp =n; n=m; m=temp; }
       m = m - n }
       return n; }
       void main( ) {
             cout<< gcd(24,18); }
       }
```

OUTPUT: 6
Method 3

```
void main( )
{
 int a ,b, gcd;
 a =b=gcd=0;
printf("\n\t Enter two numbers:");
scanf("%d %d, &a, &b);
while(a!=0)
{
        gcd =a;
        a= b% a;
```

```
                    b=gcd;
      }
   printf("GCD = %d",gcd);
   }
      }              ].
```

Q5. Enter a number from the keyboard and find out the Fibonacci series using a while loop.

   [Hint: void main( )

```
                     {
                       int a=0, b=1, c=0, size;
                     printf("\n\t Enter a range");
                     size = s;
                     printf("\n");
                     printf("Enter a and b:");
                     while(c <= size)
                       {
                            c = a +b;
                             if(c<=size)
                                   printf("%d\n", c);
                            a=b;
                            b=c;
                       }
                     }
                 }
```

OUTPUT (after running):

Enter a range

50

0

1

2

3

5

8

13

21

34].

Q6. Write a C program to read a number from the keyboard and find its factorial.

> **[Hint:**   void main( )

```
{
      int fact=1, b, c;
      printf("Enter a number:");
      scanf("%d", &b);
       c = b;
      while(c >0)
       {
             fact = fact * c;
             c--;
       }
      printf("\n   Factorial   of   b
      is:",fact);
}
    }
```

OUTPUT *(after running)*:

Enter a number: 3

The Factorial of 3 is 6.

Q7. Write a C program to check whether a given number is a palindrome.

> **[Hint:** The algorithm is given first:

1. Initialize s=0

2. Read number, num

3. Set b=num

4. Repeat through step 7 until (num > 0)

5. r=num % 10

6. s=(s*10) + r

7. num = num/10

8. If b is equal to s, then print "b is a palindrome" else print "b is not a palindrome"

9. Exit

```
/* palindrome program */
```

```
void main ( )
{
      int num, b, s=0, r;
      printf ("\n\t Enter a number:");
      scanf ("%d", &num);
      b=num;
      while (num > 0)
        {
r = num % 10;
s= (s * 10) + r;
num = num/10;
        }
          if (b = =s)
            printf("b is a palindrome");
          else
            printf("b is not a palindrome");
      }
}
```

OUTPUT (after running):

Enter a number

121

121 is a palindrome.

Run2:

Enter a number

123

123 is not a palindrome

Q8. Write an algorithm and the resulting C program to check whether a given number is an Armstrong number.

   [**Hint:** The algorithm is as follows:

1. Initialize s=0

2. Read number, num

3. Set b = num

4. Repeat through step 7 while num is greater than 0

5. r=num%10

6. s=s+(r°r°r)

7. num=num/10

8. If b is equal to s, then print "it is an Armstrong number" else print "it is not an Armstrong number"

9. Exit

The resulting program is as follows:

```
void main( )
{
        int num, b, s=0, r;
        printf( "Enter a number:");
        cin >> num;
        b = num;
        while (num > 0)
          {
                r = num % 10;
                s=s+ (r *r*r);
                num = num/10;
        }
    if ( b = =s)
        printf("b is an Armstrong number");
    else
        printf("b is not an Armstrong number");
    }
}
```

OUTPUT (after running):

Enter a number: 153

153 is an Armstrong number

Run2:

Enter a number: 15

15 is not an Armstrong number

Q9. Write a C program to check whether a given number is binary.

[**Hint:**

```
void main( )
        {
            int r=0,c=0, num, b;
```

```
                                      printf("Enter a number:");
                                      scanf("%d", &num);
                                      b = num;
                                      while(num > 0)
                                        {
                                              if((num % 10 ==0) ||
(num%10==1))

                                              c++;
                                              r++;
                                              num=num/10;
                                        }
                                      if(c= =r)
                                        printf( "b is a binary num-
ber.";

                                      else
                                        cout << b <<"is not a binary
number.");

                                        }
                          }
```

OUTPUT (after running):

Enter a number:

12345

12345 is not a binary number.

Enter a number:

11001011

11001011 is a binary number.

The do-while Loop

The general syntax of a do-while loop is as follows:

```
do
  {
  statement(s);
  } while (test-condition);
```

The do-while statement evaluates the test condition at the end of the loop. This loop guarantees that the loop will be executed at least once. **Whereas a loop is called a pretest loop or entry-controlled loop, a do-while loop is known as a posttest loop or exit-controlled loop.** A loop that uses another loop is called a **nested loop. Any type of loop may be used inside another loop. The rules for nested loops are as follows:**

Rule 1: An inner loop goes through all of its iterations for each iteration of an outer loop.

Rule 2: Inner loops complete their iterations before outer loops do.

Rule 3: To get the total number of iterations of a nested loop, multiply the number of iterations of all the loops.

Working of the do-while Loop

The do-while loop is similar to the while loop only but here the condition is evaluated after the statement is executed once. Its flowchart is as follows:

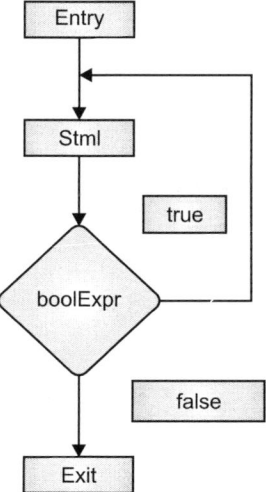

Please note that it is important to place a semicolon (;) after closing the Boolean expression in the do-while loop construct. This loop construct executes the statement part in the loop before the boolExpr is evaluated. **Also note that it is because of this reason that the minimum number of times the do-while loop is executed is one. The loop is terminated when the boolExpr yields a false value.** Because the condition is tested after execution of the body of the loop, it is also known as a **post-tested loop or bottom-tested loop.**

Notes

1. **The do-while loop is the same as the repeat-until control construct of PASCAL language except that the loop is terminated when the test condition returns a false value.**

2. **The do-while loop is a posttest loop which means its Boolean expression is tested after each iteration.**

3. **The do-while loop must be terminated with a semicolon.**

Questions

Before further discussion about the for-loop, let us solve some questions now.

Q1. Write an algorithm and hence a C program to develop a multitable program.

[**Hint:** The algorithm is as follows:

1. Initialize a=1.

2. Initialize b=1.

3. Print a°b.

4. Increment b by 1 (i.e., b = b+1).

5. Repeat steps 3 to 5 until (b <=3).

6. Increment a by 1 (i.e., a=a+1).

7. Repeat steps 2 to 7 until (a<=3).

8. Exit.

The C program is as follows:

```
void main ( )
 {
       int a, b;
       a=1;
       do
        {
             b=1;
             do
              {
        printf("\nValue of a and b is %d",
        (a *b));
             b++;
             } (while(b<=3);
             a++;
       }while(a<=3);
 }
 }
```

OUTPUT (after running):

Value of a and b is 1

Value of a and b is 2

Value of a and b is 3

Value of a and b is 3

Value of a and b is 4

Value of a and b is 6

Value of a and b is 3

Value of a and b is 6

Value of a and b is 9

Q2. Distinguish between while and do-while loops.

[**Hint:**

while loop	do-while loop
1. The test condition is evaluated first.	1. The loop is entered first and then the test condition is evaluated.
2. The minimum number of times the loop will be executed is zero.	2. The loop will be executed at least once.
3. It is also known as a pretest loop or entry-controlled loop.	3. It is also known as a posttest loop or exit-controlled loop.

4.　　　Its syntax is:
　　while(test-condition)
　　{
　　Statement(s);
　　}
	4. Its syntax is:
	do{
	statement(s);
	while(test-condition);

5. There is no need for a semicolon.	5. A semicolon is needed after the while statement in this loop.

The **for Loop**

The most common, frequently used, and versatile loop used in programs is the for loop. **It is used when a loop will be repeated a known number of times. In C, it can be used to execute for a known number of times or execute the loop repeatedly based on specific conditions.**

Syntax

```
for ( expression-1; boolExpr; expr3)
    {
```

```
            statement(s);
   }
```

Working of the for Loop

The working of the for loop is as follows:

1. First, expr1 is evaluated. It is usually used to initialize a counter.

2. Then boolExpr is evaluated to check for the condition for execution. If it returns a true value, then

   (a) **a statement in the loop is executed.**

   (b) **Expr2 is evaluated.**

   (c) **Control is then transferred to step 2.**

3. If the boolExpr returns a false value, the loop is terminated.

This means the working of the for loop is as follows:

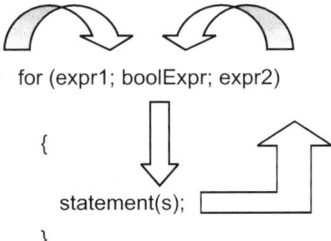

That is, first, ***expr1*** is evaluated. Then the condition is checked. If it is true, then the loop enters into the body (after the { brace) and executes the statements within it. After one iteration is over, control goes back to ***expr2*** and then again the ***boolExpr*** condition is checked. This is the process by which a for loop works. **Also note here that any one, two, or all of the three expressions can be omitted in a for loop but the two semicolons (;) must be placed separating the expressions. Also, expr1 and expr2 can be lists of expressions separated by a comma. Thus, expr1 or expr2 may become compound statements also.**

Remember the following points regarding for loops:

1. A for loop can also be written equivalently using ***while*** or ***do-while loops*** as follows:

   For loop implementation using while loop:

```
expr1;
while (boolExpr) {
    statements;
    expr2
}
```

Similarly, a for loop may be implemented by using a do-while loop also:

```
expr1;
do {
  statements;
  expr2
  }
while (boolExpr);
```

2. Any valid value can be initialized to expr1 that will act as the counter.

3. **The minimum number of times a for loop is executed is zero.**

4. It is also possible to declare the counter variable in a for loop itself—for example,

for (int count=1; count< 10; count++) {...}

5. We can also nest any of the three loops discussed so far into one another. **Such loops are called nested loops. Note that loops should not overlap each other. Also note that one type of loop construct can be nested in another type of loop construct. For instance, a for loop may be nested within a while loop or do-while loop and vice versa. This depends on the program statement that you are solving.**

6. We can also control the operation of a loop with **break and continue statements, with and without labels. The break statement immediately terminates the loop code block whereas the continue statement skips any remaining code in the block and continues with the next loop iteration.**

7. **A variable/iterator/counter variable** that is declared in a for statement can be referred to only inside the loop.

8. The following is the bare minimum for a loop (with missing parts):

for (;;){ }

9. These loops are counter-controlled loops. We can also write user-controlled loops (i.e., that allow the user to decide the number of iterations).

10. The first line of the for loop is also known as a **loop header.**

11. **Note that there is no semicolon after expr3.**

12. **A for loop is also a pretest loop as it checks for the condition before it performs an iteration.**

13. It is also possible to execute more than one statement in the initialization expression and the expr3 (increment/decrement). **Just remember that when you use multiple statements in any of the parts of the for loop header, simply separate the statements with commas. For instance,**

    for (int i=1, j=2; i<10; i--) {…}

14. The following is the for loop as an infinite loop:

    for (; ;)

15. A new feature of the for loop is that it is also able to iterate through collections without the explicit use of iterators. **Iterators are the programming patterns used to provide simple sequential access to a collection of objects without knowing a priori the type and the size of the specific collection accessed (to be discussed later).**

Rules Followed While Writing Triangle-Like Programs:

1. If values are repeated row-wise, then i is printed in printf.

2. If values are repeated column-wise, then j is printed in printf.

3. For any triangle problem, loop j will run either j<=i or j>=i.

4. There are two cases that arise (discussed below).

I. Normal Photo

That is, when the triangle looks like the following:

Rule: "In these cases, when photo will be normal, then both the loops, i and j, will run straight/normal, starting from 1 or otherwise both loops, i and j, will run in reverse. This is the rule.

II. Reverse Photo

Rule: "When photo appears reverse then one of the loops will run normal and second will run in reverse manner and vice versa."

Several examples based on these two rules like, PASCAL's triangle and FLOYD's triangle, are discussed later in this chapter.

Questions

Before further discussion, please solve the following questions.

Q1. Write a program to implement a Fibonacci series using a for loop control structure.

[**Hint:** A Fibonacci series is a series of numbers in which the first number is 0 and the second is 1. The next number is obtained by adding the previous 2 numbers:

$$F1=0$$

$$F2=1$$

$$F3= F2 + F1$$

In general, $Fn = f(n-1) + f(n-2)$ (where n is a positive number). The program follows:

```
void main( )
  {
    int i, n, f1, f2, f3;
        n=12;           /*first  12  fibonacci  numbers
        are displayed*/
        if(n <=1)
            printf("%d", n);
        else
        {
            f1 =0;
            f2 =1;
            f3 = f1 + f2;
            printf("%d", f3);
            for (i=2; i<=n; i++)
            {
```

```
                                        f3  =  f1  +  f2;
                                        f1  =  f2;
                                        f2  =  f3;
                                        printf("\t%d",  f3);
                        }
                 }
           }
     }
```

OUTPUTS *(after running):*

0	1	1	2	3	5	8	13	21	3

4   55   89   144

Dry run:

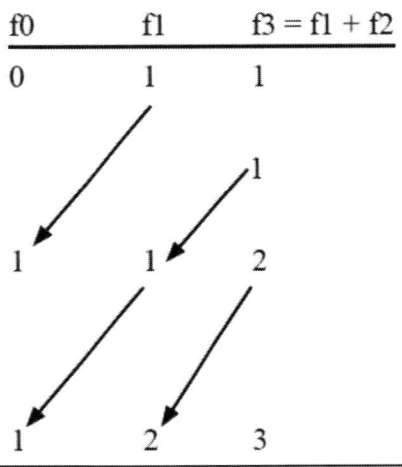

f0	f1	f3 = f1 + f2
0	1	1
		1
1	1	2
1	2	3

Let us now rewrite this program using a for loop:

```
void main( )
{
int i,  f0=0,f1=1,f2;
printf("%d %d",f0 ,f1);
for(i=3;i<=10;i++)
  {
    f2= f1 + f0;
    printf("%d",f2);
    f0 = f1;
    f1 = f2;
}
 }
}
```

OUTPUT *(after running)*:

   0   1   1   2   3   5   8   13   21   34

Q2. Write a C program using for loops to check whether the given number is Armstrong. An Armstrong number is a 3-digit number which is equal to the sum of the cubic values of the individual digits in it. For example, 153= 1 **3 + 5 **3 + 3 **3 and thus is an Armstrong number. Also modify your program to generate these types of numbers from 100 to 999.

[**Hint:** The program follows:

```
void main( ) {
string s1;
int num, n, d;
int sum =0;
printf("Enter any three digit number:");
scanf("%d", num);
n = num;
while(num!=0)
  {
    d= num % 10;
    num = num/10;
    sum = sum + d*d*d;
}
if (sum= =n)
    printf("Number is Armstrong!!!");
else
    printf("Number is not Armstrong!!!");
  }
}
```

OUTPUT *(after running)*:

Enter any three digit number

123

Number is not Armstrong!!!

OR

/*the modified program to find **Armstrong numbers** between 100 to 999 */

void main( ) {

```
int n, a, b, c;
for( int i=100; i<1000; i++) {
    a = i % 10;
    b = i % 100 / 10;
```

```
        c – i / 100;
        n = a * a * a + b * b * b + c*c*c;
        if (i= =n)
              printf("%d", i);
        }
    }
    }
```

OUTPUT (after running):

153   370   371   407

Q3. Write a C++ program to compute the factorial of an integer.

    [Hint:

```
        void main( ) {
              int n;
              printf("Enter your number:");
              scanf("%d", &n);
              long f =1;
              for (int i =1; i<=n; i++)
               f *= i;
              cout <<"Factorial is" << f);
        }
    }
```

OUTPUT (after running):

Enter your number:

4

Factorial is 24

Q4. An important series in mathematics is the sine series. Write a C program to find the value of sin(x) from the following series:

$$\textbf{Sin(x)} = x - x^3 / 3! + x^5 / 5! - x^7 / 7! + \dots$$

    [Hint:

```
    void main( ) {
      int deg, n;
      printf("Enter the number of terms: ");
      scanf("%d", &n);
      printf("Enter the angle in degrees:");
      scanf("%d", &deg);
      float x, s = 0.0f, t;
```

```
x = (float) Math.PI *deg/180;
s = x;
t = x;
for (int i=1; i<=n;i++) {
    t = (-t*x*x) / ( (2 * i) * (2*i+1) );
    s = s+t;
}
printf("Sin = %d deg= %d", deg, s);
}
}
```

OUTPUTS (after running):

Enter the number of terms:

20

Enter the angle in degrees:

90

Sin (90) = 1.000000   ].

Q5. Write a C program to generate perfect numbers. We define a perfect number as a positive integer that equals the sum of its positive integer divisors, including unity but excluding the number itself. For instance, 6 is a perfect number as 6 = 1 + 2 + 3.

[Hint:

```
void main( ) {
    int n;
    /* read n-number of prefect numbers you
want */
    printf( "Enter your n:");
    scanf("%d", &n);
    int sum, count =0;
    for (int i=4;; i++) {
        sum =0;
        for (int j=1; j<=i/2; j++) {
            if (i % j ==0)
                sum+=j;
        }
        if (sum = = i) {
          printf("sum = %d", sum);
          ++count;
```

```
                }
            if (count = =n)
                break;
            }
        }
    }
```

OUTPUTS (after running):

Enter your n:

4

6   28   496   8128

Q6. If a loop has a counter-variable, would it be normally written as a while statement or a for statement? In a for loop, which of the initialization, test, and update parts are optional? Which of the initialization, test, and update parts allow the use of commas? Give examples(s) to explain this.

Q7. Write a C program to draw the following triangle:

```
 ✿

    ✿        ✿

    ✿        ✿        ✿

    ✿        ✿        ✿        ✿

    ✿        ✿        ✿        ✿        ✿

    ✿        ✿        ✿        ✿        ✿        ✿
```

[Hint: Rule: For any triangle problem, loop j will run either j <= i or j >= i.

Let us write its algorithm first:

1. Read the *row* variable (i.e., the number of rows).

2. Initialize i=0.

3. Repeat through step 9 while i is less than *row*.

4. Initialize j=0.

5. Repeat through step 7 while j is less than or equal to i.

6. Print "✿".

7. j=j+1

8. Move to new line.

9. i=i+1

10. Stop and exit.

The program is as follows:

```
void main( )
   {
      int row, i, j;
      printf("Enter the number of rows:");
      scanf("%d", &row);
      printf("\n");
      for (i=0; i<row; i++)
        {
             for (j=0; j<=i; j++)
               {
                    printf(" * ");
               }
             printf( "\n");
        }
      }
   }
```

OUTPUT (after running):

Enter the number of rows:

6

❁

❁   ❁

❁   ❁   ❁

❁   ❁   ❁   ❁

❁   ❁   ❁   ❁   ❁

❁   ❁   ❁   ❁   ❁   ❁

Q8. Write a C program to draw the following triangle:

1

01

101

0101

10101

010101

1010101

[Hint: Let us write its algorithm first:

1. Read number of rows, *row*.

2. Initialize i=1.

3. Repeat through step 8 while i is less than or equal to *row*.

4. Initialize j=0.

5. Repeat through step 7 while is j less than i.

6. Print (i–j) % 2.

7. j=j+1

8. Move to the next line.

9. Stop and exit.

The program is as follows:

```
void main ( )
  {
    int row, i, j;
    printf("Enter the number of rows:");
    scanf("%d", &row);
    printf("\n");
    for (i=1; i<row; i++)
      {
            for (j=0; j<i; j++)
              {
                    printf("%d", (i-j) % 2);
              }
            printf("\n");
      }
  }
}
```

Q9. Write a C program to print the following triangle:

```
❀    ❀    ❀    ❀    ❀    ❀    ❀

❀    ❀    ❀    ❀    ❀    ❀

❀    ❀    ❀    ❀    ❀

❀    ❀    ❀    ❀

❀    ❀    ❀

❀    ❀

❀
```

[**Hint:** Let us develop its algorithm first:

1. Read the number of rows, *row*.

2. Initialize i = row.

3. Repeat through step 9 until i is greater than 0.

4. Initialize j=0.

5. Repeat through step 7 until j is less than i.

6. Print "❀".

7. j=j+1

8. Move to new line.

9. i=i–1

10. Stop and exit.

The program is as follows:

```c
void main ( )
  {
    int row,  i,  j;
    printf ("Enter the number of rows:");
    scanf ("%d", &row);
    for (i=row; i>0; i- - )
      {
           for (j=0; j<i; j++)
             {
                    printf (" * ");
```

```
                              }
                      printf("\n");
              }
              }
      }
```

OUTPUT (after running):

Enter the number of rows

7

```
✿      ✿      ✿      ✿      ✿      ✿      ✿

✿      ✿      ✿      ✿      ✿      ✿

✿      ✿      ✿      ✿      ✿

✿      ✿      ✿      ✿

✿      ✿      ✿

✿      ✿

✿                      ].
```

Q10.   Write a C program to print the following triangle:

1

12

123

1234

12345

123456

1234567

[Hint:

Let us develop its algorithm first:

1. Read the number of rows, *row*.

2. Initialize i=1.

3. Repeat through step 9 until i is less than or equal to *row*.

4. Initialize j=1.

5. Repeat through step 7 until j is less than or equal to i.

6. Print j.

7. j=j+1

8. Move to new line.

9. i=i+1

10. Stop and exit.

The program is as follows:

```
void main( )
  {
    int row, i, j;
    printf("Enter the number of rows:");
    scanf("%d", &row);
    for (i=1; i<=row; i++)
      {
            for(j=1; j<=i; j++)
              {
                    printf("%d", j);
              }
    printf("\n");
      }
  }
```

OUTPUT (after running):

Enter the number of rows

7

1

12

123

1234

12345

123456

1234567

Q11. Now write a C program to print the following triangle:

7777777

666666

55555

4444

333

22

1

[**Hint:** Let us develop its algorithm first:

1. Read the number of rows, *row*.

2. Initialize i=row.

3. Repeat through step 9 until i is greater than 0.

4. Initialize j=0.

5. Repeat through step 7 until j is less than i.

6. Print i.

7. j=j+1

8. Move to new line.

9. i=i–1

10. Stop and exit.

The program is as follows:

```c
void main( )
  {
    int row, i, j;
    printf("Enter the number of rows:");
    scanf ("%d", &row);
    for (i=row; i>0; i- - )
      {
            for(j=0; j<i; j++)
              {
                    printf("%d", i);
```

```
                    }
            printf ("\n");
        }
        }
    }
```

OUTPUT (after running):

Enter the number of rows

7

7777777

666666

55555

4444

333

22

1

Q12. Write an algorithm and a C program to print the following pattern:

```
          ✿
        ✿ ✿ ✿
      ✿ ✿ ✿ ✿ ✿
    ✿ ✿ ✿ ✿ ✿ ✿ ✿
  ✿ ✿ ✿ ✿ ✿ ✿ ✿ ✿ ✿
✿ ✿ ✿ ✿ ✿ ✿ ✿ ✿ ✿ ✿ ✿
```

[**Hint:** Let us develop its algorithm first:

1. Read the number of rows, *row*.

2. Initialize i=0.

3. Repeat through step 17 until i is less than or equal to row.

4. Initialize j=1.

5. Repeat through step 7 until j is less than or equal to row i.

6. Print " ".

7. j=j+1

8. Initialize j=1.

9. Repeat through step 11 until j is less than or equal to i.

10. Print "*".

11. j=j+1

12. Initialize j=1.

13. Repeat through step 15 until j is less than i.

14. Print "*".

15. j=j+1

16. Move to new line.

17. i=i+1

18. Stop and exit.

The program is as follows:

```
void main( )
    {
    int row, i, j;
    printf("Enter the number of rows:");
    scanf("%d", &row);
    for(i=0; i<=row; i++)
        {
        for(j=1; j<=row-i; j++)
            printf(" ");
        for(j=1; j<=i; j++)
            printf("*");
        for(j=1; j<=i; j++)
            printf("*");
        printf("\n");
        }
    }
```

OUTPUT (after running):

Enter the number of rows

6

```
          ✿
        ✿ ✿ ✿
       ✿ ✿ ✿ ✿ ✿
      ✿ ✿ ✿ ✿ ✿ ✿ ✿
     ✿ ✿ ✿ ✿ ✿ ✿ ✿ ✿ ✿
    ✿ ✿ ✿ ✿ ✿ ✿ ✿ ✿ ✿ ✿ ✿
```

Q13. Write a C program to draw a Pascal Triangle as follows:

```
          1
        1   1
      1   2   1
    1   3   3   1
  1   4   6   4   1
```

[**Hint:** Let us develop its algorithm first:

1. Set a=1, q=0.

2. Read the number of rows, *row*.

3. Repeat through step 15 until q is less than *row*.

4. Initialize p=30–3*q.

5. Repeat through step 7 until p is greater than *row*.

6. Print " ".

7. p=p–1

8. Initialize b=0.

9. Repeat through step 13 until b is less than or equal to q.

10. If b equals to 0 or q equals to 0 then set a=1, else set a=(a*(q–b+1)/b).

11. Print (" ");

12. Print a.

13. b=b+1

14. Move to the next line.

15. q=q+1

16. Stop and exit.

The program is as follows:

```
void main( )
{
    int a=1,p,q=0,row, b;
    printf("Enter the number of rows:");
    scanf("%d", &row);
    printf("\n Pascal Triangle\n");
    while (q<row)
        {
        for (p=30-3*q; p>0;p--)
            printf(" ");
        for (b=0;b<=q;b++)
            {
            if (b==0 || q==0)
                a=1;
            else
                a=(a*(q-b+1)/b;
            printf ("    " ,a);
            }
    printf("\n");
    q++;
    }
}
```

OUTPUT (after running):

Enter the number of rows

5

```
              1
            1   1
          1   2   1
        1   3   3   1
      1   4   6   4   1        ].
```

Q14. Write a C program to display the Floyd triangle.

[**Hint:** Let us write its algorithm first:

1. Initialize a=1.

2. Read the number of rows, *row*.

3. Initialize i=0.

4. Repeat through step 12 until i is less than *row*.

5. Initialize j=0.

6. Repeat through step 10 until j is less than or equal to i.

7. Print a.

8. If a is less than 10, print " " else print " ".

9. a=a+1

10. j=j+1

11. Move to the next line.

12. i=i+1

13. Stop and exit.

The program is as follows:

```c
void main( )
  {
    int a=1,i, j, row;
    printf("Enter the number of rows:");
    scanf("%d", & row);
    printf("\n");
    for(i=0;i<row;i++)
     {
          for(j=0;j<=i;j++)
           {
                if(a<10)
                printf("%d\t", a);
                else
                printf("%d\t", a);
                a++;
           }
          printf("\n");
          }
      }
  }
```

OUTPUT (after running):

Enter the number of rows

4

1

2   3

4   5   6

7   8   9   10   ].

Q15. Write a C program to generate a sequence of numbers using a for loop construct and print them in the following format:

1

2   3

4   5   6

7   8   9   10

11   12   13   14   15 ?

[**Hint:**

```
void main( ) {
    int k=1;
    printf("%d", k);
    for(int i=1;i<5;i++) {
        printf("%d", ++k);
        for (int j=0; j<i; j++) {
            k+=1;
            printf("%d", k);
        }
        printf("\n");
    }
}
```

OUTPUT (after running):

1

2   3

4   5   6

7   8   9   10

11   12   13   14   15].

Other Statements of C

The break Statement

When a break statement is executed inside a loop, it skips the remaining statements of that loop and control is immediately transferred outside the loop.

Syntax

     break;

For example,

```
void main ( )
  {
    int i, j;
    for(i=1;  i<=3;i++)
      {
            for(j=1;j<=3;j++)
            {
                    if(i= =j)
                        break;
                    else
                        printf("%d\t %d", i, j);
            }
        }
      }
  }
```

OUTPUT (after running):

2	1
3	1
3	2

Please note that when a break statement appears inside a loop or in a switch statement, it terminates execution at that point and transfers execution control to the statement immediately following the loop or switch statement. Thus, it does an early exit from any loop or switch statement. **Also note that when multiple statements are nested within each other, a break transfers control to the immediate outer level.**

However, break statements should be avoided in loops (whenever possible) because they bypass the loop's logic and make the code difficult to understand and debug.

Another variant of the break statement has the following syntax:

break label_name;

For example,

```
        .
        .
        .
        {
            Statement;
            break kk;
        }
        .
        kk:
        .
        .
```

Here, label_name is an identifier and not a number. There is no need for declaring these labels as they are just user-defined labels. When the compiler encounters the label (kk in this example), control jumps to the statement labeled kk and executes the statements following that label. **If these statements appear before a break statement, the flow is backward. If the statements appear after a break statement, the flow is forward.**

The continue Statement

A *continue* statement is used within loops to end execution of the current iteration and proceed to the next iteration. Thus, it provides a method of skipping the remaining statements in that iteration after the continue statement. **Please note that a continue statement should be used only in loop constructs and not in selective control constructs. Also note that using a continue statement in selective control constructs results in a compilation error.**

Continue Statement Syntax

continue;

In a while loop. The program jumps to the *Boolean expression* at the top of the loop. If the expression is still true, the next iteration begins.

In a do-while loop. The program jumps to the *boolean expression* at the bottom of the loop, which determines whether the next iteration will begin.

In a for loop. Causes the *update expression (i.e., increment/decrement part of the for loop)* to be executed and then the test expression is evaluated.

The continue statement should be used sparingly because, like the break statement, it also bypasses the loop's logic and makes the code difficult to understand and debug.

Most repetitive algorithms can be written with any of the three loops discussed above. But each loop works best in different situations.

1. **The while loop:** As we have seen, a *while loop* is a pretest loop. **This loop is ideal when you do not want the loop to iterate if the condition is false from the beginning.** It is also ideal if you want to use **a sentinel value** to terminate the loop. **A sentinel value is a special value that cannot be mistaken as a member of the list and signals that there are no more values to be entered. When the user enters the sentinel value, the loop terminates.**

2. **The do-while loop:** As we have seen, a *do-while loop* is a sort of posttest loop. **This loop is ideal for situations where you always want the loop to iterate at least once.**

3. **The for loop:** As we have seen, the *for loop* is a pretest loop that has inbuilt expressions for initializing, testing, and updating. These expressions make it very convenient to use a loop control variable as a counter. **The for loop is ideal in situations where the exact number of iterations is known.**

The return Statement

A return statement is used only in methods (functions in C and member-functions in C++ are known as methods in Java). It terminates the method's execution by transferring control to the calling method. Thus, if a method has to return a value, you may write:

return *expression;*

On the other hand, **for a void type of method that does not return any value,** the following **syntax** is used:

return;

A return statement unconditionally transfers control to the calling method from the called method. This means that all statements between the return statement and the end of the method are skipped. That is why such a statement is normally placed at the end of a method; it is also possible to use it when specific conditions apply and an early termination is required. **Using a return statement at the end of the method is essential in the case of methods that return a type different from *void.***

NOTE *For methods having a void return type, this statement can be omitted and will be implicitly added by the compiler.*

Block Statements

A group of statements enclosed within curly braces comprises a block. Thus, a block contains a statement list—a sequence of statements. **A statement in a block is called an embedded statement and it can be a label, a declaration, or a simple statement. Please note that a block is also called a compound statement.** It is valid to have no statements or an empty statement in a block. A block is syntactically similar to a single statement. **Also note that no semicolon is placed after the closing brace that ends a block.** When there is no statement in a block, it is called an **empty block. A block having an empty statement is not an empty block since it contains a valid statement.** That is,

```
{ }        //is empty block
{ ; }      //non-empty block
```

Empty statement: A statement that does nothing is known as an empty statement. It is written as a single semicolon as follows:

```
;  //empty statement
```

Remember that an empty statement is also known as a null statement. This statement helps a programmer introduce some delays in program execution. Actually, they do nothing and just bypass certain machine cycles, thereby producing delays. For example,

```
for( int i=0; i<100; i++)
   {
       ;        // null statement
   }
```

Similarly, we can use it in while and do-while loops as well.

We are in a position to solve some examples now.

Q1. Define sentinel value and explain why it is used?

Q2. Write a C program to read numbers 1 to 10 through the keyboard and display their squares in a tabular format.

[**Hint:** void main( ) {

```
{
    int number, maxValue;   //  number  is  loop
    control variable
```

```
printf("Displaying  the  table  of  numbers  and
their squares:");
/* get the maximum value to display */
printf ("Till what number you want the squares?");
scanf("%d", &maxValue);
/*display your table now */
printf("Number            Number Squares");
printf ("------------------------------");
for ( number=1; number <=maxValue; number++)
   {
printf ("%d \t\t %d", number ,number * number);
   }
}
}
```

Q3. Give the outputs of the following program snippets:

(a) int x, y;
for (x=1, y=1; x <=5; x++)
{

  cout<<x << "plus" << y << "equals" << (x + y);
}

[**Hint:** Both *x* and *y* are initialized to 1. Thus, we get the following output:

1 plus 1 equals 2

2 plus 1 equals 3

3 plus 1 equals 4

4 plus 1 equals 5

5 plus 1 equals 6   ].

(b) int x, y;
for(x=1, y=1; x<=5; x++, y++)
{
cout <<x << "plus" << y << "equals" << (x + y);
}

[**Hint:** The loop update expression is x++, y++. Thus, we get the following output:

1 plus 1 equals 2

2 plus 2 equals 4

3 plus 3 equals 6

4 plus 4 equals 8

5 plus 5 equals 10   ].

Q4. Give an example to show the use of a sentinel value.

[Hint:

while (result != -1)

    {

        result = result + 20;

    }

Here, the value –1 was chosen for the sentinel because it is not possible to have a negative result. Thus, this makes it possible for the loop to terminate immediately if the user gets –1 as the result].

Q5. Write a C program that reads the number of students and the number of test scores per student and then displays the average score for a student.

[Hint:

```
void main( )
    {
        int n,            /* number of students */
         numTests,        /* number of tests per
student*/
         score,           /* test score */
         total;           /* test scores in total
*/
        double average;        /*average test score */
        printf("TEST AVERAGING PROGRAM");
    /* read number of students */
        printf("Enter number of students:");
        scanf("%d", &n);
        /* get number of test scores per student */
        printf("How many test scores per stu-
        dent?");
        scanf("%d", &numTests);
        /* Calculate for each student */
        int student =1; student <=numStudents;
        student++)
        {
        total = 0;  /*set total to 0 */
```

```
/*get the test scores for a student */
for (int test = 1; test <=numTests; test++)
{
printf    ("Enter    score    for    student
",test,student);
scanf("%d", &score);
total += score;    /* add score to total */
}
/* calculate and display the average */
average = total / numTests;
printf("The average score for student is"
, average);
  }
 }
}
```

OUTPUT (after running):

TEST AVERAGING PROGRAM

Enter number of students: 2

How many test scores per student? 3

Enter score 1 for student 1: 80

Enter score 2 for student 1: 85

Enter score 3 for student 1: 90

The average score for student 1 is 85.0

Enter score 1 for student 2: 60

Enter score 2 for student 2: 80

Enter score 3 for student 2: 80

The average score for student 2 is 73.3   ].

Q7. Write a nested loop that displays 5 rows of '#' characters. There should be 10 '#' characters in each row.

Q8. Do as directed:

(a) **Convert the while loop to a do-while loop in the code below:**

```
int x=1;
while (x >0)
  {
```

```
        printf("Enter a number:");
        scanf("%d", &x);
    }
```

(b) **Convert for loop to a while loop in the code below:**

```
for( int i = 10 ; i > 0; i--)
  {
        printf( "%d seconds to go", i);
  }
```

(c) **Write an input validation loop that asks a user to enter a number in the range of 1 through 100.**

(d) **Write a C++ program that displays a table of centigrade temperatures 0 to 50 and their Fahrenheit equivalents. The formula used is:**

$$C = 5/9 \ (F{-}32)$$

where C and F have their usual meanings. Try to use a loop to display your table.

Q9. Develop a program to find the roots of a given quadratic equation. Use switch statements and loops to display your roots.

[Hint: Refer to page 267].

Q10. The distance a body travels in free fall is given by the formula:

S= $-gt^2$

where s is the distance traveled in feet,

T is the time in seconds to travel the distance s,

G is a constant and is equal to 32.2 feet per second^2.

Write a C program for this equation.

Q11. Write a C program to read a number from the keyboard and to add each of its digits.

[Hint:

```
void main( )
  {
        int r, sum=0, num;
        printf("Enter a number:");
        scanf("%d", &num);
        while(num > 0)
```

```
            {
                r = num % 10;
                sum = sum + r;
                num = num /10;
            }
        printf("The sum of digits is= %d", sum);
    }
}
```

OUTPUT (after running):

Enter a number

123

The sum of digits is = 6].

Q12. Give and discuss the output of the following code:

```
int price;
for (int width =11; width <=20; width++) {
    for(int length =5; length <=25;  length +=5) {
    price = width * length * 19;
    printf(" \t%d ", price);
    }
    //finished one row; now move on to the next row
    printf(" ");
}
```

[**Hint:** The outer for statement is set to range from the first row (width=11) to the last row (width=20). For each repetition of the outer for, the inner for statement is executed, which ranges from the first column (length=5) to the fifth column (length=25). The loop body of the inner for computes the price of a single item and prints out this price. So, the complete execution of the inner for loop, which causes its loop body to be executed 5 times, completes the output of one row. The following shows the sequence of values for the 2 control variables:

	width	length
11		
		5
		10
		15
		20

25 (this completes the printing of the first row)

12

5

10

15

20

25 (this completes the printing of the first row)

13

5

10

:

:

].

Q13. What will be the value of sum after the following nested for loops are executed?

(a)
```c
int sum =0;
for (int i = 0; i < 5; i++) {
    sum = sum + i;
    for (int j = 0; j < 5; j++) {
        sum = sum + j;
    }
}
```

(b)
```c
int sum =0;
for( int i = 0; i < 5; i++) {
sum = sum + i;
for(int j = i; j < 5; j++) {
  sum = sum +j;
}
}
```

Q14. What is wrong with the following nested for loop?
```c
int sum = 0;
for (int i = 0; i < 5; i++) {
  sum = sum + i;
    for (int i = 5; i > 0; i- -) {
    sum = sum + j;
  }
}
```

2.12 STORAGE CLASSES: AUTO, STATIC, EXTERN, AND REGISTER

Variables in C have a data type. But they also have a storage class that provides information about their location and visibility. The storage class divides the portion of the program within which the variables are recognized. The following are the storage classes:

I. Auto

The auto storage class is a local variable known only to the function in which it is declared.

Auto is the default storage class. The auto keyword places the specified variable into the stack area of memory. This is usually implicit in most variable declarations like int i;

The default storage class for all local variables is **auto**.

For example,

> int counter;

> auto int i;

Both the variables are here defined with the same storage class; auto can only be used within functions (i.e., local variables).

II. Static

The static storage class is a local variable which exists and retains its value even after control is transferred to the calling function.

A static variable is the one that does not get initialized again and again. The static keyword is useful for extending the lifetime of a particular variable. **Please note that if you declare a static variable inside a function, the variable remains even after the function call is long gone** (the variable is placed in the alterable area of memory). **Also note that the static keyword is overloaded.** It is also used to declare variables to be private to a certain file only when declared with global variables. Static variables can also be used with functions, making those functions visible only to the file itself. **Static is the default storage class for global variables.**

For example,

static int count;

Static variables can be seen within all functions in this source file. At link time, the static variables defined here will not be seen by the object modules that are brought in. Note that static can also be defined within a function. If this is done the variable is initialized at runtime but is not reinitialized when the function is called. This *inside a function static variable* retains its value during various calls.

For example,

```
void func(void)
static count=10; /* global variable- static is the
default */
main( )
  {
    while (count - - )
      {
          func( );
      }
  }
void func(void)
  {
    static i = 5;
    i++;
    printf("i is %d and count is %d\n", i, count);
  }
```

OUTPUT (after running):

i is 6 and count is 9

i is 7 and count is 8

i is 8 and count is 7

i is 9 and count is 6

i is 10 and count is 5

i is 11 and count is 4

i is 12 and count is 3

i is 13 and count is 2

i is 14 and count is 1

i is 15 and count is 0

NOTE *Here, the keyword void means function does not return anything and it does not take any parameter. Static variables are initialized to 0 automatically.*

III. Extern

We know that global variables are known to all functions in the file. The extern keyword makes the specified variable access the variable of the same name from some other file. This is very useful for sharing variables in modular programs; **extern** is used to give a reference of a global variable that is visible to all program files. When you use extern the variable cannot be initialized as all it does is point the variable name at a storage location that has been previously defined. **Please note that when you have multiple files and you define a global variable or function, which will be used in other files also, then *extern* will be used in another file to give reference of the defined variable or function. Also note that *extern* is used to declare a global variable or function in another file.**

For example,

File 1: main.c

```
int count = 10;
main( )
  {
    write_extern( );
  }
```

File 2: write.c

```
void write_extern(void)
extern int count;
void write_extern(void)
  {
    printf("count is %i\n", count);
  }
```

Here, the ***extern*** keyword is being used to declare a count in another file. Now compile these two files as follows:

gcc main.c write.c –o write

This creates a write file that can be used to produce a result by executing it. The count in **main.c** will have a value of 15. If **main.c** changes the value of the count, **write.c** will see the new value.

IV. Register

The keyword **register** refers to the social variables that are stored in the register. It suggests that the compiler place the particular variable in the fast register memory located directly on the CPU. Most compilers these days (like gcc) are so smart that suggesting registers could actually make your programs slower. **Please note that *register* is used to define local variables that should be stored in a register instead of RAM. Also note that this means that the variable has a maximum size equal to the register size (usually one word) and can't have the unary '&' operator as it does not have a memory location.**

For example,

register int u;

The register keyword should only be used for variables that require quick access such as counters. **Also understand that defining *register* does not mean that the variable will be stored in a register; rather, it means that it might be stored in a register—depending on hardware and implementation restrictions.**

Before we close this chapter, let us write some programs now.

Q1. Write a C program to convert a binary number to a decimal number.

Ans. 1: The program is as follows:

```c
#include<stdio.h>
main( )
  {
    int binary, bin, digit, decimal=0, base=0;
    printf("\n\t Enter any binary number:");
    scanf("%d", &binary);
    bin = binary;
    while (binary !=0)
      {
        digit = binary % 10;
        digit = digit << base;
        decimal = decimal + digit;
        base++;
        binary = binary / 10;
      }
printf("\n Decimal equivalent of binary number %d = %d",
bin, decimal);
  }
```

OUTPUT *(after running)*:

Enter any binary number: 11111

Decimal equivalent of binary number 11111 = 31

Q2. Write a C program to sum the following series:

$$\textbf{Sin } (x) = x - x^3 / 3! + x^5 / 5! + x^7 / 7! + \dots + x^n / n!$$

Ans. 1: The program is as follows:

```
#include<stdio.h>
main( )
 {
    float x, num, sum;
    long int n, den, i, sn;
    printf("\nEnter the value of x and n:");
    scanf("%f %ld", &x, &n);
    x= x * 3.1412 / 180;    /* changing x into radians */
    sn = 1;
    sum = x;
    num = x;
    den = 1;
    i = 1;
    while (i < n)
      {
        num = num * x * x;
        den = den * (2 * i) * (2 * i +1);
        sn = -sn;
        sum = sum + (num/den) * sn;
        i++;
      }
    printf("Sin(%2.2f) = %f", xx, sum);
 }
```

OUTPUT *(after running)*:

Enter the value of x and n: 45 6

Sin(45.00) = 0.707037

Enter the value of x and n: 90 8

Sin(90.00) = 1.000000

Q3. Give the output of the following C program:

```
#include<stdio.h>
#include<conio.h>
main( )
 {
   int i, j;
   for (i = 1; i<=5; i++)
    {
      printf ("\n i= %d \n", i);
      for (j=10; j<=20; j = j+3)
       printf("\t J= ");
      i++;
    }
 }
```

Ans. 3: The output is as follows:

I = 1

        J=   10   13   16   19

I = 2

        J=   10   13   16   19

I = 3

        J=   10   13   16   19

I = 4

        J=   10   13   16   19

I = 5

        J=   10   13   16   19

Q4. Write a C program to display the following pyramid:

        a

       ab

      abc

     abcd

    abcde

Ans. 4: The program is as follows:

```c
#include<stdio.h>
main ( )
 {
    int i, blanks = 20;
    char ch1, ch2;
    for (ch1 = 'a'; ch1 <= 'e'; ch1++)
      {
        printf("\n");
        for (i=1; i<=blanks; i++)
        printf(" ");
        for (ch2 = 'a'; ch2 <= ch1; ch2++)
            printf("%c", ch2);
        blanks - - ;
      }
 }
```

Q5.   Write a C program to display all prime numbers from 1 to 100.

Ans. 5: The program is as follows:

```c
#include<stdio.h>
main ( )
 {
    int n, flag, i
    for (n=1; n <=100; n++)
    {
    i = 2;
    flag = 0;
    while (i <= n/2)
      {
        if (n % i = = 0)
          {
            flag = 1;
            break;
          }
        i++;
      }
    if (flag = =0)
        printf("%d" \t", n);
 }
 }
```

OUTPUT (after running):

1	2	3	5	7	11	13	17	19
23	29	31	37	41	43	47	53	59
61	67	71	73	79	83	89	97	

Q6. What points are to be kept in mind while using switch statements?

Ans. 6: The following points must be kept in mind:

1. You can use *case* labels in random order.

2. Case values cannot be expressions.

3. Case labels cannot be repeated within a switch statement.

4. You can mix integer and character constants in different cases of a single switch statement.

Q7. When is a while loop preferred over a for loop?

Ans. 7: A while loop is preferred over a for loop when it is not known in advance how many times the loop is going to execute.

Q8. What is meant by lifetime and scope regarding variables?

Ans. 8: The lifetime of a variable is the length of time it retains a particular value. The scope of a variable refers to those parts of a program that will be able to recognize it.

Q9. Using the ternary operator of C, write a program to find the largest of two numbers.

Ans. 9: The program is as follows:

```c
#include<stdio.h>
main( )
 {
    int num1, num2, large;
    printf("Enter any two numbers:");
    scanf("%d %d", &num1, &num2);
    printf("%5d %5d\n", num1, num2);
    large = num1 > num2 ? num1 : num2;
    printf("\n Larger of the two is %5d \n", large);
 }
```

OUTPUT (after running):

Enter any two numbers: 11 22

Larger of the two is 22

Q10. With the help of a flowchart, explain the working of a nested if-else statement.

Ans. 10: The following is the flowchart for a nested if-else statement:

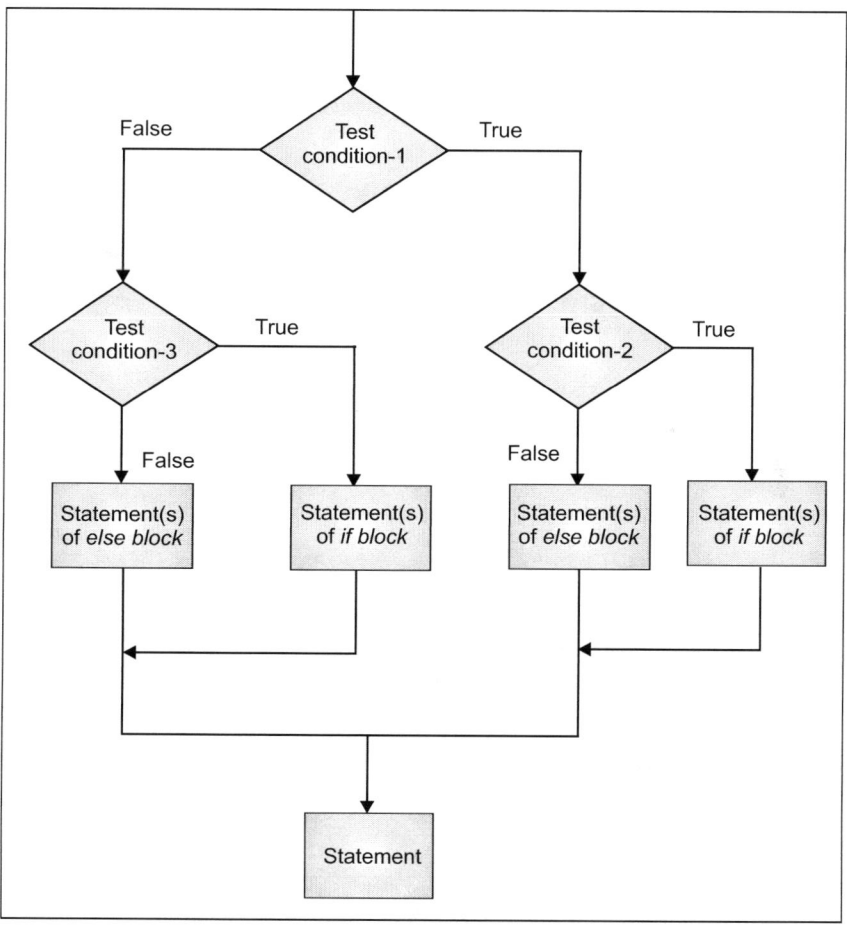

Here, if test condition-1 results in True then the if-else statement, which is embedded in the if block, is executed and the other if-else statement, which is embedded in the else block, is skipped. On the other hand, if test condition-1

results in False then the if-else statement, which is embedded in the if block, is skipped and the other if-else statement, which is embedded in the else block, is executed.

Q12. Write a C program to find the power of x raised to y (xy).

Ans. 12: The program is as follows:

```
#include<stdio.h>
main( )
  {
    int x, y, i, power =1;
    printf("\n Enter the value of a and y =");
    scanf("%d %d", &x, &y);
    if (y = =0)
       printf("\n Power of %d to %d is = %d", x, y, power);
    else
      {
        while (y > = 1)
          {
            power = power * x;
            y - - ;
          }
          printf("\n Power of %d to %d is = %d", x, y, pow-
er);
      }
  }
```

OUTPUT (after running):

Enter the value of x and y = 2 3

Power of 2 to 3 is = 8

Q13. Write a C program to generate the Fibonacci series that continues till n.

Ans. 13: The program is as follows:

```
#include<stdio.h>
main( )
  {
    int i, n, f1, f2, f3;
    printf("\n \t Enter the value of n: ");
    scanf("%d", &n);
    if (n <= 1)
     printf("%d", n);
```

```
    else
     {
       f1 = 0;
       f2 = 1;
       f3 = f1 + f2;
       printf("%d\t", f3);
       for (i=2; i<=n; i++)
        {
          f3 = f1 + f2;
          f1 = f2;
          f2 = f3;
          printf("%d\t", f3);
        }
       }
     }
```

Please note here that in a for statement, you can have more than one expression in the initialization part of the statement and more than one expression in the update part. To separate multiple initializations and updating, we use commas to separate them. Also note that the C language strictly allows only one test condition and no more than that in a for statement.

Q14. Write the output of the following C code:

```
#include<stdio.h>
main( )
  {
    int x = 4;
    x *= x + 4;
    printf("%d", x);
  }
```

Ans. 14: The output is as follows: 32

This is so because we have x = x * (x + 4) = 4 * (8) = 32.

Q15. What is a variable declaration and what is a variable definition?

Ans. 15: extern int a is a declaration whereas int a=100 is a definition.

Q16. What are different types of linkages?

Ans. 16: There are three different types of linkages: external, internal, and none.

External linkage means *global*, nonstatic variables and functions.

Internal linkage means *static variables* and functions with file scope.

No linkage means *local variables*.

Q17. Give the output of the following C code:

```
main ( )
  {
    int i = 1;
    while ( )
      {
        printf ("%d", i++);
        if ( i > 10)
          break;
      }
  }
```

Ans. 17: error: the condition in the while loop is necessary.

Q18. Give the output of the following code:

```
#include<stdio.h>
main ( )
  {
    int i = 4;
    printf ("%d", printf ("%d %d", i, i));
  }
```

Ans. 18: 4   43

Q19. Why is goto not a preferred method?

Ans. 19: goto cannot take control to a different function.

Q20. Can we use a switch statement to switch on strings?

Ans. 20: No, the cases in a switch must have integer constants or constant expressions.

Q21. Rewrite the following statement so that 30 is used only once:

a<= 20 ? b = 30 : c=30;

Ans. 21: *((a<=20) ? &b : &c) = 30;

Q22. Give the output:

```
main ( )
  {
```

```
    int sc, sv;
    sc= 012;
    sv = 0x28;
    sc << 1;
    sv << 2;
 printf("%d %d", sc, sv);
 }
```

Ans. 22:   024   0xA0h

Why? We are given that:

sc = (012)8 = (000 001 010)2

sv = (0x28)16 = (0000 0010 1000)2

So, sc << 1 = 000 001 010 = 0128

= (000 010 100)2 = 0248 (after left shift)

Similarly, sv << 2 = (0000 0010 1000) = 028h

So, sv << 1 = (0000 0101 0000) = 050h

And sv << 1 = (0000 1010 0000) = 0(10)0h = 0A0h

So, the output is (024 0xA0h) = (20d 160d)

NOTE *In shifting, bits are lost, whereas in rotation, bits are not lost (i.e., LSBs become MSBs and vice versa).*

Q23. How many times is the following loop executed?

for (l=0; ++l <10; l++)

(a) 10 times

(b) 9 times

(c) 5 times

(d) none of the above

Ans. 23: 9 times

l	++l	execution
0	1<10	1
1	2<10	2
2	3<10	3

3	4<10	4
4	5<10	5
5	6<10	6
6	7<10	7
7	8<10	8
8	9<10	**9 times.**
9	10<10 (is false).	

Q24. Give the output of the following program:

```
main( )
 {
   int m, n;
   m = 14;
   n = 15;
 printf("m & n = %d", m & n);
 }
```

Ans. 24: Now, m= 14 d = $(1110)_2$

n = 15d = $(1111)_2$

So, 1110

& 1111

1110

And $1110 = 0 * 2^0 + 1 * 2^1 + 1 * 2^2 + 1 * 2^3 = 0 + 2 + 4 + 8 = 14_{10}$

Q25. Give the output of the following program:

```
#include<stdio.h>
#include<conio.h>
main( )
 {
   int i = 7;
   int res;
   clrscr( );
   res = i++ * i++;
   cout << "Result is: " << res;
   getch( );
 }
```

Ans. 25:   49

Q26. Give the output of the following program:

```
main ( )
  {
    int i =7;
    int res;
    res = ++i * ++i;
    printf ("%d", res);
}
```

Ans. 26: 81 (as unary has higher precedence, i is incremented twice first and then multiplied.

Q27. Give the output of the following program:

```
void main ( )
  {
    int i = 7;
    int res;
    res = i++ * ++i;
    printf ("%d", res);
  }
```

Ans. 27: **64** (unary has higher precedence, and first i is incremented once (i.e., 8 and then 8 * 8 gives 64).

Q28. Give the output of the following program:

```
#include<stdio.h>
#include<conio.h>
#define value 1+2
void main ( )
  {
  printf ("Value is %d", value);
  printf ("Value of expressions are %d %d:", value/value,
value * 3);
  }
```

Ans. 28: The value is 3.

Value of expressions are 5 7

Why? value/ value = 1+ 2/1 + 2, 1+2*3

$$= 1+2+2, 1+6$$

$$= 5, 7$$

Q29. Differentiate between a constant and a variable.

Ans. 29. The following table gives the differences:

Constant	Variable
A constant does not change during the execution of the program.	A variable varies during the execution of the program.
A constant is a quantity that is fixed. It may be numbers, characters, or strings.	A variable is the named memory location where a constant is stored.
A constant does not store in memory.	A variable stores in memory.
For example, 7.8, 3.1417 are constants.	For example, u, v are variables.

Q30. Distinguish between the getchar( ) and scanf( ) functions of C.

Ans. 30. The following table gives the differences:

getchar( )	scanf( )
getchar( ) is an unformatted input function.	scanf is a formatted input function.
It is used to accept only characters from the keyboard in a fixed format.	It is used to accept any data from the keyboard.
Only a single character is input in this function.	Any type of data (such as integer, character, float, etc.) can be entered using this function.
A format string is not placed in this function.	Format strings are placed.
No arguments are passed to this function.	A number of arguments are passed here.
Syntax: getchar( );	**Syntax:** scanf("format string", arguments);

Q31. Distinguish between the getch( ) and getche( ) functions of C.

Ans. 31. The following table gives the differences:

getch( )	getche( )
This function reads a character from the keyboard. This character is not echoed on the screen.	This function also reads a character from the keyboard but the character is echoed on screen.
It is used where the user does not want to show the input.	It is used where the user wants to show the input entered.

Q32. Distinguish between the gets( ) and puts( ) functions of C.

Ans. 32. The following table gives the differences:

gets( )	puts( )
This function reads a string from a standard input device.	This function prints a string on the standard output device.
This function is used as an input function for a string.	This function is used as an output function for a string.
No message can be printed with this function.	With this function any message can also be printed.

Q33. Distinguish between switch and nested-if.

Ans. 33. The following table gives the differences:

Switch	Nested-if
The expression used in switch can return an integer or character constant. Also, 0 and 1 are included in these values.	The expression used in nested-if returns a true (1) or false (0) value.
It has more flexibility and a cleaner way of programming.	It has poor flexibility and a complex format.
It is easier to handle.	It is difficult and complex to handle.
It needs a break statement after every case.	It does not need a break statement.
There is no need to put multiple statements of a case into braces.	Multiple statements of nested-if must be written within braces.
The keywords switch, case, and default are used.	The keywords if and else are used.

Summary

In this chapter, we have examined how a C program reads and writes inputs and outputs from a standard input device like a keyboard. We have seen that C provides a facility for decision making by using different types of control statements like the if, if-else, and switch statements. We have explored how if-else can be nested and the switch statement as a multi-way selection statement. We have also seen how loops are used and the functioning of different loops like the while loop, do-while loop, and for loop. We have looked at break and continue statements and have studied modifiers and qualifiers in C.

Exercises

Q1. What are the major data types available in C? Using a suitable example, discuss enumerated data types.

Q2. Write short notes on bitwise operators in C.

Q3. Can we replace a for loop with a while loop? If yes, explain with an example.

Q4. Write a loop that will generate every third integer beginning with i=2 and continuing for all integers that are less than 100. Calculate the sum of those integers that are evenly divisible by 5.

Q5. Explain briefly all storage classes used in C.

Q6. What does the storage class of a variable mean and how would you define the scope of a variable within a program. Also explain how an automatic variable is defined and initialized? What happens if an automatic variable is not explicitly initialized within a function?

Q7. Write a C program to sum the following exponential series:

$$e^x = 1 + x + x^2/2! + x^3/3! + \ldots x^n/n!$$

[**Hint:**

1. Read x and n.

2. Initialize t=1 and sum =1.

3. for i ← 1 to n do

4. prod = i.

5. t = t ° x/prod.

6. sum = sum + t

7. Print sum.   ].

Q8. Write a C program to find the factorial of a number using for loops.
[**Hint:**
```
fact =1.
for(i=1; i<=n; i++)
fact = fact * i.
printf fact.                    ].
```
Q9. Write a C program to compute the 100th triangular number. A triangular number is obtained by adding the integers from 1 up to 100.

[**Hint:**
```
main( )
   {
      int n, triangular_number;
      triangular_number = 0;
```

```
for( n=1; n <=100; n = n + 1)
triangular_number = triangular_number + n;
printf("The 100th triangular number is %d\n", trian-
gular_number);
}                                                    ].
```

Q10. Modify the program in Q9 to generate the table of triangular numbers.

Q11. Write a C program to find the GCD of two numbers, u and v.

[**Hint:**

```
/* say two numbers are u and v */
while ( v != 0)
  {
    temp = u % v;
    u = v;
    v = temp;
  }
  printf("GCD is %d, u);
```
].

Q12. Write a C program to reverse the digits of a number.

[**Hint:**

1. read a number.

2. right_digit = number % 10.

3. print right_digit.

4. number = number /10   ].

Q13. Write a C program to generate and display a table of n and n2 and n3 for integers ranging from 1 to n.

Q14. Write a C program to generate and print the table of the first 10 factorials.

Q15. Write a C program to show what happens when a minus is placed in front of a field width specification.

[**Hint:** The field is displayed left-justified].

Q16. Write a C program to calculate the average of a set of grades and to count the number of failing test grades.

[**Hint:**

```
main( )
  {
```

```
int number_of_grades, i, grade;
int grade_total = 0;
int failure_count = 0;
float average;
printf("How many grades will you be entering? ");
scanf("%d", &number_of_grades);
for (i=1; i<= number_of_grades; ++i)
  {
    printf("Enter grade %d", i);
    scanf("%d", &grade);
    grade_total = grade_total + grade;
    if (grade < 50)
       ++failure_count;
  }
average = (float) grade_total / number_of_grades;
printf("\n Grade average = %.2f \n", average);
printf("\n Number of failures = %d \n", failure_count);
}
```

Q17. Write a C program to find out whether a given number is even or odd.

Q18. Write a C program to implement the sign function. That is,

if number < 0 then sign = −1

else if number = 0 then sign is 0

else sign = 1

Print sign value.

Q19. Write a C program to categorize a single character read from the keyboard.

[Hint:

1. Read a character c.

2. If c >= 'a' and c <= 'z' or c >= 'A' and c <= 'Z' then print 'It is a character'.

3. Else if c >= '0' and c <= '9' then print 'It is a digit'.

4. Else print ' It is a special character'.   ].

Q20. What are the largest positive and negative numbers that can be stored? How are they determined?

[Hint: The largest positive number that can be stored into n bits is $2^{n-1} - 1$. So, in 8-bits, we can store up to $2^7 - 1$ or 127. Similarly, the smallest negative number that can be stored in n bits is -2^{n-1}, which in an 8-bit comes to −128. **Please note that these two values are not the same.** This is applicable to characters, as they take 1 byte or 8 bits.

On the other hand, integers take 2 bytes or 16 bits in computer memory, so the largest possible value that can be stored into such an integer is $2^{15}-1$ or 32,767, whereas the smallest negative number that can be stored is −32,768.].

Q21.   Why do unsigned integers take values from 0 to 65,535?

[**Hint:** We know that an unsigned modifier can be used to increase the accuracy of a variable. This is because the leftmost bit is no longer needed to store the sign of the number, since we are only dealing with positive integers. This **extra bit** is used to increase the magnitude of the value stored in that variable by a factor of 2. Please note that n bits can now be used to store values up to 2^n-1. Also note that on a machine that stores integers in 16 bits, this means that unsigned integers can range in value from 0 through 65,535.].

CHAPTER 3

ARRAYS AND POINTERS

3.0 INTRODUCTION

S ay we wish to store the marks of 3000 students at our college; if I use variables, more than 3000 variables are required. This is very tedious and cumbersome. So to solve this type of problem, we use an array that has a common name with a subscript representing the index of each element. Thus, **an array is an ordered sequence of finite data items of the same data type that share a common name.** The common name **is the array name and** each individual data item **is known as an element of the array.**

An array is defined as a set of a similar type of elements that are stored contiguously in memory. This means that the elements of an array are stored in the subsequent memory locations starting from the first memory location of the block of memory created for the array. Each element of an array can be referred to by an array name and a subscript or an index. **Please note that all elements of an array should be of similar type.** Arrays can have one of more dimensions—one-dimensional (1D), two-dimensional (2D), or multidimensional. **A one-dimensional array uses a single index and a two-dimensional array uses two indexes, and so on. A 1D array can be used to represent a list of data items and is also known as a vector or a list. Similarly, a 2D array can be used to represent a table of data items consisting of rows and columns. It is also known as a matrix. A 3D array can be used to represent a collection of tables. The concept can go beyond three dimensions also.**

The dimension of the array is known as its rank. For instance, a 1D array has rank 1, a 2D array has a rank of 2, and so on. **The number of subscripts is determined by the rank of an array. The size or length of each dimension is represented by an integral value greater than or equal to 0. The total number of elements in an array is the product of the sizes of each dimension in an array. If any one or more of the dimensions of an array have size 0, the array is known as an empty array.** An array may be *regular or ragged.* **A ragged/jagged array** is a 1D array which contains arrays as elements. **A regular array** is a multidimensional array where each dimension contains the same number of elements, which is not generally true for jagged arrays.

NOTE   *2D regular arrays are also known as rectangular arrays.*

Note that the size of an array is not part of the array data type.

The overall classification of arrays in C is shown in Figure 3.1.

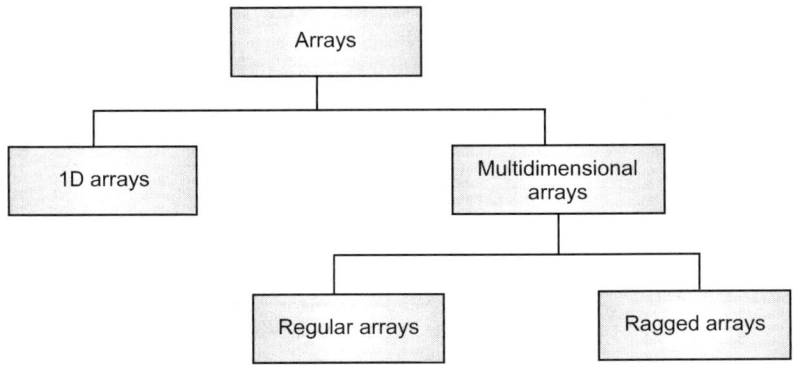

Figure 3.1: Types of Arrays

A regular array results in a regular shape whereas a ragged array results in an irregular shape.

3.1 1D, 2D, AND 3D ARRAYS

An array must be created before using its elements in a program. There are two steps:

(a) Declare an array

(b) Instantiate an array

The syntax for declaration of an array depends on the shape and number of dimensions. Only declared arrays can be instantiated. It is worth mentioning here that it is also possible to combine declaration and instantiation in a single statement.

In C, a one-dimensional array is declared as follows:

datatype   arrayname[ ];

For example, the following statements declare an array of integers:

int marks[ ];

Note that this statement just declares that 'marks' is an array variable; no array actually exists.

Arrays can also be initialized (for example, the first 6 elements) as follows:

int marks [ ] = {10, 20, 30, 40, 50, 60};

Please note that in this case the array will automatically be created large enough to hold the number of elements that you specify in the array initializer. Also note that there is no need of using new operator when you initialize an array. You can access an array element by specifying its index within square brackets. For example, you can access the fourth element of an array 'marks' as marks[3].

Remember the following points:

1. The square brackets follow the data type and not the array name.

2. It is also possible to have the square brackets follow the array name.

3. The above syntax declares references to the arrays of a specific data type.

4. These references are initialized with default null values.

5. Thus, memory is not allocated for an array by the declaration alone.

6. The data type of elements and the rank of the array are identified from the declaration.

7. The size of an array representing the length of dimension is not part of the array's type. That is why the size of the array is not mentioned it its declaration.

8. The declaration also does not enclose any integer value between the opening and closing square brackets.

9. **Note here that in C array indexing starts from 0 and uses integer expressions.**

10. An array having a size equal to 0 is known as an **empty array.**

11. **Once an array is created, its size cannot be changed.**

12. **The subscript of the last element in an array is one less than the total number of elements in the array.**

13. In C, array initialization suffers from two drawbacks:

    (a) There is no simple way to initialize only the selected elements.

    (b) There is no shortcut method to initialize a large number of elements.

14. To alleviate indexing problems, the sizeof( ) expression is commonly used when coding loops that process arrays—that is,

```
int i;
short a[ ] = {1,2,3,4,5};
for (i=0; i< (sizeof(a) / sizeof(short)); ++i)
{
    ........
}
```

In the preceding code snippet, the size of the array was not explicitly specified. The compiler knows to size it as 5 as there are 5 elements in the list 'a'. *Adding an additional value to the list will cause it to be sized to 6 and because of the sizeof expression in the for loop, the code automatically adjusts to this change.*

For example,

```
void main( )
  {
    int a[ ] = {2,4,6,8,10};
    int i;
    for ( i = 0; i < 5; i ++)
          printf ("The array elements are: ", a[i]);
  }
}
```

OUTPUT (after running):

2   4   6   8   10

Please note here that C strictly checks to make sure that you do not try to store or reference values outside of the range of the array. C's runtime system does all this work. If you try to go outside the array boundary C reports an error as follows:

Exception in "main" 'Array Index is Out Of Bounds...'

So we have to be careful while using arrays in C.

As already explained earlier, regular arrays may be 1D or multidimensional. Those beyond 3D arrays are rarely used. The regular array is the simplest form of 1D array. It is also created using the two steps mentioned at the beginning of the chapter.

Say we want to add 100 elements of an array. We can write as follows:

```
sum = 0.0;
for(i=0; i<100; ++i)
  sum = sum + a[i];
```

Note that in addition to integer constants, integer-valued expressions can also be used inside the brackets to reference a particular element of the array. So if low and high were defined as integer variables, then the statement

next_value = sorted_data[(low + high)/2];

would assign to the variable next_value indexed by evaluating the expression (low+high)/2.

If low is equal to 1 and high is equal to 9, the value of sorted_data[5] would be assigned to the next_value; and

If low is equal to 1 and high is equal to 10, the value of sorted_data[5] would also be referenced.

Also note that, like variables, arrays must be declared before they are used. The declaration of an array involves the type of the element that will be contained in the array, such as int, float, or char, as well as the maximum number of elements that will be stored inside the array.

How to Read an Array from the Keyboard

Consider the following code snippet:

```
int i;               //n = 10 = size of array
int a[10];
printf(" Enter total number of elements in array:");
for (i =0; i<n; i++)
  scanf("%d", &a[i]);
```

The Issue of Copying Arrays

An array is an object. There is a difference between an array and the variable that references it. Thus, that array and the reference variable are two separate entities. This difference becomes essential when you wish to copy the contents of one array to another. The following is the **wrong way** of copying an array:

```
int a1[ ] = {1, 3, 5, 7};
int a2[ ] = a1;   //error, no copying will be done.
```

These two statements will not copy the contents of a1 to a2. Instead a copy of the address stored in a1 is stored in a2. Thus, after this statement executes, both the a1 and a2 variables will reference the same array. Recall that this is also known as shadow copying.

Correct Method

We observed from the preceding example that we **cannot copy** an array by merely assigning one array reference variable to another. **Please remember that to copy an array you need to copy the individual elements of one array to another as follows:**

int [ ] firstArray = { 1, 2, 3, 4, 5, 6, 7, 8, 9};

int [ ] secondArray [9];

for(int i=0; i < n; i++)

secondArray[i] = firstArray[i];

The loop in this code copies each element of *firstArray* to the corresponding element of *secondArray*.

Before we discuss multidimensional arrays, let us summarize arrays as follows:

1. Do not index into an array with an invalid index.

2. Not initializing all of the values of an array results in errors.

3. Saying a=10; will not assign 10 to each element of the array 'a'. This is not syntactically correct **because the left-hand side is not an integer variable whereas the right-hand side is an integer expression.**

4. You must differentiate between an array index and the values stored in an array at a particular index.

5. An array may hold at most the number of elements specified by its size. **It may hold no data if the size is 0.**

6. An array name followed by a subscript enclosed within the square brackets refers to the individual elements in it.

7. The subscript can be *byte, short, char,* or *int.* it cannot be **long type.**

8. The elements are stored in **consecutive/successive memory locations.**

9. **Subscripted array variables are treated as ordinary variables.**

10. **Subscripted array variables use the subscript enclosed within square brackets whereas ordinary variables do not have any subscript.**

11. By incrementing the value of the subscript by 1, the data stored in the subsequent memory location is obtained. **Please note here that this is not true of ordinary variables.**

12. Accessing an array element is similarly easy irrespective of the size of the array. **The value of the subscript gives the position of the element in the array.**

13. Arrays may be one-dimensional **or multidimensional.**

14. Arrays may be **regular or ragged.**

15. In 2D regular arrays, all rows have the same number of columns.

16. A 1D ragged array may have rows with equal or different column sizes.

17. An array instance created is always an array type.

18. When an instance of an array is created, the rank and size of each dimension are specified and **remain constant throughout the lifetime of the instance. It is not possible to change the rank and size of the dimensions of an existing array.**

19. **Sizes must be constant values.**

20. An array is a reference data type.

21. The data type of elements, the shape of an array, and the number of dimensions are part of the type of array. Thus, an array contains only these details in its declaration.

22. Array size is not part of the array's type. Thus, the declaration of an array does not contain its size.

23. An array declaration does not reserve any memory.

24. An instance of the array is created dynamically using **new operator.**

25. **It is only in array creation using** *new operator* that the values within square brackets mention the size. In other places, they refer to the indices or subscripts only. **The subscript must be an integral constant.**

26. **The size of the array must be an integer greater than or equal to 0.** After creation of arrays, the values of the subscripted variables assume default values if there are no initializers.

27. **The array subscripts must always start at zero.**

28. **The last array variable's subscript is always [size -1] (i.e., one less than the size of the array).**

29. You cannot index an array backward (like a[-1], a[-2], etc.). **Also note that it is illegal to refer to elements that are out of array bounds. For example,** for an array of size 8, the array bound is from a [0] to a [7] only. The **C compiler checks on the array bounds and report errors, if any, at compile time.**

30. While executing a program, a value of an array type can be null or a reference to an instance of that array type.

31. Initialization of an array may be combined with instantiation by using initializers.

32. **Array elements are initialized to their default values,** if they are not explicitly initialized by using initializers, when an instance is created.

We are in a position to solve some questions based on 1D arrays now.

Q1. Write a C program that reads 10 integer elements and displays them.

Solution 1: The program is as follows:

```
#include<stdio.h>
main( )
{
    int val[10];
    int i;
    printf("\n\tEnter the array elements:");
    for (i =0; i<10; i++)
     scanf("%d", &val[i]);
    printf("\n\tArray elements are: ");
    for (i = 0; i <10; i++)
       printf("\n%d", val[i]);
}
```

OUTPUT (after running):

Enter the array elements: 1 2 3 4 5

Array elements are:

1

2

3

4

5

Q2. Write a C program that finds the sum and average of 10 real numbers and displays them.

Solution 2: The program is as follows:

```
#include<stdio.h>
main( )
{
    int num [10], i, large;
    float average, sum;
    int i;
    printf("\n\tEnter the array elements:");
    for(i=0; i<10; i++)
        scanf("%f", &num[i]);
    sum = 0;
    for(i=0;i<10;i++)
     sum = sum + num[i];
    average = sum / 10.0;
    printf("\n\tSum of 10 real number is=%f", sum);
```

```
    printf("\n\tAverage of 10 real numbers is=%f", average);
    }
```

NOTE *Students should run this program on their own.*

Q3. Write a C program to show the passing of an entire array.

Solution 3: The program is as follows:

```
#include<stdio.h>
main( )
{
    int val[10];
    int max, i,n;
    printf("\n\tPlease enter the array size:");
    scanf("%d", &n);
    printf("\n\tPlease enter the array elements:");
    for(i=0; i<n;i++)
      scanf("%d", &val[i]);
    max = large(val, 10);   /*passing the entire array
'val' */
    printf("\n\tLargest elements is %d", max);
}
large(int val[ ] , int n)
{
    int temp, i;
    temp = val[0];
    for(i=1;i<n;i++)
      {
        if (temp < val[i])
            temp = val[i];
      }
    return temp;
}
```

OUTPUT (after running):

Enter the size of the array: 10

Enter the array elements: 1 2 3 4 5 8 9 10 20 30

Largest element is: 30

Please note here that when an array is passed as an argument then the base address of the array (i.e., the address of the first element) is passed. Also note that by default the array is passed by reference only.

Q4. Write a C program that reads 10 integer elements, reverses them, and then displays them.

Solution 4: The program is as follows:

```
#include<stdio.h>
void main( )
{
    int a[10], i;
    clrscr( );
    printf("\n\tEnter your 10 array elements:");
    for(i=0; i<10; i++)
        scanf("%d", &a[i]);
    printf("\nThe list in reverse order is:");
    for(i=9; i>=0; i- -)
        printf("%d", a[i]);
    getch( );
}
```

OUTPUT (after running):

Enter the 10 array elements: 1 2 3 4 5 6 7 8 9 10

The list in reverse order is: 10 9 8 7 6 5 4 3 2 1

Q5. Write a C program that reads an array, finds the greatest element, and prints this number and its position in that array.

Solution 5: The program is as follows:

```
#include<stdio.h>
#include<conio.h>
void main( )
{
    int a[90], big, pos, i, n;
    clrscr( );
    printf("\nEnter the size of the array:");
    scanf("%d", &n);
    printf("\nEnter the array elements:");
    for (i =0; i<n; i++)
        scanf("%d", &a[i]);
    big = a[0]; /*assume 1st element is the largest one */
    pos = 0;    /*set the position of big as 0 */
    for (i=1; i<n; i++)
      {
        if (a[i] > big)
```

```
        {
          big = a[i];
          pos = i;
        }
    }
      pos++;  /*increment  pos  by  1  as  array  is  counted
  from 0 */
      printf("\nLargest  number  =%d  is  stored  at  position
  = %d", big, pos);
      getch( );
    }
```

OUTPUT (after running):

Enter the size of the array: 5

Enter the array elements: 1 2 3 4 5

The largest number = 5 is stored at position = 5

Q6. Write a C program using an array of, say, 10 elements, to interchange its even-position elements with odd-position elements.

Solution 6: The program is as follows:

```
#include<stdio.h>
#include<conio.h>
void main( )
{
    int a[10], i, t;
    clrscr( );
    printf("\n\tEnter a list of 5 elements:");
    for(i=0; i<5; i++)
        scanf("%d", &a[i]);
    /*Interchange eve elements with odd elements position
wise */
    for(i=0; i< 5; i+=2)
      {
        t = a[i];
        a[i] = a[i+1];
        a[i+1] = t;
      }
    printf("\nThe final list is:");
    for(i=0; i<5; i++)
        printf("%d\t", a[i]);
    getch( );
}
```

OUTPUT (after running):

Enter a list of 5 elements: 2 4 6 -8 10

The final list is: 4 2 -8 6 10

Q7. Write a C program to convert a binary number to a decimal number.

Solution 7: The program is as follows:

```
#include<stdio.h>
#include<conio.h>
#include<math.h>
void main( )
{
    int i, r, count=0;
    long b, n =0, b1;
    clrscr( );
    printf("\nEnter a binary number: ");
    scanf("%ld", &b);
    b1 = b;
    while(b > 0)
      {
        r = b % 10;
        n = n + r * pow (2, count);
        count = count + 1;
        b = b/10;
      }
    printf("\nDecimal value of binary %ld = %ld", b1, n);
    getch( );
}
```

OUTPUT (after running):

Enter a binary number: 0010

Decimal value of binary 0010 = 2

NOTE *Students should attempt the reverse program (i.e., convert a decimal number to its binary form).*

Q8. Write a C program to search a given number from a list of n numbers and to print its location also.

Solution 8: The program is as follows:

```
#include<stdio.h>
#include<conio.h>
void main( )
{
    int a[80], i, s, n, loc;
    clrscr( );
    printf("\nEnter number of elements in the array: ");
    scanf("%d", &n);
    printf("\nEnter the array elements:");
    for(i=0; i<n; i++)
        scanf("%d", & a[i]);
    printf("\nEnter the element you want to search:");
    scanf("%d", &s);
    for(i =0; i <n; i++)
      {
        if (s = = a[i])
      {
      loc = i + 1;
      printf("\nElement %d is present at %d location", s,
loc);
      break;
      }
      }
      if (i = =n)
      printf("\nElement %d is not present in the list", s);
      getch( );
      }
```

OUTPUT (after running):

Enter number of elements in the array: 10

Enter the array elements: 10 20 30 40 50 60 70 80 90 100

Enter the element you want to search: 90

Element 90 is present at 9 location

Q9. Write a C program to read n values from the keyboard and compute their mean standard deviation (SD) and variance (VAR).

[**Hint:** The formulas to be used are as follows:

$$AM = 1/n \ \Sigma x_i \text{ where } i \rightarrow 1 \text{ to } n$$

$$VAR = 1/n \ [\Sigma \ (x_i - AM)^2 \ ]$$

and SD = sqrt(VAR)].

Multidimensional Arrays

A multidimensional array is an array having more than one dimension (2d, 3d, etc.)

Two-Dimensional Arrays

A two-dimensional array is basically a collection of similar types of elements which are organized in two dimensions. They are used to represent a table with rows and columns. Real-life examples of 2d arrays include chess boards, tic-tac-toe boards, and so on.

How to Declare 2d Arrays in C

Declaring a 2d array uses the following syntax:

datatype arrayname [m][n];

Here, **arrayname** is the name of a two-dimensional array that contains the elements of the **datatype** mentioned and has 'm' number of rows and 'n' number of columns. **For example,**

int a[10][20];

It declares that 'a' is a two-dimensional array with dimensions of (10 * 20).

How to Access 2d Arrays in C

An individual data item of a 2D array is accessed by specifying the row and column of a 2d array as follows:

a[i] [j];

where 'i' refers to the row number and 'j' refers to the column number.

For example, a[1][2] refers to the data item in the 2nd row and 3rd column (noting that indexing in C starts from 0).

How to Read Elements into a 2d Array in C

We read in the values of 2d arrays by using two nested for loops as follows:

```
for(i=0;  i<m;  i++)
  {
    for(j=0;j<n;j++)
        scanf("%d", &num[i][j]);
  }
```

How to Display Elements from a 2d Array in C

We use nested loops to display the array elements (i.e., one for the row and one for the column) as follows:

```
for(i=0; i<m; i++)
 {
    for(j=0;j<n;j++)
      printf("%d\n", num[i][j]);
 }
```

How to Initialize a 2d Array in C

Like a 1d array, we can also initialize a 2d array during its declaration as follows:

```
int a[3][4] = {
      {10, 20, 30, 40},
      {50, 60, 70, 80},
      {90, 100, 110, 120}
      };
```

We can also initialize it as follows in a single line:

int a[3][4] = {10,20,30,40,50,60,70,80,90,100,110,120};

Please note that when we initialize 2d arrays, the declaration of the first dimension (row) is optional but the second dimension (column) declaration is compulsory. Also note that the user has to explicitly mention size of column during the initialization of a 2d array.

The following statement is **valid in C**:

int a[ ][4] = {10,20,30,40,50,60,70,80,90,100,110,120};

On the other hand, the following declarations are **invalid**:

int a[ ][ ] = {10,20,30,40,50,60,70,80,90,100,110,120};

int a[3][ ] = {10,20,30,40,50,60,70,80,90,100,110,120};

Matrices are the best example of 2d arrays.

We are in a position to write some programs now.

Example 1: **Write a C program to add two matrices, giving keyboard entries.**

Solution 1: *Two matrices are added when they have similar dimensions (i.e., both matrices must have the same number of rows and the same number of columns).* The program is as follows:

```c
#include<stdio.h>
main( )
{
    int a[10][10], b[10][10], c[10][10];
    int i, j, row1, row2, col1, col2;
    printf("\n\tEnter the number of rows and columns of
    first matrix:");
    scanf("%d%d", &row1, &col1);
    printf("\n\tEnter the number of rows and columns of
    second matrix:");
    scanf("%d%d", &row2, &col2);
    if ((row1 = = row2) && (col1 = = col2))
      {
        printf("\nEnter the elements of first matrix (*d *
        %d)", row1, col1);
        for(i=0; i<row1; i++)
          {
            for(j=0; j<col1; j++)
                scanf("%d", &a[i][j]);
          }
printf("\nEnter the elements of second matrix (*d * %d)",
row2, col2);
        for(i=0; i<row2; i++)
          {
            for(j=0; j<col2; j++)
                scanf("%d", &b[i][j]);
          }
        for(i=0; i<row1; i++)
          {
            for(j=0; j<col1; j++)
                c[i][j] = a[i][j] + b[i][j];
          }
        printf("\nAddition of two matrices is:");
        for(i=0; i<row1; i++)
          {
            printf("\n");
            for(i=0; i<col1; i++)
              {
                    printf("%d", c[i][j]);
              }
          }
      }
}
```

```
      else
        {
          printf("\nDimensions  of  both  matrices  do  not
          match");
          printf("Please enter same dimensions of both ma-
          trices");
        }
      }
```

OUTPUT-1 (after running):

Enter the number of rows and columns of first matrix: 3 4

Enter the number of rows and columns of second matrix: 4 4

Dimensions of both matrices do not match.

Please enter same dimensions of both matrices.

OUTPUT-2 (after running):

Enter the number of rows and columns of first matrix: 3 4

Enter the number of rows and columns of second matrix: 3 4

Enter the elements of first matrix (3 ° 4):

5	5	5	5
5	5	5	5
5	5	5	5

Enter the elements of second matrix (3 ° 4):

5	5	5	5
5	5	5	5
5	5	5	5

Addition of two matrices is:

10	10	10	10
10	10	10	10
10	10	10	10

Example 2: **Write a C program to multiply two matrices, giving keyboard entries.**

Solution 2: *Two matrices are multiplied when the number of columns of the first matrix matches with the number of rows of the second matrix.* The program is as follows:

```
#include<stdio.h>
main( )
{
    int a[10][10], b[10][10], c[10][10];
    int i, j, k, row1, row2, col1, col2;
    printf("\n\tEnter the number of rows and columns of
    first matrix:");
    scanf("%d%d", &row1, &col1);
    printf("\n\tEnter the number of rows and columns of
    second matrix:");
    scanf("%d%d", &row2, &col2);
    if (col1 = = row2)
      {
        printf("\nEnter the elements of first matrix (%d *
        %d)\n",                        row1, col1);
        for (i=0; i<row1; i++)
          {
            for(j=0; j<col1; j++)
              {
                    scanf("%d", &a[i][j]);
              }
          }
        printf("\nEnter the elements of second matrix (%d
                %d)\n", row2, col2);
  *     for (i=0; i<row2; i++)
          {
            for(j=0; j<col2; j++)
              {
                    scanf("%d", &b[i][j]);
              }
          }
        for(i=0; i<row1; i++)
          {
            for(j=0; j<col2; j++)
              {
                    c[i][j] = 0;
                    for(k=0; k<col1; k++)
                        c[i][j] += a[i][k] * b[k][j];
              }
```

```
    }
    printf("\nMultiplication of two matrices is: ");
    for(i=0; i<row1; i++)
      {
        printf(\n");
        for(j=0; j<col2; j++)
          {
              printf("%d\t", c[i][j]);
          }
      }
    }
    else
      {
      printf("\nColumns of first matrix and rows of second
      ma trix do not match");
      printf(\nPlease re-enter correct dimensions of both
      the matrices");
      }
    }
```

OUTPUT (after running):

Enter the number of rows and columns of first matrix: 2 4

Enter the number of rows and columns of second matrix: 4 3

Enter the elements of first matrix (2 * 4):

2	4	5	6
1	6	3	8

Enter the elements of second matrix (4 * 3):

5	3	8
9	0	1
3	5	7
4	6	1

Multiplication of two matrices is:

85	67	61
100	66	43

Example 3: **Write a C program to find the transpose of a given matrix.**

Solution 3: *The transpose of a matrix is found by changing all rows to columns and vice versa. So in our program we need to set the elements of a[i][j] to b[j][i].* The program is as follows:

```c
#include<stdio.h>
main( )
{
    int a[10][10], b[10][10];
    int i, j, row, col;
    printf("\n\tEnter the number of rows and columns of the
    matrix:");
    scanf("%d%d", &row, &col);
    printf("\nReading array elements:");
    for(i=0; i<row; i++)
      {
        for(j=0; j<col; j++)
           scanf("%d", &a[i][j]);
      }
    printf("\nEchoing…..");
    for(i=0; i<row; i++)
      {
        for(j=0; j<col; j++)
           printf("%d", a[i][j]);
      }
    for(i=0; i<col; i++)
      {
        for(j=0; j<row; j++)
           b[i][j] = a[j][i];
      }
    printf("\nTranspose of a given matrix:");
    for(i=0; i<col; i++)
      {
        printf("\n");
        for(j=0; j<row; j++)
           printf("%d", b[i][j]);
      }
}
```

OUTPUT (after running):

Enter the row and column of a matrix: 3 3

Echoing ...

1 2 3

4 5 6

7 8 9

Transpose of a given matrix:

1 4 7

2 5 8

3 6 9

Example **4: Write a C program to find the largest and the smallest elements of a matrix.**

Solution 4: The program is as follows:

```
#include<stdio.h>
#include<conio.h>
void main( )
{
    int a[10][10], r, c, i, j, big, small, locbi, locbj,
    locsi, locsj;
    clrscr( );
    printf("\n\tEnter the number of rows and columns of the
    matrix:");
    scanf("%d%d", &row, &col);
    printf("\nReading array elements:");
    for(i=0; i<row; i++)
      {
        for(j=0; j<col; j++)
            scanf("%d", &a[i][j]);
      }
        big = a[0][0];
        small = a[0][0];
    for(i=0; i<r; i++)
      {
        for(j=0; j<c; j++)
          {
            if (a[i][j] > big)
```

```
            {
                 big = a[i][j];
                 locbi = i +1;
                 locbj = j + 1;
            }
          if (a[i][j] < small)
            {
                 small = a[i][j];
                 locsi = i +1;
                 locsj = j + 1;
            }
      }
    }
    printf("\nLargest element is %d", big);
    printf("\nLargest element is stored at %d row %d
    column",                 locbi, locbj);
    printf("\nSmallest element is %d", small);
    printf("\nSmallest element is stored at %d row %d
    column", losci, locsj);
    getch( );
}
```

OUTPUT (after running):

Enter the row and column of a matrix: 3 3

Echoing …

1 2 3

4 5 6

7 8 9

Largest element is 9

Largest element is stored at 3 row and 3 column

Smallest element is 1

Smallest element is stored at 1 row and 1 column

Example 5: Write a C program to print Pascal's triangle—that is,

1

1   1

1   2   1

1	3	3	1	
1	4	6	4	1 ?

Solution 5: The program is as follows:

```c
#include<stdio.h>
#include<conio.h>
void main( )
{
    int a[10][10], i, j, n;
    clrscr( );
    printf("\nHow many rows you want?");
    scanf("%d", &n);
    for (i =1; i< = n; i++)
      {
        for (j=1; j <=i j++)
          {
            if (j = = 1 | | j = = i)
                  a[i][j] = 1;
            else
                  a[i][j] = a[i-1][j] + a[i-1][j-1];
            printf("%d\t", a[i][j]);
          }
        printf("\n");
      }
    getch( );
}
```

OUTPUTS (after running):

How many rows you want? 5

1

1 1

1 2 1

1 3 3   1

1 4 6   4   1

What Is an Array of Characters

Like a number array, we can also define and use character arrays, which are declared as follows:

char array_name[size];

Here, *array_name* is the name of the array storing character-type data and *size* is the total number of characters in **array_name.**

For example,

char name[80];

Here, name is an array that can hold upto 80 characters. Again, array indexes start from 0. So the fifth element of name[ ] array is referred to as:

name[4];

Similarly, entire array elements can be accessed using loops.

How to Read Characters into a Character Array

The procedure is the same as that for integer arrays, but you should know that a character takes 1 byte, so an array of characters storing 10 characters will have a size of 10 bytes. Here is the loop:

for(i=0; i<size; i++)

scanf("%c", &name[i]);

How to Write Characters from a Character Array

Again the procedure is same as that for integer arrays; the loop to write is as follows:

for (i=0; i<size; i++)

printf("%c", name[i]);

Before further discussion, attempt to write the following programs.

Q1. Write a C program to read your name using the concept of array of characters.

Solution 1: The program is as follows:

```
#include<stdio.h>
main( )
{
    char name[10]'
    int i;
    printf("\nPlease enter your name:");
    for(i=0; i< 10; i++)
        scanf("%c", &name[i]);
```

```
        printf("\nEchoing…..");
        for(i=0;  i<10;  i++)
            printf("%c", name[i]);
}
```

OUTPUT (after running):

Please enter your name: Dr. RAJIV

Echoing … Dr. RAJIV

How to Initialize a Character Array

Like an array of ints or floats or doubles, we can also initialize an array of chars during its declaration as follows:

> char name[10] = {'D', 'r', '.', 'R', 'A', 'J', 'I', 'V' };

We can also write the following:

> char name[ ] = {'D', 'r', '.', 'R', 'A', 'J', 'I', 'V' };

Please note that during array declaration, if the subscript (array size) is omitted, it is assumed to be the size of the data with which the array is initialized. This means that the size declaration is optional in array declaration. Also note that it is the duty of the user to remember the number of characters stored in the array.

What Are Strings in C?

A string is a special character array which is terminated by a NULL character. This NULL character is represented by '\0' (ASCII value of NULL is 0). Strings in C are enclosed in double quotes.

For example,

> "Dr. Rajiv Chopra is a Ph.D. in Computer Science"

Each character is stored in 1 byte. The last character is a NULL character.

How Are Strings Initialized?

A string in C is initialized character by character as follows:

> char name[10] = {'D', 'R', '.', 'R', 'A', 'J', 'I', 'V', '\0' };

Please note here that it is necessary to insert the NULL character at the end of the string. But it is also possible to initialize a string as follows:

> char name[10] = "Dr. RAJIV";

Here the NULL character is appended automatically by the C compiler. **Also note that while declaring char as a string, the size of string should be declared one character longer.** It implies that if an array of characters can hold 10 characters, then it can store 9 characters as a string because the last character stored in the string is a NULL character.

How to Read and Write Strings

The format specifier used in scanf is '%s' for strings.

For example,

```
#include<stdio.h>
main( )
{
    char name1[ ] = "Dr.";
    char name2[ ] = "Rajiv";
    printf("\nFirst name is %s", name1);
    printf("\nSecond name is %s", name2);
}
```

This results in:

First name is Dr.

Second name is Rajiv

For another example,

```
#include<stdio.h>
main( )
{
    char name1[15], name2[15];
    printf("\nPlease enter your first name:");
    scanf("%s", name1);
    printf("\nPlease enter your second name:");
    scanf("%s", name2);
    printf("\nFirst name is %s", name1);
    printf("\nSecond name is %s", name2);
}
```

This results in:

Please enter your first name: RAJIV

Please enter your second name: CHOPRA

First name is: RAJIV

Second name is: CHOPRA

But please note here that the %s format specifier has some limitations:

1. The first limitation of using the format specifier '%s' is that the programmer has to remember the size of the character array.

2. The second limitation is that it cannot receive multiwords strings from the keyboard.

3. That is, in the above program, if we enter the input name string as DR. RAJIV then it would only display Dr. When it encounters a space bar, it will automatically terminate the string.

The gets( ) and puts( ) Functions in C

In C, we have the standard function gets( ) to receive multiword strings from the keyboard and the function puts( ) to print multiwords strings on the screen.

For example,

```
#include<stdio.h>
main( )
{
    char name1[50][name2[50];
    printf("\nEnter the first name: ");
    gets(name1);
    printf("\nEnter the second name: ");
    gets(name2);
    printf("\nFirst name is:");
    puts(name1);
    printf("\nSecond name is:");
    puts(name2);
}
```

OUTPUT (after running):

Enter the first name: Dr. RAJIV

Enter the second name: CHOPRA

First name is: Dr. RAJIV

Second name is: CHOPRA

But there are some limitations. We can receive and display one and only one string by using the gets( ) and puts( ) functions. Thus, the following statements are absolutely invalid:

gets(name1, name2)   /* invalid */

puts (name1, name2) /* invalid */

Along similar lines, we can display only one string on the screen using the puts( ) function.

Let us see how:

```
#include<stdio.h>
main( )
{
    puts("\nDr. RAJIV");
    puts("\nCHOPRA");
    getch( );
}
```

OUTPUT (after running):

Dr. RAJIV

CHOPRA

Before further discussion, let us write some programs.

Example **1: Write a C program to convert an uppercase string into a lowercase string.**

Solution 1: Remember that the ASCII values of uppercase letters (A, B, C, etc,) fall between 65 and 90 and the values of lowercase letters (a, b, c, etc.) fall between 97 and 122. **The difference between each uppercase letter and its corresponding lowercase letter is 32.** Keeping this in mind, we write the following program:

```
#include<stdio.h>
main( )
{
    char name[80];
    int i =0;
    puts("\nEnter any upper case string:");
    gets(name);
    puts("\nEchoing....);
    puts(name);
    while (name[i] != '\0')
{
    if (name[i] >=65) && (name[i] <=90))
        name[i] = name[i] + 32;
    i++;
}
```

```
puts("Converted lower case string is");
puts(name);
}
```

OUTPUT *(after running):*

Enter any uppercase string: DR. RAJIV CHOPRA

Echoing …

DR. RAJIV CHOPRA

Converted lowercase string is:

dr. rajiv chopra

Inbuilt String Functions and the "string.h" Header File

C provides an inbuilt library of string manipulating functions. **These inbuilt functions are defined in a header file named <string.h>.** Inclusion of this file is necessary if you use any of the following inbuilt string functions:

> I. **The strlen( ) function**
>
> II. **The strcpy( ) function**
>
> III. **The strcmp( ) function**
>
> IV. **The strcat( ) function**
>
> V. **The strrev( ) function**
>
> VI. **The strlwr( ) and strupr( ) functions**

I. The strlen( ) Function

The strlen( ) function returns the total number of characters (excluding the null character) in a string.

Syntax

strlen(str);

Here, *str* is any string constant or a string variable name.

For example,

```
#include<stdio.h>
#include<string.h>
main( )
{
    char name[20];
```

```
    int len;
    printf("\nEnter any string:");
    gets(name);
    len = strlen(name);
    printf("The length of a given string is %d", len);
}
```

OUTPUT (after running):

Enter any string: Dr. Rajiv Chopra

The length of a given string is 16

NOTE   *Each space is counted as 1 byte (even '.' is counted as 1 byte).*

II. The strcpy( ) Function

The strcpy( ) function copies the contents of one string into another string.

Syntax

strcpy(dest, source);

Here, the contents of string *source* are copied into string *dest*.

For example,

```
#include<stdio.h>
#include<string.h>
main( )
{
    char name[20], dupname[20];
    printf("\nEnter your string:");
    gets(name);
    strcpy(dupname, name);
    printf("Duplicated string is %s", dupname);
}
```

OUTPUT (after running):

Enter your string: DR. RAJIV

Duplicated string is: DR. RAJIV

III. The strcmp( ) Function

The strcmp( ) function compares the contents of one string to another string. It returns an **integer value.**

Syntax

strcmp(str1, str2);

Here str1 and str2 are the string constants or string variables. *The function returns 0 if they are equal, returns a negative if str1 is less than str2, and returns a positive if str1 is greater than str2.* **Remember that this comparison is case sensitive.**

For example,

```
#include<stdio.h>
#include<string.h>
main( )
{
    char name1[80], name2[80];
    printf("\nEnter your first string:");
    gets (name1);
    printf("\nEnter your second string:");
    gets (name2);
    if (strcmp(name1, name2) = = 0)
       printf("Both strings are equal");
    else
       printf("Both strings are not equal");
}
```

OUTPUT (after running):

Enter your first string: DR. RAJIV

Enter your second string: DR. RAJIV

Both strings are equal

OUTPUT-2 (after running):

Enter your first string: DR. RAJIV

Enter your second string: dr. rajiv

Both strings are not equal

IV. The strcat( ) function

The strcat( ) function appends the characters of the second argument to the end of the first argument.

Syntax

strcat (str, str);

Here the contents of string str2 are appended to string str1.

For example,

```
#include<stdio.h>
#include<string.h>
main( )
{
    char str1[20], str2[20], str3[20];
    printf("\nEnter your first string:");
    gets(str1);
    printf("\nEnter your second string:");
    gets(str2);
    strcpy(str3, str1);
    strcat(str3, str2);
    printf("Concatenated string is %s", str3);
}
```

OUTPUT (after running):

Enter your string: DR. RAJIV

Enter your second string: CHOPRA

Concatenated string is: DR. RAJIV CHOPRA

V. The strrev( ) Function

The strrev( ) function reverses the string.

Syntax

strrev(str);

Here the contents of string str are reversed and stored in str.

Before continuing the discussion, please write the following programs.

Example 1: **Write a C program to find whether a given string is a palindrome.**

Solution 1: Any number or word or string that reads the same from left-to-right as it does from right-to-left is a palindrome (e.g., 121, TOOT, MADAM, etc.). The program is as follows:

```
#include<stdio.h>
#include<string.h>
main( )
{
    char name1[80], name2[80];
    printf("\nEnter your string:");
    gets (name1);
    strcpy(name2, name1);
    strrev(name1);
    if (strcmp(name1, name2) = = 0)
        printf("Given string is a palindrome");
    else
        printf("Given string is not a palindrome");
}
```

OUTPUT (after running):

Enter your string: DR. RAJIV

Given string is not a palindrome.

Enter your string: TOOT

Given string is a palindrome

VI. The strlwr( ) and strupr( ) functions

The strlwr( ) function changes the characters of a string into lowercase and the **strupr( ) function** changes the characters of a string into uppercase.

Syntax

strlwr (str1);

strupr (str);

For example,

```
/*Program to convert any string into lowercase characters
and uppercase characters.
#include<stdio.h>
#include<string.h>
main( )
{
    char name1[80], name2[80];
    printf("\nEnter your string:");
    gets (name1);
    strcpy(name2, name1);
```

```
    strlwr(name1);
    strupr(name2);
    printf("Equivalent lowercase string is %s", name1");
    printf("Equivalent uppercase string is %s", name2");
}
```

OUTPUT (after running):

Enter your string: Dr. Rajiv

Equivalent lowercase string is dr. rajiv

Equivalent uppercase string is DR. RAJIV

Arrays of Strings/2d Array of Characters

An array of strings is also known as two-dimensional array of characters.

Syntax

char arrayname[row][col];

Here, 'arrayname' is the name of a 2d array of strings, 'row' contains the number of strings, and 'col' contains the number of columns reserved for each string.

For example,

char days[7][10];

Here, 'days' is the name of the array having 7 strings (or rows) and 10 is the number of columns reserved for each string/row. We can also initialize the array of strings during its declaration as follows:

char days[7][10] = {

```
              { 'M', 'O', 'N', 'D', 'A', 'Y', '\0' },
              { 'T', 'U', 'E', 'S', 'D', 'A', 'Y', '\0' },
              { 'W', 'E', 'D', 'N', 'E', 'S', 'D', 'A',
              'Y', '\0' },
              { 'T', 'H', 'U', 'R', 'S', 'D', 'A', 'Y',
              '\0' },
              { 'F', 'R', 'I', 'D', 'A', 'Y', '\0' },
              { 'S', 'A', 'T', 'U', 'R', 'D', 'A',
              'Y', '\0' },
              { 'S', 'U', 'N', 'D', 'A', 'Y', '\0' },
        };
```

Or you can also initialize the array of strings as follows:

```
char days[7][10] = {
            "MONDAY",
            "TUESDAY",
            "WEDNESDAY",
             "THURSDAY",
             "FRIDAY",
             "SATURDAY",
             "SUNDAY"
            };
```

This is simpler than the previous one.

Now if we want to display the contents of arrays of strings named as days[ ] [ ], we use the following statements:

```
for(i=0; i<6; i++)

        printf("\n%s", days[i]);
```

Yet another way of doing this is:

```
for(i=0; i<6; i++)

        printf("\n%s", days[i] [0]);
```

Similarly, if we want to read strings into an array from the keyboard, we use the following statement:

```
for(i=0; i<6; i++)

        scanf("\n%s", days[i]);
```

Let us write a complete program now to display weekday name according to a given weekday number.

```
#include<stdio.h>
main( )
{
char days[7][10] = {
            "MONDAY",
            "TUESDAY",
            "WEDNESDAY",
             "THURSDAY",
             "FRIDAY",
             "SATURDAY",
             "SUNDAY"
            };
```

```
    int choice;
    printf("\nEnter any week day number:");
    scanf("%d", &choice);
    if ((choice >=1) && (choice <=7))
    printf("\nYou have entered %s", days[choice - 1]);
    else
        printf("\nYou have entered wrong number");
}
```

OUTPUT (after running):

Enter any week day number: 4

You have entered THURSDAY.

We are in a position to write some programs now.

Example 1: **Write a C program to show the concept of pass by value in C. Then rewrite that same program using the concept of call by reference.**

Solution 1: Like any other arguments (data), array elements can also be passed by value and by reference. In the pass by value method, the array elements are passed while in pass by reference addresses of the array elements are passed. Let us write these two programs now.

```
/* using pass by value or call by value in C */
#include<stdio.h>
#include<conio.h>
void main( )
{
    int m [ ] = {10, 20, 30, 40 50}, i;
    clrscr( );
    for(i =0; i< 5; i++)
        show(a[i]);
    getch( );
}
    show (int marks)
     {
        printf("\t%d", marks);
     }
```

OUTPUTS (after running):
10 20 30 40 50

On the other hand, in call by reference or pass by reference:

```
/* using pass by reference or call by reference in C */
#include<stdio.h>
#include<conio.h>
void main( )
{
    int m [ ] = {10, 20, 30, 40 50}, i;
    clrscr( );
    for(i =0; i< 5; i++)
        show(&a[i]);
    getch( );
}
    show (int *marks)
      {
        printf("\t%d", *marks);
      }
```

OUTPUTS *(after running):*

10 20 30 40 50

Example **2: How will you modify the above program to pass an entire array in C?**

Solution 2: The program is as follows:

```
#include<stdio.h>
#include<conio.h>
void main( )
{
    int a[ ] = {10, 20, 30, 40 50}, i;
    clrscr( );
    show(a, 5); /* a is the starting address of the array
*/
    getch( );
}
show (int *a, int n)
{
    int i;
    for (i=0; i<n i++)
      {
        printf("\t%d", *a);
        a ++;
      }
}
```

OUTPUTS (after running):
10 20 30 40 50

Example 3: **Write a C program to sort an array of integers using the bubble sort method.**

Solution 3: The program is as follows:

```c
#include<stdio.h>
#include<conio.h>
void main( )
{
    int a[10], i, j, n, temp;
    clrscr( );
    printf("\n\tEnter the size of your array:");
    scanf("%d", &n);
    printf("\n\tEnter your array elements:");
    for(i =0; i<n; i++)
     scanf("%d", &a[i]);
    printf("\n\tEchoing array elements....");
    for(i =0; i<n; i++)
     printf("%d", a[i]);
    /*sorting now */
    for(i =0; i<n; i++)
     for(j= 1; j< n-1; j++)
     if( a[i] > a[j]) 3 cs. right
       {
          temp = a[i];
          a[i] = a[j];
          a[j] = temp;
       }
    printf("\n\tThe sorted array is:");
    for(i =0; i<n; i++)
     printf("%d", a[i]);
    getch( );
}
```

OUTPUTS (after running):

Enter the size of your array: 10

Enter the array elements: 20 10 40 50 30 60 70 90 80 100

Echoing the array… 20 10 40 50 30 60 70 90 80 100

The sorted array is 10 20 30 40 50 60 70 80 90 100

***Example* 4: Give the output of the following C code:**

```
#include<stdio.h>
main( )
{
    int i, j, Num=1;
    for (i =1; i <=100; i++)
      {
        for (j=1; j<1=100; j++)
            Num +=1;
        printf("%d\n", Num);
      }
}
```

Solution 4: Let us see the contents of the Num, i, and j variables by giving it a dry run:

Num		i	j
1	1	1	
2		2	
.		3	
.		..	
..		..	
..		99	
..		100	
101			

OUTPUT:

101

201

301

401

501

601

701

801

901

1001

...

Example **5: Write a C program to evaluate a polynomial using an array.**

Solution 5: The program is as follows:

```c
#include<stdio.h>
void main( )
{
    int a[40];
    int x, n, i, res;
    printf("\nEnter the maximum power of x: \n\t");
    scanf("%d", &n);   /* maximum size of array is read */
    printf("\nEnter the coefficents of the polynomial:\n");
    for(i=0;  i<=n;  i++)
      {
        printf("\nEnter the coefficient of X^ %d = \t", i);
        scanf("%d", &a[i]);
      }
    printf("\nEnter the value of X= \t");
    scanf("%d", &x);
    /*calculating polynomials value */
    res = a[n];
    for(i = n-1; i >=0; i- - )
        res = res * x + a[i];
    printf("\nValue of polynomial = %d\n", res);
}
```

OUTPUTS (after running):

Enter the maximum power of x: 2

Enter the coefficients of the polynomial:

Enter coefficient of X ^ 0 = 1

Enter coefficient of X ^ 1 = 2

Enter coefficient of X ^ 2 = 3

Enter the value of X = 2

Value of polynomial = 17

Example 6: **Write a C program to copy its input to its output, replacing each string of one or more blanks by a single blank.**

Solution 6: We will be using the getchar( ) and putchar( ) functions of C.

I. The getchar Function: getchar( );

The getchar function reads a single character from standard input. It takes no parameters and it returns the input character. In general, a reference to the getchar function is written as:

variable = getchar( );

For example,

char c;

c = getchar( );

Please note here that the second line causes a single character to be entered from the keyboard and then assigned to c. If an end-of-file condition is encountered when reading a character with the getchar function, the value of the symbolic constant EOF will automatically be returned. Also note that this function can also be used to read multi-character strings by reading one character at a time within a multipass loop.

II. The putchar Function: putchar(variable | constant);

The standard C function that prints or displays a single character by sending it to standard output is called **putchar.** This function takes one argument which is the character to be displayed.

For example,

putchar('R'); will display the character 'R'.

or

char var = '$';

putchar(var); displays the character $.

Let us first write the algorithm for this program:

Step 1: Read a character.

Step 2: If entered character is non-blank, print it.

Step 3: else print the first blank character and skip all consecutive blanks.

Step 4: Repeat steps 1 to 3 till the entered character is a newline character.

The program is as follows:

```c
#include<stdio.h>
#include<string.h>
void main( )
{
    char c;
    printf("\nEnter the text:");
    c= getchar( );
    printf("The output text is: ");
    while (c!= '\n')
      {
        if (c = = ' ' || c= = '\t')
          {
            c = ' ';
            putchar( c );
          }
        while(c = = ' ' | | c = = '\t')
        {
          c = getchar( );
        }
        putchar(c );
        c = getchar( );
      }
    printf("\n");
}
```

OUTPUTS *(after running):*

Enter the text: DR. RAJIV   CHOPRA

The output text is: DR. RAJIV CHOPRA

Example 7: **Write a C program to input N integer numbers in ascending order in a single-dimensional array and then perform a binary search for a given key integer number and display proper messages.**

Solution 7: Let us write the algorithms first:

Step 1: Read the array size n.

Step 2: Read the array elements.

Step 3: Read the key element to be searched.

Step 4: If the key element is equal to the middle element of the array,

> Print 'search is successful'.

Else if the element is greater than the middle element,

> Perform binary search in the second half of the array

Else

> Perform binary search in the first half of the array.

Step 5: Stop.

And the program in C is as follows:

```c
#include<stdio.h>
#include<process.h>
void main( )
{
    int i, n, a[10], key, low, high, mid;
    printf("\nEnter the number of elements:");
    scanf("%d", &n);
    printf("\nEnter %d elements in ascending order", n);
    for(i=0;i < n; i++)
        scanf("%d", &a[i]);
    printf("\nEnter the element to search (key): ");
    scanf("%d", &key);
    low = 0;
    high = n - 1;
    while(low <= high)
      {
        mid = (low + high) / 2;
        if (key = = a[mid])
          {
            printf("\n\nSearch successful.");
            exit(0);
        }
        else if(key > a[mid])
            low = mid + 1;
        else
```

```
        high = mid - 1;
    }
    printf("\nUnsuccessful Search");
}
```

OUTPUTS (after running):

Enter the number of elements: 10

Enter 10 elements in ascending order:

1

2

3

4

5

6

7

8

9

10

Enter the key element to search: 5

Search successful.

Example 8: **Write a C program to compare two strings without using the strcmp( ) function.**

Solution 8: The program is as follows:

```
#include<stdio.h>
#include<string.h>
void main( )
{
    char a[100], b[100];
    int result;
    printf("\nEnter the first string:");
    gets(a);
    printf("\nEnter the second string:");
    gets(b);
    result = compare(a, b);
```

```
        if (result = = 0)
         printf("\nEntered strings are equal.\n");
        else
         printf("\nEntered strings are not equal.\n");
    }
int compare(char a[ ] , char b[ ] )
{
    int c = 0;
    while (a[c] = = b[c])
      {
        if (a[c] = = '\0' || b[c] = = '\0')
         break;
        c++;
      }
    if (a[c] = = '\0' && b[c] = = '\0')
     return 0;
    else
     return -1;
}
```

OUTPUTS (after running):

Enter the first string: DR. RAJIV

Entered the second string: DR. RAJIV

Entered strings are equal.

OUTOUTS 2 (after running):

Enter the first string: DR. RAJIV

Entered the second string: CHOPRA

Entered strings are not equal.

Example 9: **Write a C program to count the frequency of occurrence of a character in a given string.**

Solution 9: The program is as follows:

```
#include<stdio.h>
#include<string.h>
void main( )
{
char str[100], ch;
int i, count = 0, length;
```

```
printf("\nEnter the string:");
gets(str);
printf("\nEnter the character to be searched:");
scanf("%c", &ch);
length = strlen(str);
(i=0; i< length; i++)
{
if (str[i] = = ch)
count++;
}
printf("\n The frequency of the occurence of %c is
%d\n\n", ch, count);
}
```

OUTPUTS (after running):

Enter the string: DR. RAJIV

Enter the character to be searched: A

The frequency of occurrence of A is 1

OUTPUTS 2 (after running):

Enter the string: C Programming

Enter the character to be searched: m

The frequency of occurrence of m is 2

Example 10: **Write a C program to find the norm of a matrix where norm of a matrix is defined as the square of the sum of squares of the elements of the matrix.**

Solution 10: The program is as follows:

```
#include<stdio.h>
#include<math.h>
void main( )
{
    int i, j, m, n;
    float norm, a[10][10];
    float nrm( );
    print("Enter row and column of A matrix: \n");
    scanf("%d %d", &n, &m);
    printf("%d %d\n",n ,m);
    printf("Input A-matrix\n");
```

```
     for(i=0;  i<n;  ++i)
      for(j=0;  j<m;  ++j)
        scanf("%f",  &a[i][j]);
     /*print A-matrix in matrix form */
     for(i=0;  i<n;  ++i)
       {
       for(j=0;  j<m;  ++j)
         scanf("%6.2f",  a[i][j]);
       printf("\n");
       }
     norm = nrm(a,  n,  m);
     printf("Norm=%6.2f\n",  norm);
       }
/* norm  of  a  matrix  =  square  root  of  the  sum  of  the
squares  of  the  elements  of  the  matrix */
float nrm(a,  n,  m)
int m,  n;
float a[10][10];
{
    int i,  j;
    float sum = 0.0;
    for(i=0;i<n;  ++i)
     for(j=0;  j<m;  ++j)
       sum = sum + a[i][j] * a[i][j];
     printf("Sum=%6.2f\n",  sum);
     return (sqrt((double) sum));
}
```

OUTPUTS (after running):

Enter row and column of A-matrix: 3 3

Input A-matrix:

1.00	2.00	3.00
4.00	5.00	6.00
7.00	8.00	9.00

Sum = 285.00

Norm = 16.88

Example 11: **Write a C program to delete duplicate elements in a vector.**

Solution 11: The program is as follows:

```c
#include<stdio.h>
main( )
{
    int i, j, k, n, num, flag=0;
    float a[80];
    printf("Enter the size of vector: ");
    scanf("%d", &n);
    printf("%d", n);
    num = n;
    printf("\nEnter the vector elements:\n");
    for (i=0; i<n;i++)
        scanf("%f", &a[i]);
    for(i=0; i<n;i++)
        printf("%f", a[i]);
    printf("\n);
    /* removing duplicates */
    for (i=0; i<n-1; i++)
      for (j=i+1; j<n; j++)
        {
            if (a[i] = = a[j])
              {
                    n= n - 1;
                    for (k =j; k<n; k++)
                        a[k] = a[k+1];
                    flag = 1;
                    j = j-1;
              }
        }
    if ( flag = = 0)
        printf ("\n No duplicates found in the vector");
    else
      {
        printf ("\nVector has %d duplicates \n\n", num -
n);
        printf ("Vector after deleting duplicates");
        for (i=0; i<n; i++)
            printf ("%f", a[i]);
        printf ("\n");
      }
    }
```

OUTPUT (after running):

Enter the size of vector: 6

Enter the vector elements: 1.00 2.00 1.00 3.00 2.00 4.00

Vector has two duplicates

Vector after deleting duplicates

1.00 2.00 3.00 4.00

Example 12: Write a C program to insert an element into the vector array.

Solution 12: The program is as follows:

```
#include<stdio.h>
main( )
{
    int i, j, k, n, pos;
    float a[80], item;
    printf("\nEnter the size of vector: ");
    scanf("%d", &n);
    printf("%d", n);
    printf("\n Enter the vector elements:\n");
    for (i=0; i<n;i++)
        scanf("%f", &a[i]);
    for(i=0; i<n;i++)
        printf("%f", a[i]);
    printf("\n);
    /* inserting element */
    printf("\n Enter the element to be inserted:");
    scanf("%d", &item);
    printf("%d", item);
    printf("\n Enter the position of insertion:");
    scanf("%d", &pos);
    printf("%d", item);
    /* pushing down the elements */
    n++;
    for (k = n; k>=pos; k- - ) {
     a[k] = a[k - 1];
     }
    a [- - pos] = item;        /* item inserted */
    printf("\n");
    printf ("\n Vector after insertion: ");
```

```
for ( i = 0; i < n; i++)
    printf ("%f", a[i]);
printf ("\n");
}
```

OUTPUT (after running):

Enter the size of vector: 6

Enter the vector elements: 1.00 2.00 1.00 3.00 2.00 4.00 5.00 6.00

Enter the element to be inserted: 10.00

Enter the position to insert: 1

Vector after insertion:

10.00 1.00 2.00 1.00 3.00 2.00 4.00 5.00 6.00

NOTE   *Attempt to write a program now to select an element from the vector.*

Example **13: Write a C program to find the row sum and column sum of a matrix.**

Solution 13: The program is as follows:

```
#include<stdio.h>
main ( )
{
    int a[10][10], i, j, m, n;
    printf("\n Enter the number of rows and column:");
    scanf("%d%d", &n, &m);
    printf("Enter matrix elements:");
    for (i=1; i< n + 1; ++)
     for(j=1; j < m+1; ++j)
        scanf("%d", &a[i][j]);
    /* find row sum */
    for (i =1; i < n+1; ++i)
     {
        a[i][m+1] = 0;
        for (j=1; j < m+1; ++j)
         {
            a[i][m+1] = a[i][m+1] + a[i][j];
         }
     }
    * find col sum */
```

```
    for (j =1; j < m+1; ++j)
     {
       a[n+1][j] = 0;
       for (i=1; j < n+1; ++i)
         {
            a[n+1][j] = a[n+1][j] + a[i][j];
         }
     }
    /* print matrix's column sum and row sum */
    printf("col-sum (last row) and row-sum (last col-
umn):");
    for (i=1; i < n+1; ++i)
     {
       for (j=1; j< m+2; ++j)
        printf("%d", a[i][j]);
       printf("\n");
     }
    /* last row (col-sum) is printed to suppress element,
a[n+1]
[m+1] */
    i = n + 1;
    for (j=1; j < m+1; ++j)
       printf("%d", a[i][j]);
     printf("\n");
     }
```

OUTPUT (after running):

Enter the size of vector: 3 3

Enter the matrix elements:

Matrix elements   col-sum and row sum

1	2	3	6
4	5	6	15
7	8	9	24
12	15	18	

Example 14: **Write a C program to sum the elements above and below the main diagonal of a matrix.**

Solution 14: The program is as follows:

```
#include<stdio.h>
```

```
main( )
{
    int a[50][50], i, j, n, csum, dsum;
    printf("Enter the size of your array:");
    scanf("%d", &n);
    printf("%d", n);
    printf("Enter matrix elements:");
    for (i=1; i< n + 1; ++)
     for(j=1; j < n+1; ++j)
        scanf("%d", &a[i][j]);
    printf("Echoing given matrix:");
    for (i=1; i< n + 1; ++)
      {
      for(j=1; j < n+1; ++j)
      {
        printf("%d", a[i][j]);
      }
        printf("\n");
}
/* add elements above the main diagonal of a matrix */
    csum = 0;
    for (i=1; i< n+1; ++i)
{
for (j=1; j< n+1; ++j)
{
    if (i < j)
       csum = csum + a[i][j];
    }
}
printf ("Sum of elements above the main diagonal: %d\n",
csum);
/* add elements below the main diagonal of a matrix */
dsum = 0;
for (i=1; i< n+1; ++i)
{
    for (j=1; j< n+1; ++j)
      {
      if (i > j)
        dsum = dsum + a[i][j];
      }
}
printf ("Sum of elements below the main diagonal: %d\n",
```

```
dsum);
  }
```

OUTPUT (after running):

Enter the size of your array: 3

Enter the matrix elements:

1 2 3

4 5 6

7 8 9

Sum of elements above the main diagonal: 11

Sum of elements below the main diagonal: 19

***Example* 15: Illustrate the process (using dry runs) of searching for an element 6 in a given array A, with elements as 1, 2, 3, 4, 5, 6, 7, 8, 9, 10, using a binary search.**

Solution 15: The following is the dry run:

Step 1: Given:

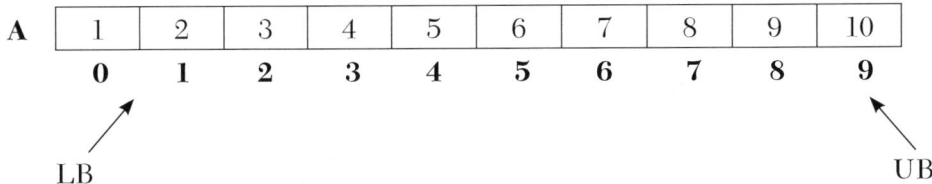

Thus, mid = LB + UB / 2 = 0 +9 /2 = 4

Therefore, A[mid] is not equal to item as 5!=6

Step 2: As A[mid] < item, so

LB = mid + 1 = 4 + 1 = 5

Thus, the array part to search now is from A[5]:

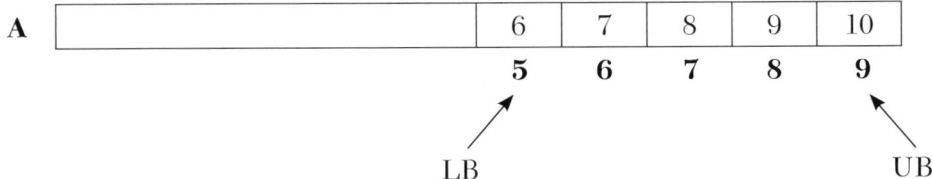

Thus, now mid = LB + UB /2 = 5 + 9 /2 = 7

Again, A[mid] = A[7] = 8

And item = 6

So, 8!=6

Thus, we go to step 3 now.

Step 3: As A[mid] > item (i.e., 8 > 6),

Thus, UB = mid – 1 = 7 – 1 = 6

Now, mid = LB + UB /2 = 5 + 6/2 = 5

Therefore, UB= 6 and LB= 5

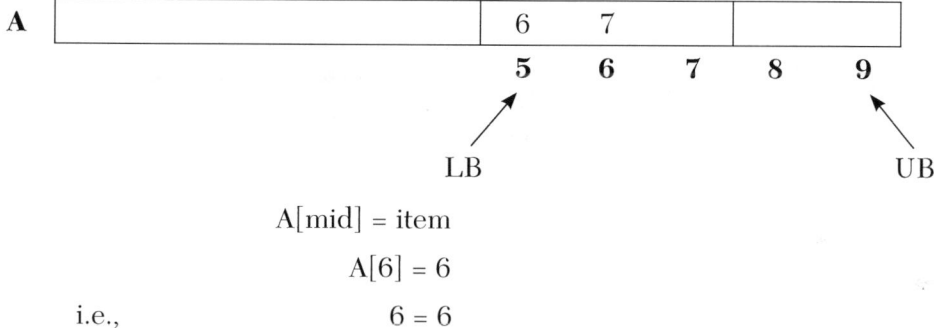

A[mid] = item

A[6] = 6

i.e.,   6 = 6

The item is found.

***Example* 16: Write a C program to do the following operations:**

(a) Find the length of a string without using the inbuilt string length function of C.

(b) Copy one string to another without using the inbuilt string copy function of C.

(c) Concatenate two strings without using the string concat function of C.

(d) Check whether two strings are the same without using the string comparison function of C.

(e) Reverse a string without using the string reversal function of C.

Solution 16: Let us write the programs one by one.

(a) The length of a string **without using strlen( )** can be found as follows:

```c
#include<stdio.h>
#include<conio.h>
#include<string.h>
void main( )
{
    char s1[20];
    int i=0, length = 0;
    clrscr( );
    printf ("Enter your string:");
    scanf ("%s", s1);
    while (s1[i] != '\0')
      {
        length ++;
        i++;
      }
    printf("The length of the string is %d", length);
    getch( );
}
```

(b) Copying a string **without using strcpy( )** can be done as follows:

```c
#include<stdio.h>
#include<conio.h>
#include<string.h>
void main( )
{
    char s1[20], s2[20];
    int i=0;
    clrscr( );
    printf ("Enter your string:");
    scanf ("%s", s1);
    while (s1[i] != '\0')
      {
        s2[i] = s1[i];
        i++;
      }
    s2[i] = '\0';
    printf("The copy of the string is %s", s2);
    getch( );
}
```

(c) Concatenating two strings **without using strcat( )** can be done as follows:

```
#include<stdio.h>
#include<conio.h>
#include<string.h>
void main( )
{
    char s1[20], s2[20], s3[40];
    int i=0, j = 0, k=0;
    clrscr( );
    printf ("Enter two strings:");
    scanf ("%s %s", s1,s2);
    while (s1[i] != '\0')
      {
        s3[k] = s1[i];
        k++;
        i++;
      }
    while (s2[j] != '\0')
      {
        s3[k] = s2[j];
        k++;
        j++;
      }
    s3[k] = '\0';
    printf("Concatenation of two strings is %s", s3);
    getch( );
}
```

(d) Comparing two strings **without using strcmp( )** can be done as follows:

```
#include<stdio.h>
#include<conio.h>
#include<string.h>
void main( )
{
    char s1[20], s2[20];
    int i=0;
    clrscr( );
    printf ("Enter two strings:");
    scanf ("%s %s", s1, s2);
    while (s1[i] != '\0' && s2[i] != '\0')
```

```
     {
        if (s1[i] = = s2[i])
          {
            flag = 0;
            i++;
          }
          else
            {
              flag = 1;
              break;
            }
     }
       if (flag = = 0)
       {
       printf (" Strings are same.");
       }
       else
         {
            printf ("Strings are not same");
         }
getch( );
}
```

(e) Reversing a string **without using strrev( )** can be done as follows:

```
#include<stdio.h>
#include<conio.h>
#include<string.h>
void main( )
{
    char s1[20], s2[20];
    int i=0, j;
    clrscr( );
    printf ("Enter your string:");
    scanf ("%s", s1);
    j = strlen(s1) - 1;
    while (j >= 0)
      {
        s2[i] = s1[j])
        i++;
        j- -;
      }
       s2[i] = '\0';
```

```
        printf (" The reverse string is: %s", s2);
getch ( );
}
```

***Example* 17: Write a C program to traverse a matrix helically.**

Solution 17: The program is as follows:

```
#include<stdio.h>
main ( )
{
    int a[20][20], n, i, j;
    printf("\n\t Enter the order of a matrix");
    scanf("%d", &n);
    printf("%d", n);
printf("\n\t Enter you array elements:");
for(i=1; i < n+1; ++i)
{
    for(j=1; j< n+1; ++j)
        scanf("%d", &a[i][j]);
}
/*traversing helically */
printf("The required traversal is: ");
i = 1;
while (n > 0)
{
    for(j = i; j < n+1; j++)
printf("%d", a[i][j]);
    for(j = i +1; j < n+1; ++j)
     printf("%d", a[j][n]);
    for(j = n-1; j> i - 1; j- - )
     printf("%d", a[n][j]);
    for(j = n-1; j>I ; j - - )
     printf("%d", a[j][i]);
i = i +1;
n = n - 1;
}
printf("\n");
}
```

OUTPUT (after running):

Enter the size of your array: 3

Enter the matrix elements:

1 2 3

4 5 6

7 8 9

The required traversal is: 1 2 3 6 9 8 7 4 5

Practice Programs

Q1. Write a C program to sort a matrix row-wise.

Q2. Write a C program to sort a given matrix column-wise.

Q3. Write a C program to check whether a given matrix is a magic square. A magic square is one in which

$$Column \; sum = row \; sum = diagonal \; sum$$

and all elements in the matrix are *distinct*.

For example, the matrix given below is a magic square matrix:

4	3	8
9	5	1
2	7	6

On the other hand, the following matrix is not a magic square matrix:

3	3
3	3.

Q4. Write a C program to modify a matrix.

***Example* 18: Write a C program to print the upper and lower triangle of a matrix.**

Solution 18: The program is as follows:

```c
#include<stdio.h>
main( )
{
    int a[10][10], i, j, m, n;
    printf ("\n\t Please enter the number of rows and col-
umns of a matrix:");
    scanf ("%d %d", &n, &m);
    printf ("%d%d", n, m);
    printf("\n\t Enter the matrix elements:");
```

```
for (i=0; i<n; i++)
 for (j=0; j<m; j++)
    scanf("%d", &a[i][j]);
/* Echoing array…. */
for (i=0; i<n; i++)
 {
 for (j=0; j<m; j++)
    printf("%d", a[i][j]);
 printf("\n");
 }
printf("\n\t Lower triangular matrix:");
for (i =0; i<n ;i++) {
 for (j=0; j<m; j++) {
    if ( i< j) printf(" ");
    if (i >=j) printf("%d", a[i][j]);
 }
 printf("\n");
 }
printf("\n\t Upper triangular matrix:");
for (i =0; i<n ;i++) {
 for (j=0; j<m; j++) {
    if ( i> j) printf(" ");
    if (i <=j) printf("%d", a[i][j]);
 }
 printf("\n");
 }
}
}
```

OUTPUT (after running):

Please enter the number of rows and columns of a matrix: 3 3

Enter the matrix elements:

1 2 3

4 5 6

7 8 9

Lower triangular matrix:

1

4 5

7 8 9

Upper triangular matrix:

1 2 3

5 6

9

Example 19: Write a C program to find the saddle point in a matrix.

Solution 19: The program is as follows:

```
#include<stdio.h>
main( )
{
    int a[5][5], i, j, m, n, min, max, flag=1, p, q;
    printf ("\n\t Please enter the number of rows and col-
umns of a matrix:");
    scanf ("%d %d", &m, &n);
    printf ("%d %d", m, n);
    printf("\n\t Enter the matrix elements:");
    for (i=0; i<m; i++)
     for (j=0; j<n; j++)
       scanf("%d", &a[i][j]);
    /* Echoing array…. */
    for (i=0; i<m; i++)
     {
     for (j=0; j<n; j++)
       printf("%d", a[i][j]);
     printf("\n");
     }
    /*find the minimum element in a row */
    for (i =0; i <m; i++) {
       min = a[i] [0];
       p = i;
       q= 0;
    /*to check whether 'min' is the maximum in column */
    for (j=0; j<n; j++) {
       if (min > a[i][j]) {
          min = a[i][j];
          p = i;
          q = j;
        }
       }
    for (j=0; j <m; j++)
```

```
    {
       if (a[j][q] > a[p][q])
          flag = 0;
    }
    if (flag)
    {
       printf("Saddle point a[%d][%d] = %d\n", p+1, q+1,
a[p][q]);
    else
       printf("No saddle point in row %d\n", i+1);
     flag = 1;
    }
}
```

OUTPUT (after running):

Please enter the number of rows and columns of a matrix: 3 3

Enter the matrix elements:

7 5 5

10 5 8

6 3 3

Saddle point a[1][2] = 5

Saddle point a[2][2] = 5

No saddle point in row 3

Example 20: **Write a C program to check whether a given matrix is orthogonal.**

Solution 20: The program is as follows:

```
#include<stdio.h>
main( )
{
    int a[5][5], b[5][5], c[5][5];
    int i, j, m, k, flag=0;
    printf ("\n\t Enter the order of matrix:");
    scanf ("%d", &m);
    printf ("%d * %d", m, m);
    printf("\n\t Enter the matrix elements:");
    for (i=0; i<m; i++)
     for (j=0; j<m; j++)
```

```c
      scanf("%d", &a[i][j]);
   /* Echoing array…. */
   for (i=0; i<m; i++)
    {
    for (j=0; j<m; j++)
      printf("%f", a[i][j]);
    printf("\n");
    }
   /*transpose the given matrix */
   for (i=0; i<m; i++)
    for (j=0; j<m; j++)
      b[i][j] = a[j][i];
   printf("Transpose is:");
   for (i=0; i<m; i++) {
    for (j=0; j<m; j++)
      printf("%f", b[i][j]);
      printf("\n");
   }
/* if matrix A * transpose of A = identity matrix */
for (i=0; i<m; i++) {
for (j=0; j<m; j++) {
   c[i][j] = 0;
   for(k=0; k<=m; k++) {
      c[i][j] + = a[i][k] * b[k][j];
   }
}
}
for (i=0; i<m; i++)
{
for (j=0; j<m; j++)
{
   if ((int) c[i][i] = = 1 && (int) c[i][j] = = 0)
      flag = 1;
}
printf("Matrix A * transpose of A");
for (i=0; i<m; i++) {
for (j=0; j<m; j++)
   printf("%f", c[i][j]);
   printf("\n");
}
if (flag = = 1)
   printf ("Matrix A * Transpose of A = Identity Ma-
```

```
trix");
    printf ("The given matrix is orthogonal\n");
else
    printf ("Matrix A * Transpose of A < > Identity Ma-
trix");
    printf ("The matrix is not orthogonal");
}
```

OUTPUT (after running):

Enter the order of the matrix: 3° 3

Enter the matrix elements:

0.0 0.0

1.0 0.0

0.0 1.0

Transpose is

0.0 0.0

1.0 0.0

0.0 1.0

Matrix A ° Transpose of A = Identity Matrix

The given matrix is orthogonal

Practice Programs:

Q1. Write a C program to find whether a given matrix is singular. It is said that if the determinant is 0, the matrix is singular.

Q2. Write a C program to find whether a given matrix is symmetric.

[Hint:

```
#include<stdio.h>
main( )
{
    int a[5][5], b[5][5], c[5][5];
    int i, j, m, k, flag=0;
    printf ("\n\t Enter the order of matrix:");
    scanf ("%d", &m);
    printf ("%d * %d", m, m);
    printf("\n\t Enter the matrix elements:");
```

```
for (i=0; i<m; i++)
 for (j=0; j<m; j++)
   scanf ("%d", &a[i][j]);
/* Echoing array…. */
for (i=0; i<m; i++)
 {
 for (j=0; j<m; j++)
   printf("%f", a[i][j]);
 printf("\n");
 }
/*transpose the given matrix */
for (i=0; i<m; i++)
 for (j=0; j<m; j++)
   b[i][j] = a[j][i];
printf("Transpose is:");
for (i=0; i<m; i++) {
 for (j=0; j<m; j++)
   printf("%f", b[i][j]);
   printf("\n");
 }
/*to check for symmetry of a matrix */
   for (i=0; i<n; i++)
{
   for (j=0; j<n; j++)
     if (a[i][j] != b[i][j])
       flag = 1;
   }
   if (flag)
     printf("Matrix is not symmetric");
   else
     printf("Matrix is symmetric");
   }                                        ].
```

Q3. Write a C program to find the rank of a matrix. Check that the principal diagonal element is not zero, and then make all elements above and below the current principal diagonal element zero. Else if principal diagonal element is zero, find the nonzero element in the same column. If no nonzero element exists, check that all elements in this column are zero. Exchange it with the last column and reduce the number of columns.

Q4. Write a C program to find the inverse of a matrix.

Examples

We are in a position to write some programs on strings now.

Example **21:** **Write a C program to write a given figure in words. Use the switch statement.**

Solution 21: The program is as follows:

```
#include<stdio.h>
main( )
{
    int digit[10], num, temp, i, j, k;
    printf("\n\t Enter your number:");
    printf("%d\n", num);
    temp = num;
    i = 0;
    while (num != 0)
      {
        digit[i++] = num - num/10 * 10;
        num = num/10;
      }
    j = - - i;
    printf ("\nThe number in words is:");
    for (k=j; k>=0; k - - )
      {
        switch (digit[k])
          {
            case 1:
                    printf("one");
                    break;
            case 2:
                    printf("two");
                    break;
            case 3:
                    printf("three");
                    break;
            case 4:
                    printf("four");
                    break;
            case 5:
                    printf("five");
```

```
                break;
        case 6:
                printf("six");
                break;
        case 7:
                printf("seven");
                break;
        case 8:
                printf("eight");
                break;
        case 9:
                printf("nine");
                break;
        case 10:
                printf("ten");
                break;
        default:
                break;
         }
        }
        printf("\n");
    }
```

OUTPUT (after running):
Enter your number: 567321
The number in words is: five six seven three two one

Example 22: **Write a C program to count the number of vowels, consonants, words, white spaces, and other characters in a line of text.**

Solution 22: The program is as follows:

```
#include<stdio.h>
main( )
{
    char line[80], c;
    int i, vow, cons, dig, word, whites, other;
    i =vow = cons = dig = word = whites = other = 0;
    printf ("\n\t Enter a line of text");
    scanf("%[^\n]", line);
    printf("%s", line);
    while ((c = tolower(line[i++])) != '\0')
      {
        if (c = = 'a' || c = = 'e' || c = = 'i' || c = = 'o'
|| c        = ='u')
            ++vow;
        else if (c >= 'a' && c<= 'z')
```

```
    ++cons;
else if (c >= '0' && c <='9')
    ++dig;
else if (c = = ' ') {
    ++word;
    ++ whites;
    while ((line[i] = = ' ' || line[i] = = '\t'))
      {
            i++;
            whites++;
      }
  }
  else
        ++other;
  }
    ++word;
printf("\n\n--------------------");
printf("\n\nTotal number of: ");
printf("\n\n--------------------");
printf("Vowels = %d\n", vow);
printf("Consonants = %d\n", cons);
printf("Digits = %d\n", dig);
printf("Other characters = %d\n", other);
printf("Words = %d\n", word);
printf("White spaces = %d\n", whites);
}
```

OUTPUT (after running):

Enter a line of text: Dr. Rajiv Chopra has written 23 books!

Total number of:

Vowels = 9

Consonants = 21

Digits = 2

Other characters = 1

Words = 7

White spaces = 6

NOTE *Observed that in the scanf statement in this program we have used the ^ character also. Its meaning can be clarified with an example. If we write:*

$$\%[A - Z]$$

in scanf, it will catch all uppercase inputs. On the other hand, if we write:

$$\%[^a - c]$$

in scanf, it will catch all ASCII except 'a', 'b', and 'c'.

Example **23: Write a C program to search for a substring within a string and to display its position.**

Solution 23: The program is as follows:

```c
#include<stdio.h>
main( )
{
char mainstr[50], patstr[50];
int i, j, k, len1, len2, diff, flag;
/*strings taken till newline character */
printf("Enter the main string\n");
scanf("%[^\n]", mainstr);
printf("%s", mainstr);
for(len1=0; mainstr[len1] != '\0'; len1++)
printf("\n Length of main string is %d\n", len1);
printf("\n Enter pattern string \n");
scanf("%s",patstr);
printf("%s", patstr);
for(len2=0; mainstr[len2] != '\0'; len2++)
printf("\n Length of pattern string is %d\n", len2);
/*index */
flag = 0; /*set flag */
j=0;
for (i=0; i<len1, j <len2; i++)
if (mainstr[i] != patstr[j])
   flag = 1;
else {
      flag = 0; /* reset flag */
      j ++;
   }
```

```
    if (flag = = 0)
        printf("\n Pattern found at position %d\n", i-len2+1);
    else
        printf("\n Pattern not found");
}
```

OUTPUT (after running):

Enter the main string:

Dr. Rajiv Chopra has a Ph.D.

Length of main string is 25

Enter pattern string

Chop

Length of pattern string is 4

Pattern found at position 24

Practice Programs:

Q1. Write a C program to insert a substring into a string.

Q2. Write a C program to replace a portion of a string.

Example 24: Write a C program to sort a string of names.

Solution 24: The program is as follows:

```
#include<stdio.h>
main( )
{
    char names[20][10], temp[10], c;
    int i, j, k, n;
    n=0;
    printf("\n Enter names one [er line \n");
    printf("Terminate with string END\n");
    scanf("%s", names[n]);
    while (strcmp(names[n], "END") > 0) {
        n++;
        scanf("%s", names[n]);
    }
    printf("\n");
    for (i=0; i<n; i++)
        printf("%10s", names[i]);
    printf("\n");
```

```
printf("\n");
printf("Total names = %d\n", n);
/*selection sorting is used */
for (i=0; i<n - 1; i++)
  for (j = i +1; j<n; j++) {
    if (strcmp(names[i], names[j]) > 0) {
        strcpy(temp, names[i]);
        strcpy(names[i], names[j]);
        strcpy(names[j], temp);
        }
    }
printf("\n Sorted Names: \n");
for(i=0; i<n; i++)
    printf("%10s", names[i]);
printf("\n");
getch( );
}
```

OUTPUT (after running):

Enter names one per line

Terminate with string END

     Krish   Rajiv   Ajay   Mayur   Diksha

Total names = 5

Sorted Names:

     Ajay   Diksha   Krish   Mayur   Rajiv

3.2 THE CONCEPT OF SUBPROGRAMMING

When a problem to be solved is very complex, we first need to divide that complex problem into smaller, simpler problems. Then we try to find the subsolutions to these subproblems. Finally, we integrate (combine) all these subsolutions to get a complete solution. **This approach is called the modular approach and such programming is called modular programming.** An advantage here is that parallel coding can be done for these modules. A library of modules may be created and these may be reused when needed by another program and called by the user. They behave like inbuilt modules. Debugging and maintenance of modules is simpler than ever, as module sizes are usually small. Bigger programs, called monolithic programs, should therefore be avoided.

Characteristics of a Module

1. A module contains a series of program instructions in some programming language.

2. A module is terminated by some special markers required by the syntax of the language.

3. A module as a whole has a unique name.

4. A module has only one entry point to which control is transferred from the outside and only one exit point from which control is returned to the calling module.

5. Structured programming involves modularization of a program structure.

Top-down analysis is a method of problem solving and problem analysis. It involves two main tasks:

(a) Subdivision of a problem

(b) Hierarchy of tasks

The top-down method carries out a process of division and subdivision, creating a hierarchy of tasks until these tasks can no longer be decomposed (i.e., they become atomic).

3.3 FUNCTIONS

As noted, a module is developed to make a program more approachable. In languages like PASCAL, we call these modules procedures, FORTRAN calls them subfunctions and subprocedures, but C calls them functions. **A subprogram or function is a name given to a set of instructions that can be called by another program or a subprogram.** This simplifies the programming process as functions can be called again and again as desired. **Understand that a function is a complete program in itself, similar to the C main( ) function, except that the name main( ) is replaced by the name of the function that is given by the programmer.**

Syntax

```
<type> name (arguments)
  {
    …….. .
    …….. .
    <statements>
    ……
  }
```

'**type**' is the value returned by the function. If no value is returned back from the function, then the keyword **void** is used.

'**name**' is the user-defined name of the function. A function can be called from anywhere with this name only.

'**arguments**' is a list of parameters. If there are no parameters, then just two parentheses ( ) are placed.

The program segment enclosed within the opening and closing brace is called a function body.

For example, in C every program starts with a main( ). **The program of every program within C also starts with main( ) only.** All functions that you define must be called from main( ), or else they will not work.

Example

```
name( )
  {
    printf("\n My name is Dr. Rajiv Chopra");
  }
void main( )
  {
    clrscr( );
    printf("\nGood Morning");
    name( ); /* function call */
    getch( );
  }
```

Here, too, program execution starts from main( ). It displays the message "Good Morning" and then calls the function name( ). Control goes to the function name( ). It displays "My name is Dr. Rajiv Chopra". And then control goes back to the main program.

Working of Functions and main( )

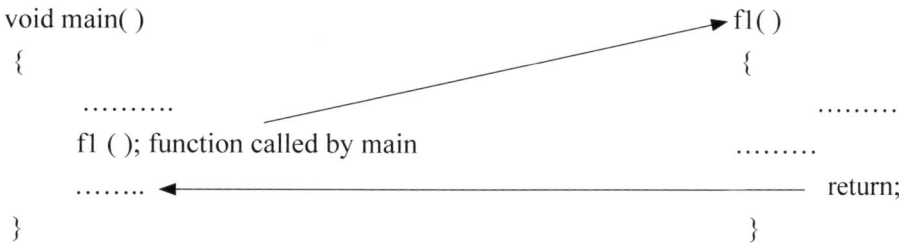

```
void main( )                                              fl( )
  {                                                         {
      ..........                                              .........
      f1 ( ); function called by main              .........
      ........                                                return;
  }                                                         }
```

That is, when the program control reaches the function call f1( ) then it transfers control to the function f1( ) (on the right-hand side), where on encountering a return statement, control returns back to the main( ) function.

Why We Need Functions

1. It is easier to write and debug functions than with a large monolithic program.

2. There is no repetition of code, as we can call functions wherever we want.

3. Functions are portable and can be run on any system.

4. A lot of time and memory resources are saved.

5. Modularization is achieved easily.

6. Program length becomes smaller.

Types of Functions

Functions can be of two types:

(a) Library or inbuilt functions.

(b) User-defined functions.

Library functions are the inbuilt functions that are predefined in the compiler of a language and stored in a special library file. For example, we include the math.h header file for mathematical functions.

On the other hand, **user-defined functions** are those defined and created by the programmer. Each is a self-contained block of statements that carries out some well-defined task as specified by the user.

Please remember the following points regarding functions:

1. A C program is a collection of one or more functions.

2. A function gets called when the function name is followed by parentheses and a semicolon.

3. Note that in the statement 'int name' 'name' is an integer variable, name[10] is an array, whereas name( ) is a function, in spite of the similarity in names.

4. Any function can be called from any other function.

5. A function once written can be called any number of times. Even main( ) is a function that can be called again and again. This is called **recursion.**

6. The order of function called and function defined may be different. It makes no difference.

7. There are two types of functions—library functions like sqrt( ), printf( ), scanf( ), sin( ), and cos( ), etc., whereas the name( ) function defined above is a user-defined function.

The syntax of the function definition has already been shown. Let us now take an example,

Defining a Function

1. int gcd(int u, int v)

2. {

3. int temp;

4. temp = u % v;

5. u = v;

6. v = temp;

7. return (v);

8. }

In this function, observe that:

1. **Line 1 is a function header and by rule a function header is always formal and the arguments within it are known as formal arguments or dummy arguments.**

2. **The arguments that are passed from main( ) are known as actual arguments. The actual arguments may be constants, variables, or more complex expressions.**

3. **Each actual argument must be of the same type as its corresponding formal argument.**

4. **It is the value of each actual argument that is transferred into the function and assigned to the corresponding formal argument.**

5. If the return type of the function is not specified, then by default it is assumed to be of type *int*.

6. Formal arguments cannot be constants or expressions.

7. Rules for naming a function are the same as for variable names.

8. The return type in the main or in the function must be of the same type.

9. The function is known as a **called function** while the main( ) function that calls it is known as a **calling function**.

Just as variables are declared, similarly functions needs to be declared as follows:

<type> <name> (arguments);

This is essentially a **function prototype.** If you are working in C on a UNIX platform, it may not be necessary to write the prototype first, but if you are running your program with a C++ compiler, it is necessary. Every C program can be run on a C++ compiler, too, as C is subset of C++.

For example,

fact(int n);

Here, 'n' is an actual argument and there is no return value in this function call. It ends with a semicolon. On the other hand, consider

result = fact(int n);

This function call will return some value in the 'result' variable.

We can even write the following:

fact( );

This means that the function has nothing to return now and has no arguments.

The return Statement (in Functions)

The return statement is used to return program control back to the main program.

Syntax

return (exp);

where 'exp' can be a constant, variable, or an expression. Even the parentheses around exp are optional.

A return statement has two tasks:

1. It transfers control back to the calling program.

2. It returns a value after return to the calling program.

Please note that the return statement may not always be at the end of the called function. There is no restriction on the number of return statements that are present in a function. **Also note that a function can return only one value.**

User-Called Functions

There are five types of functions that can be created by the user and then called.

I. Functions with No Arguments and No Return Value

A function without arguments or return value is the simplest way of writing a user-defined function in C. There is no data communication between a calling portion of a program and a called function block. The function is invoked by a calling environment by not feeding any formal arguments and the function does not return back anything to the caller.

For example,

```
main( )
{
    int x, y;
    ......... .
    ......... .
    message( );      //function is invoked
}
message( )
{
```

```
    //body of the function
}
```

These functions receive no argument and return no value. Such functions may take data from either external or internal sources.

It is also possible to eliminate the function declaration, but only if the function is defined before its first call. For example,

```
message( )                        //function definition
{
   printf("\nI am in function now");
}
main( )
{
   printf("\n Now I am in function main");
   message( );          //function is invoked
   printf("\n Back in main...");
}
```

Output:

Now I am in function main( )

I am in function now

Back in main …

Understand that this approach is simpler for short programs, because in larger programs it is difficult to arrange all the functions so that each appears before it is called by the other.

II. Functions with Arguments and No Return Value

Those functions that receive arguments from the calling function but do not return any value to the calling programs fall into the next category of functions.

For example,

```
main( )
  {
    ............
    void power (int , int); //function declaration
    ............
    ............
  }
void power (int x, int y)
  {
```

```
            //body of the function
            //no values will be transferred back to the
            caller
        }
```

Here we are calling one power ( ) function from the main function. In the power function, we are passing two parameters or two variables as x and y. These values are collected into the local copies of the called function. **This process is known as call by value. Note that if you make any changes in the local copies of the function, that change is not reflected in the values of the arguments of the calling function. Also note that void indicates that we are not returning any values.**

III. Functions with No Arguments but with a Return Value

The third category of functions receives no arguments from some calling function but does return some value.

For example,

```
#include<iostream.h>
void main ( )
  {
    int add (void);
    int sub (void);
    int mul (void);
    int x;
    x = add ( );
    printf("The addition of two numbers:");
    x = sub ( );
    printf("The difference of two numbers:");
    x = mul ( );
    printf("The product of two numbers:");
  }
int add ( )
  {
    int a, b, c;
    printf("\n Enter two numbers for addition:");
    scanf("%d %d", &a, &b);
    c = a + b;
    return ( c) ;
  }
int sub ( )
  {
```

```
    int a, b, c;
    printf("\nEnter two numbers for difference:");
    scanf("%d %d", &a, &b);
    c = a - b;
    return ( c) ;
  }
int mul( )
  {
    int a, b, c;
    printf("\nEnter two numbers for multiplication:");
    scanf(%d %d", &a, &b);
    c = a * b;
    return ( c) ;
  }
```

OUTPUT (after running):

Enter two numbers for addition: 20 40

The addition of two numbers: 60

Enter two numbers for difference: 80 40

The difference of two numbers: 40

Enter two numbers for multiplication: 50 90

The product of two numbers: 4500

Explanation: In this program, we have called three functions—add( ), sub( ), and mul( )—from the main( ) function. **Note that since we are not passing any values to these three functions and just receiving value, in their prototypes declaration it is therefore necessary to include void in parenthesis and int as their return types.** If a function prototype specifies its return type as void then it is terminated by the closing brace of its definition. If you want to return some value from a function, you must use the return statement with a value within its body. The return statement returns only one value at a time. A void returning function can use the return statement with no value as:

```
void example( )
  {
    printf("\n Thanks to God");
    return;
  }
```

Also note that the return statement can appear anywhere in the function body. It means that the programmer is free to use it before the closing brace of the function body.

For example,

```
#include<iostream.h>
void main( )
{
    void test( );
    test( );
}
void test( )
{
    int u;
    printf("Enter your number: ");
    scanf(%d", &u);
    if ( u < 0)
      {
        printf("\n It is a negative number");
        return;
      }
    else
      {
        printf("\n It is a positive number");
        return;
      }
}
```

OUTPUT (after running):

Enter your number: -80

It is a negative number

NOTE

If you call a value-returning function and use it in a context in which no value is expected, say, you are not assigning the return value to anything, actually nothing unusual happens. There is no warning message by the compiler. The function executes correctly and it returns its value. The caller function can use it or ignore it.

IV. Functions with Arguments and a Return Value

Those functions that receive some arguments from the calling function and return some value are put under the next category. Here we use the call-by-value method, which is discussed in Section 3.4.

V. Recursions

Recursion is defined as a process in which a function calls itself again and again. It is a technique of defining a problem in terms of one or more smaller versions of the same problem. The solution to the problem is built on the results from the smaller versions. A recursive function is one which calls itself directly or indirectly to solve a smaller version of its task until a final call which does not require a **self-call.**

For example,

```
Add ( )
  {
    Add ( );
  }
```

This means that the function add( ) calls itself.

Advantages of Recursion

1. Recursion makes **the program compact.**

2. For complex problems, recursions can lead to solutions that are much clearer and easier to write.

3. It is very simple and quite apt for data structures like stacks, queues, trees, and so on.

4. During recursion, the system takes care of the internal stack.

5. It is useful for problems in which there is some repetition.

Disadvantages of Recursion

1. It is slower as far as speed and execution time.

2. It takes more memory space as variables are created again and again during every function call.

3. It needs extra runtime overhead.

4. For most problems recursion is difficult to implement.

5. Too many recursive calls will result in stack overflow.

There are two conditions for recursion:

1. **The function must call itself again and again.**

2. **The function must have an exit condition.**

Iteration is different from recursion. Table 3.1 lists the differences.

Table 3.1: Differences between Recursion and Iteration

Recursion	Iteration
(1) It is slower as compared to iteration.	(1) Iteration is faster than recursion.
(2) It takes more memory, as variables are created again and again during every function call.	(2) It takes less memory, as variables are declared only once.
(3) These algorithms may require extra overhead for multiple function calling.	(3) No overhead is involved in these algorithms.
(4) In some scenarios, recursion is simple to use (like tree traversal); otherwise, it is difficult.	(4) For some scenarios, iteration is difficult to implement; sometimes it is easy to implement.
(5) The system takes care of the internal stack.	(5) The user must take care of the internal stack.

Let us now write a program to find the factorial of a number using each of these methods (i.e., recursion and iteration).

Iterative Method:

An iterative loop to find the factorial of a number is as follows:

$$\vdots$$

$$\vdots$$

$$\vdots$$

```
fact = 1;
for (i =1; i <=n; i++)
fact = fact * i;
printf("\n The factorial of %d = %d", n, fact);
```

Recursive Method:

As we know

$$n! = n * (n - 1)!$$

$$= n * (n - 1) * (n - 2)!$$

We continue this process till the end (i.e., 0! = 1). We can generalize now:

fact (n) = 1 if n = 0

    n * fact (n – 1) if n > 0

Thus, we write:

```
fact (int n)
  {
    if ( n = = 0)
        return ( 1);
    else
        return ( n * fact (n - 1));
  }
```

The function fact is being called by itself but with parameter n replaced by n-1. **This ability of a function to call itself again and again is known as recursion.**

Working of a factorial function:

Say we want to compute the factorial of 4, the recursive calls would be:

fact(4) returns (4. Fact (3)

    which returns (3. Fact (2)

        which returns (2. Fact (1)

            which returns (1. Fact 0)

                which returns (1)))))

or we can also say that:

4! = 4.3!

  3! = 3.2!

    2! = 2.1!

      1! = 1.0!

        0! = 1

      1! = 1.1 = 1

    2! = 2.1 = 2

  3! = 3.2 = 6

4! = 4.6 = 24

Thus, we get the answer 4! = 24.

This process is repeated for any factorial that you want to find. **But please remember that this program will work up until, say, 8! or 9! or 10! Higher numbers may result in stack overflows. Therefore, we need to modify the preceding program by changing integer-type variables to either long int or even doubles. This is because the register sizes now needed are larger than for the smaller values of n (whose factorial you want).**

Also keep the following points in mind while using recursions:

1. Determine the specific variable which will be responsible for the termination of the algorithm (i.e., key variable).

2. Determine the value of the key variable that will terminate the algorithm (i.e., base value).

3. Ensure that the key variable always approaches the base value.

4. When the key variable equals the base value, the algorithm must terminate.

We are in a position to write some programs on recursions now.

Example 1: **Write a C program to generate a Fibonacci series to n using recursion.**

Solution 1: The program is as follows:

```c
#include<stdio.h>
#include<conio.h>
void main( )
  {
    int n, i, t;
    clrscr( );
printf("\n Enter the number of terms to be generated");
    scanf("%d", &n);
    printf("\n\t The Fibonacci series is:");
    for (i =1; i <=n; i++)
      {
        t = fib (i);
        printf("\t %d", t);
      }
    getch( );
  }
fib (int n)
  {
```

```
    if (n = = 1)
        return 0;
    else
        if ( n = = 2)
                return ( 1);
        else
                return (fib (n - 1) + fib (n -2));
    }
```

OUTPUT *(after running)*:

Enter the number of terms to be generated: 5

The Fibonacci series is:

0   1   1   2   3

***Example* 2: Write a C program to find the GCD of two numbers using recursion.**

Solution 2: The program is as follows:

```
#include<stdio.h>
#include<conio.h>
void main( )
  {
    int a, b, res;
    clrscr( );
    printf("\n Enter the two numbers to find their
    gcd:");
    scanf("%d %d", &a, &b);
    if ( a > b)
        res = gcd(a, b);
    else
        res = gcd (b, a);
     printf("\n The GCD of %d and %d = %d", a, b, res);
    getch( );
    }
gcd( int x, int y)
  {
    int r;
    r = x % y;
    if ( r = = 0)
            return (y);
    else
            return (y, r);
  }
```

OUTPUT (after running):
Enter the two numbers to find their gcd: 22   11
The GCD of 22 and 11 = 11

3.4 PARAMETER TRANSMISSION TECHNIQUES— CALL BY VALUE AND CALL BY REFERENCE

There are two ways in which data can be made available to a program. One way is to declare global data. This type of data will be available throughout the program. The other method is by passing data through and across functions. This method is better than the first one as in the first method (global variables) the privacy of the data is lost.

The ultimate aim of the program is that data should be available to other functions. This can be done two ways—one is to declare data (variables) as global variables and the other way is to pass the data to the functions.

Arguments can generally be passed to functions in one of two ways:

(a) Sending the values of the arguments

(b) Sending the addresses of the arguments

Three methods are used: pass by value, pass by address, and pass by reference.

I. Pass by Value
We know that the function header is always formal and thus its arguments are called formal arguments. Whenever a portion of the program is calling a function with a formal argument, control will be transferred from the main to the calling function and the value of the actual argument is copied into the function. Within the function, the actual value copied from the calling portion of the program may be altered or changed. **Please note that when control is transferred back from the function to the calling portion of the program, the altered values are not transferred back. This way of passing formal arguments to a function is called call by value.** The only limitation of call by value is that the value of the actual argument remains unchanged. This situation is useful where we do not want to change the values of the arguments. In other situations call by value is not as appropriate.

For example,

```cpp
#include<iostream.h>
#include<conio.h>
void main( )
{
    clrscr( );
    int a = 10;
    int b = 20;
    swapv (a, b);
    printf("\na is:", a);
    printf("\nb is:",b);
    getch( );
}
swapv (int x, int y)
{
    int t;
    t = x;
    x = y;
    y = t;
    printf("x is:",x); //values are exchanged here but no
impact on the main( ) above.
    printf("y is:", y);
}
```

OUTPUT (after running):

x = 20

y = 10

a = 10

b = 20

Explanation: In this first method, the 'value' of each actual argument in the calling function is copied into the corresponding formal arguments of the called function. With this method, changes made to the formal arguments in the called function have no effect on the values of the actual arguments in the calling function. **Also note that the values of 'a' and 'b' remain unchanged even after exchanging the values of 'x' and 'y'.** We are passing 10 and 20 from the main ( ) into the swapv function. In the swapv function, the values are exchanged (i.e., x and y become 20 and 10 after exchange but this change is NOT reflected back in the main program).

II. Pass by Address

In pass by address, the addresses of actual arguments in the calling function are copied into formal arguments of the called function. This means that using the formal arguments in the called function we can make changes in the actual arguments of the calling function.

For example,

```
#include<iostream.h>
#include<conio.h>
void main( )
{
    clrscr( );
    int a = 10;
    int b = 20;
    swapr (&a, &b);
    printf("\n a is:", a);
    printf("\n b is:", b);
    getch( );
}
swapv (int *x, int *y)
{
    int t;
    t = *x;
    *x = *y;
    *y = t;
    printf("x is:",x);        //values  are  exchanged  here
but now impact is on the main( )
    //above.
    printf("y is:", y);
}
```

OUTPUT (after running):

x = 20

y = 10

a = 20

b = 10

Explanation: Here we must understand the concept of pointers. **A pointer is a variable that holds the memory address of another variable.** For example, int a =10;

int *ptr = &a;

That is, 'ptr' is an integer pointer that holds the memory address of another integer variable, 'a'. We must declare a pointer variable also. Many pointer variables can be declared on a single line, such as

int *ptr1, *ptr2, *ptr3;

We can even have an array of pointers and so on but we shall study this a bit later. **Remember the following rule: "Always store the address of a data type into a pointer of the same data type. We cannot store the address of a variable of one type into a pointer variable of another type. This means that the integer pointer can hold the address of an integer variable, the float pointer can hold the address of a float variable, and so on."** In the call by address technique, we pass addresses of actual arguments to the called function. These addresses are stored in formal arguments, which are nothing but pointer variables. Now whatever changes are made in the formal arguments are reflected directly to the actual arguments.

III. Pass by Reference

In call (or pass) by reference, a function passes a reference as an argument to another function. *In this method, the called function works on the caller's copy of parameters and not on a local copy.* **A reference is defined as an alias (or copy) that is an alternate name for another variable.** Like pointers, the reference enables us to pass a large amount of data without the overhead of copying them. References are much like pointers. You can do anything with a reference that you can do with a pointer. C reference variables can give various similar problems until you understand them, but they also have advantages over pointers. A reference is indicated when following the type specifier with the address-of (&) operator, such that it can be said that the '&' operator identifies a reference variable. A reference must be initialized when it is declared.

For example,

int u = 89;

int &v = u;

Here we have declared 'u' as an integer variable that has another name, 'v'. **Please note that a reference can't be made to refer to another variable and this is the reason why it must be initialized.** If you make any change to a reference, then that change is actually applied to the variable to which the reference refers. As a result, all references to either name have the same effect.

For example,

v+ = 1;

will add 1 to 'u', the variable referred to by 'b'. **Also note that each definition of a reference must be preceded by the address-of operator—that is, & (ampersand).**

For example,

```
#include<iostream.h>
void main( )
 {
   int a = 100;
   int &b = a;
   printf("\n a= %d b= %d" , a, b);
   b = 200;
   printf("\n a= %d b= %d" , a, b);
   a = 300
   printf("\n a= %d b= %d" , a, b);
   }
```

OUTPUT (after running):

a= 100 b = 100

a= 200 b = 200

a= 300 b = 300

Please note here that 'b' is called as a reference to 'a' and note that the 'a' variable and its reference are so closely interlinked that if one changes, the other will automatically change. Also remember that even the address of 'a' and 'b' are the same. From the output it is also observed that a reference is neither a copy nor a pointer to the object to which it refers. Instead it is just another name.

However, there is a difference between a normal reference and a const reference. **A const reference can be initialized to a variable of a different data type. There is a conversion from one type to another, as well as to some constants.**

For example,

  float u = 99.90;

  const int &a = u;

Note that these initializations are completely invalid for non-const references and thus they result in compile-time errors. When it is initialized to a variable type then the compiler must generate a temporary object that the reference actually addresses. But, unfortunately, the user has no access to it. So the previous two statements are internally transformed as follows:

  float u = 99.90;

  int temp = u;

  const int &a = temp;

We have already written swap functions for the call by value and call by address methods. Now let us write one for the call by reference method.

```
#include<iostream.h>
void main( )
  {
    int u, v;
    printf("\n Enter your two numbers:");
    scanf("%d %d", &u, &v);
    printf("Before calling swapref( ) function.");
    printf("\n u=%d \t v= %d", u, v);
     swapref(u, v);
    printf("After calling swapref( ) function.");
    printf("\n u=%d \t v= %d", u, v);
  }
void swapref (int &aa, int &bb)
  {
    int temp;
    temp = aa;
    aa = bb;
    bb = temp;
  }
```

OUTPUT (after running):

Enter your two numbers: 11 55

Before calling swapref( ) function.

u = 11 v = 55

After calling swapref( ) function.

u = 55 v = 11

3.5 POINTERS

Programming languages like C and C++ make use of pointers whereas the JAVA2 language is free of pointers. A pointer is a variable that holds the memory address of another variable. It allows us to do an indirect manipulation of that variable because it holds the address of that variable where it has been stored in memory. Pointers have many applications and if used with care they can improve the efficiency of our programs. Let us explore this and other concepts in this section.

Pointers and Addresses

As we have already seen, when we initialize a variable, it is stored in a contiguous memory location, at some address. **For example,**

> **int u = 80;**

This declaration tells the compiler to do three things:

(a) Declare an integer variable u

(b) Initialize it with a value of 80

(c) Assign 2 bytes to this integer (an integer takes 2 bytes)

The compiler does the following:

$$u \quad \boxed{\quad 80 \quad} \quad 20A0$$

Here the address of 20A0 is assigned to the variable 'u' with a value of 80 in it. **Note here that the address itself is an integer (in HEX form).**

Now when we say 'u', the reference is to the value at 'u' whereas if we say '&u', the reference is to its address, which is 20A0 in memory. This is done by the operating system itself. And if now I say '*(&u);' it means the value or contents of the location referred to by 'u' (i.e., 80). **It means that first the parentheses are evaluated—that is, the address (&) of 'u' and then its**

contents (by *). So if we write the following three print statements:

printf("\n Address of u:", &u);

printf("\n Value of u: %d", u);

printf("\n Value of u: %d", *(&u));

we will get the following output:

Address of u: 20A0

Value of u: 80

Value of u: 80

Also note here that printing the value of *(&u); is the same as printing the value of 'u'.

Pointer Variables

We can store the addresses of variables in a special type of variable known as a **pointer variable. We can define a pointer variable as a variable that holds the address of a variable or a function.**

Syntax

data-type   *pointer-name;

Here, 'pointer-name' is the name of the pointer variable and 'data-type' is any valid C++ data type. The asterisk operator or star operator (*) means "pointer to". In C, we can write:

int *ptr;

But in C++ we can also write:

int* ptr;

Note here that both will work, as spaces are optional. **Also note here that the result of the pointer operator (*) does the reverse of the operator &. The pointer operator (*) returns the value of the variable stored at the address following it.** So to access the value stored at an address, we will use the pointer operator. **Also note that, like integer pointers, we can also have char pointers or float pointers.**

For example,

    char *ptr1;

    float *ptr2;

This means that *ptr1 and *ptr2 are pointing to float value and char value, respectively. It does not mean that *ptr1 contains a char value or *ptr2 contains a float value. Actually, pointer variables are of uniform size regardless of what they point to.

Just like ordinary variables, we can also write multiple pointer declarations in one line as follows:

    int *ptr1, *ptr2, *ptr3;

But please remember that we store the address of a data type into a pointer of the same data type. This means that an integer pointer can hold the address of an integer variable, a float pointer can hold the address of a float variable, and so on.

For example,

```
#include<iosteam.h>
void main( )
{
    int i = 100;
    float *ptr;
    ptr = &i;
    printf("value of ptr is %d", *ptr);
}
```

After compilation, we get the following error:

'cannot convert "int" to "float"'

Why? This is so because 'ptr' is a float pointer and we have stored the address of an integer variable to a float pointer. Therefore, the pointer variable must always point to the correct data type. But there is an exception to this rule in C++ as C++ provides a void pointer to overrule this limitation.

void Pointers

A void pointer is a pointer that can point to any type of variable. It is declared as follows:

    void *vptr;

Here 'vptr' is called a *pointer to void type* that can point to *any type of variable,* say, an int, a float, and so on. **Thus, we can also define a void pointer as a general-purpose pointer that can point to any data type.**

Applications of Void Pointers

Void pointers are used as parameters to functions that can operate on any type of memory. It is also possible to return void pointers to assign to any of several different types of pointers. **Remember that you cannot use a void pointer to dereference a variable unless you provide a type cast. It means that if 'vptr' contains an address of an integer variable, then you cannot display its value as:**

printf("void pointer is", *vptr);

A void pointer can point to any data type but the reverse is not true—that is, the following program statement would result in an error:

ptr1 = vptr; //error

To remove this error, you would have to type cast it explicitly as follows:

ptr = (int *) vptr;

Also remember that if you have to perform arithmetic on a void pointer, it is not possible without a type cast.

Arithmetic View of Pointers

A pointer is an unsigned integer variable. Thus, a pointer contains a numeric unsigned value, using which it is possible to add integer values and even subtract them from a pointer. **Please note that you cannot multiply or divide two pointers.** The main difference between a normal integer and an integer pointer is that pointer arithmetic adds and subtracts the size of the data type to which the pointer points.

For example, when we say add 1 to any integer pointer, it is incremented by the size of an integer variable. **Also note that each integer datum occupies 2 bytes in memory, so if we add 1 to an integer pointer, then actually we are adding 2 to it.**

For example,

int *ptr;

ptr = ptr + 2;

If 'ptr' holds 2000 (address), then after the execution of the second statement, 'ptr' gets 2002. Subtraction works similarly.

A character pointer also works like this, except its size is different now. When we increment or decrement a character pointer variable, its value is incremented/decremented by 1. This is because a character occupies 1 byte in memory. Along similar lines, a float pointer variable's value, when incremented/decremented, increases/decreases by 4. **In other words, in pointer arithmetic, all pointers increase and decrease by the length of the data type they point to. And remember that regardless of the pointer type, the pointer holds the address of the very first byte of the memory location. And this address of the very first byte is known as the base address. Every time a pointer is incremented, it points to the immediate next location of its type.**

So we can use them as follows:

    int i = 75;

    int *ptr;

    ptr = &i;

Also we can say that:

    int *ptr = 0;

    int *ptr1 = &i;

And we can even write:

    ptr = ptr1;   // is OK

But the following is invalid:

    ptr = i;

This implies that one should always set a pointer to a definite and appropriate address before applying the dereference operator (*) to it.

In a nutshell, we can say:

1. Addition of a number to a pointer is allowed.

2. Subtraction of a number from a pointer is allowed.

3. Addition of two pointers is not allowed.

4. Multiplying a pointer with a number is not allowed.

5. Dividing a pointer with a number is not allowed.

6. Accessing array elements by pointers is always faster than accessing them by subscripts, because internally subscripts are converted into pointers.

7. **Please note that the following two statements mean the same thing:**

   display(&num[0], 10);

   display(num, 10);

8. When we say a[i], the C++ compiler internally converts it to $*(a +i)$. The same thing happens with 2D arrays.

9. In memory, whether it is a 1D array or a 2D array, the elements are stored in one continuous chain.

10. Just as num[i] is the same as $*(num + i)$, similarly, $*(num[2] +1)$ is the same as $*(*(num +2) +1)$.

11. So a[i], $*(a +i)$, $*(i + a)$, and i[a] all refer to the same element—the ith element from the base address.

12. The expression $*(a + i) = a[i] + i[a]$ is nothing but a[i] = a[i] + a[i];

3.6 RELATIONSHIP BETWEEN ARRAY AND POINTER

Internally all arrays (of any dimension) make use of pointers for their implementation. In C/C++, the array name is treated as the address of its first element.

For example,

   int a[20];

Here, 'a' is the name of the array that holds 80 integer numbers and the value of 'a' is the address of num[0] (i.e., the address of the first element of the array); then, (a + 1) contains the address of the 2nd element, (a +2) contains an address of the 3rd element, and so on. This is because the C++ compiler internally reserves 40 words for a 20-array element. However, you can also access the address of array elements as &a[0], &a[1], &a[2], and so on. **Just remember** that data items/elements of an array are stored in consecutive memory locations (i.e., a[0] contains an element and (a + 0) contains an address of this element). So, if we apply pointer operator (*) on it, it will give the value stored at this address—that is,

*(a + 0) = the value stored at the 0th location

So,

*(a + 0) is equivalent to a[0]

*(a + 1) is equivalent to a[1]

Please note that internally C converts a[i] as *(a + i). Therefore, the following notations refer to the same element:

a[i];

*(a + i);

*(i + a);

i[num];

These are all the same.

Note that we cannot write the following statement:

***(a++); //is invalid**

This is because you cannot increment an address. But you can increment a pointer that holds an address. Here, 'a' holds the address of the first element of the array. So if we increment the base address, the compiler cannot determine the first location of this array. **Therefore, we cannot change a pointer constant.** If you want to increment the address, it is necessary to store the base address into a pointer variable first and then increment this pointer.

Note: There is a difference between *ptr++ and *(ptr++); this difference lies in the precedence of the operators. The ++ operator has a lower precedence than the * pointer operator. So, in the first expression, the value at the address ptr is retrieved first and increments its value. In the second expression, the pointer is incremented first and then the value is retrieved from this new address. The parentheses override the default precedence. The precedence rules apply equally to auto decrement operators too.

For example, consider the following program:

```
#include<stdio.h>
void main( )
 {
    int a[ ] = {10, 20, 30, 40, 50};
    int i, j;
    int *ptr = a;
    i = *ptr + 1;
    j = *(ptr + 1);
    printf(" \n Value of i is %d and j is %d");
 }
```

Here we might think that the output should be the same. But it isn't. This is because the expression considers the precedence of the pointer operator and the arithmetic operators. In the first assignment statement, 'i' gets the integer value to which ptr points and adds 1 to its value and thus the value of 'i' is displayed as 11. In the second assignment statement, the address ptr is incremented by an int value of 1. So it is incremented by 2. Thus, the value of 'j' is displayed as 20. Thus, the output of the above program after running is:

Value of i is 11 and j is 20

Remember the following points regarding arrays:

1. The bracket [ ] tells the compiler that we are dealing with an array.

2. An array is a collection of similar elements.

3. The first element in an array is numbered 0 and hence the last element is 1 less than the size of the array.

4. However big an array may be, its elements are always stored in contiguous memory locations.

5. If array elements are not initialized, then they are said to contain garbage values.

3.7 ARGUMENT PASSING USING POINTERS

In the method of pass by address, the addresses of actual arguments in the calling function are copied into formal arguments of the called function. This means that using the formal arguments in the called function, we can make changes in the actual arguments of the calling function.

For example,

```
#include<iostream.h>
#include<conio.h>
void main( )
{
    clrscr( );
    int a = 10;
    int b = 20;
    swapr (&a, &b);
    printf("\n a is:", a);
    printf("\n b is:", b);
    getch( );
}
swapv (int *x, int *y)
{
    int t;
    t = *x;
    *x = *y;
    *y = t;
    printf("x is:",x);  //values  are  exchanged  here  but
now impact                                    is  on  the
main( )
                //above.
    printf("y is:", y);
}
```

OUTPUT (after running):

x = 20

y = 10

a = 20

b = 10

Explanation: Let us review the concept of pointers. **A pointer is a variable that holds the memory address of another variable.** For example,

int a =10;

int °ptr = &a;

That is, ptr is an integer pointer that holds the memory address of another integer variable, 'a'. We must declare a pointer variable also, many of which can be declared on a single line, as in the following:

int °ptr1, °ptr2, °ptr3;</dsp>

Remember the following rule regarding pointers: "**Always store the address of a data type into a pointer of the same data type. We cannot store the address of a variable of one type in a different type of pointer variable. This means that the integer pointer can hold the address of an integer variable, the float pointer can hold the address of a float variable, and so on.**" In the call by address technique, we pass addresses of actual arguments to the called function. These addresses are stored into formal arguments, which are nothing other than pointer variables. Now whatever changes are made in the formal arguments are reflected directly to the actual arguments.

3.8 ARRAY OF POINTERS

Like a normal data-type array, we can also create an array of pointers. If we want to store the addresses of 5-integer variables, we write:

int *ptr[5];

This declaration reserves 10 bytes of contiguous memory for 5 pointers.

For example, consider the following program:

```
#include<stdio.h>
void main( )
  {
    int a = 10, b= 20, c=30,d= 40,e= 50};
    int ptr[5];
    ptr[0] = &a;
    ptr[1] = &b;
    ptr[2] = &c;
    ptr[3] = &d;
    ptr[4] = &e;
    for(int i=0; i<5;i++)
       printf("\nValue stored at address=", *ptr[i]);
  }
```

OUTPUT (after running):

Value stored at address = 10

Value stored at address = 20

Value stored at address = 30

Value stored at address = 40

Value stored at address = 50

3.9 PASSING ARRAYS AS ARGUMENTS

Just like ordinary variables, we can also pass a complete array by using its base address.

For example,

```c
#include<stdio.h>
void main( )
  {
    int a[5];
    void aread(int *, int);
    void adisplay(int*, int);
    printf("\nEnter any 5 integers:");
    aread(a, 5);
    printf("Array elements are :");
    adisplay(a, 10);
  }
void aread(int *aptr, int n)
  {
    for (int i=0; i<n; i++)
       scanf("%d", &aptr[i];
  }
void adisplay(int *ptr, int n)
  {
    for (int i=0; i<n; i++)
       printf("\n Array Elements:", aptr[i]);
  }
```

OUTPUT (after running):

Enter any 5 integers: 1 2 3 4 5

Array elements are:

1

2

3

4

5

Explanation: Here we have used two functions—aread( ) and adisplay( )—to read an integer array and to display its elements, respectively. Their prototypes are as follows:

```
    void aread(int *, int);
    void adisplay(int *, int);
It is said to be the pointer variable notation. You can also
use the following notations while declaring an array pointer
parameter:-
    void aread(int aptr[ ] , int n)
      {
        for(int i=0; i<n; i++)
         scanf("%d", &aptr[i];
      }
    void adisplay(int aptr[ ] , int n)
      {
        for(int i=0; i<n; i++)
         scanf("%d \n",& aptr[i]);
      }
```

NOTE

There is no difference between the earlier notations and the later notations. They both work in the same way. The only difference between the former and latter notation is that in the former:

void aread(int *, int);

void adisplay(int *, int);

The pointer is an integer pointer. On the other hand, in the latter example:

void aread(int [ ] , int);

void adisplay(int [ ], int);

This parameter is a pointer to an int array. However, if you declare a pointer parameter with an array dimension, such as:

void aread(int [5], int);

void adisplay(int [5], int);

the compiler ignores the dimension. In this program, aptr contains an address of the first element and sees that there is no & operator in their call statement.

It is also possible to pass 2D arrays just as we can pass 1D arrays to functions. But please remember that the only mandatory condition is that when we pass 2D arrays, it is necessary to mention the column size in the function prototype as well as in the function definition. On the other hand, the size of the row is optional. This is because a 2D array is an array of arrays. Therefore, the function does not need to know how many rows there are in such a 2D array, but the length of each row (i.e., column) is mandatory.

We are in a position to solve an example now.

Example 1: **Write a C program to find the trace of a 2D matrix.**

Solution 1: Trace of a matrix is defined as the sum of its diagonal elements. The program is as follows:

```c
#include<stdio.h>
void main( )
{
    void readarray(int a[ ] [4], int n);
    void trace(int a[ ] [4], int n);
    void display(int a[ ] [4], int n);
    int a[4][4];
    readarray(a, 4);
    display(a, 4);
    trace(a, 4);
}
void readarray(int a[ ] [4], int n)
{
    int i, j;
    printf("\nEnter the elements of 2D matrix:\n)";
    for (i =0; i<4; i++)
      {
        for(j=0; j<4;j++)
           scanf("%d", &a[i][j]);
      }
}
void display(int a[ ] [4], int n)
{
    int i, j;
    printf("\nMatrix is:");
    for (i =0; i<n; i++)
      {
        printf("\n");
        for(j=0; j<n; j++)
           printf(" Array is:\t", a[i] [j]);
      }
```

```
    }
    void trace(int a[ ] [4], int n)
    {
        int diagonal_sum = 0;
        // trace calculated now
            for (int i =0; i<n; i++)
                diagonal_sum += a[i][j];
            printf("\n Trace=", diagonal_sum);
    }
```

OUTPUT *(after running):*

Enter the elements of 2D matrix:

1	2	3	4
5	6	7	8
9	10	11	12
13	14	15	16

Matrix is:

1	2	3	4
5	6	7	8
9	10	11	12
13	14	15	16

Trace = 34

We are in a position to write some programs now.

***Example* 1:** Give the output of the following C program:

```
#include<stdio.h>
main( )
  {
    static int a[ ] = {1, 2, 3, 4 };
    int *ptr;
    ptr = a;
    *(a + 3) = (*ptr++) + *(ptr++);
    printf("\n\t\t Elements are:", *(a + 3);
    printf("\n\t\t", a[0], a[1], a[2], a[3]);
    getch( );
  }
```

Solution 1: Elements are: 1   2   3   2

Example 2: Give the output of the following C program:

```
#include<stdio.h>
main( )
  {
     int a, b;
     a = 10,11;
     b = (10, 11);
     clrscr( );
     printf("\n a and b are:", a, b);
     getch( );
  }
```

Solution 2: 10   11

Example 3: Whenever we give the array name we refer to its base address. It is also said that the array has decayed into a pointer. Will this happen in all situations?

Solution 3: Decaying of an array into a pointer does not take place in two situations:

(a) When the array name is used with the sizeof operator

(b) When the array name is an operand of the & operator

If we pass the name of a 1d int array to a function, it decays into a pointer to an int. But if we pass the name of a 2d array of integers to a function, then it decays into a pointer to an array and not a pointer to a pointer.

Example 4: Give the output:

```
void main( )
  {
     printf("%c", "abcdefgh"[5] );
  }
```

Solution 4: f is the output.

Example 5: How will you display \n as an output?

Solution 5: Simply write:

printf("\\n");

***Example* 6: Give the output:**

```
void main( )
  {
    char ch = 'R';
    printf ("%d %d", sizeof (ch), sizeof ('R'));
  }
```

Solution 6: The output is: 1   2

***Example* 7: Give the output:**

```
void main( )
  {
    printf( 5 + "RajivChopra");
  }
```

Solution 7: The following is the output:

hopra

***Example* 8: Say an array c is defined as follows:**

char c[ ] = "Rajiv";

What would sizeof(c) and strlen(c) return?

Solution 8: sizeof(c) will return 5 and strlen (c) will return 4. This implies that sizeof uses '\0' (i.e., null terminator) whereas the strlen( ) function does not.

***Example* 9: Write a C program to calculate the factorial of a given integer number using the call-by-value method.**

Solution 9: The program is as follows:

```
#include<stdio.h>
#include<conio.h>
void main( )
{
    long fact (int);  /* function prototype */
    int num;
    long f;
    clrscr( );
    printf(\n Enter your number:");
    scanf("%d", &num);
    f= fact (num);
    printf("\nFactorial of %d = %ld", num, f);
    getch( );
}
```

```
long fact (int n)
{
    int i;
    long f1 = 1;
    for (i=1; i<=n;i++)
        f1 = f1 * i;
    return (f1);
}
```

OUTPUT (after running):

Enter your number: 3

Factorial of 3 = 6

***Example* 10: Write a C program to sum the following series:**

> **Sum = 1 + 2 + 3 + 4 + 5 + ... n**

Solution 10: The program is as follows:

```
#include<stdio.h>
#include<conio.h>
void main ( )
{
    int n, sum;
    clrscr ( );
    printf("\nEnter the last term of the series");
    scanf("%d", &n);
    sum = series (n);
    printf("\nSum of series = %d", sum);
    getch ( );
}
series (int last)
{
    int i, s=0;
    for (i=1; i<=last; i++)
        s+ = I;
    return (s);
}
```

NOTE   *Please run this program yourself.*

***Example* 11: Write a C program to find the sum of the digits of an integer number. Use functions only.**

Solution 11: The program is as follows:

```
#include<stdio.h>
#include<conio.h>
void main( )
{
    int s;
    long n;
    clrscr( );
    printf("\nEnter your number");
    scanf("%ld", &n);
    s = sumdig (n);
    printf("\n Sum of digits of %ld = %d", n, s);
    getch( );
}
sumdig (long num)
{
    int d, sum = 0;
     while (num > 0)
     {
          d= num % 10;
          num = num /10;
          sum += d;
     }
        return (sum);
}
```

OUTPUT *(after running):*

Enter your number: 246

Sum of digits of 246 = 12

***Example* 12: Write a C program to compute the bionomial coefficient $^nC^r$ using functions:**

$$^nC_r = n! / r! (n - r)!$$

Solution 12: The program is as follows:

```
#include<stdio.h>
#include<conio.h>
void main( )
{
    int ncr;
    long n, r;
```

```
    clrscr( );
    printf("\n Enter value of n and r");
    scanf("%ld%ld", &n, &r);
    ncr = fact(n) / (fact (r) * fact(n - r));
    printf("\n Value of ncr = %d", ncr);
    getch( );
}
fact (int num)
{
    int i;
    long f = 1;
    for (i =1; i <= num; i++)
        f = f * i;
    return (f );
}
```

NOTE   *Please run the program yourself.*

Example 13: **Write a C function to reverse a number.**

Solution 13: The program is as follows:

```
reverse (int n)
  {
    int r, rev = 0;
    while (n > 0)
      {
        r = n % 10;
        n = n/10;
        rev = revr * 10 + r;
      }
    return (rev);
}
```

Example 14: **Write a C program to sum the following series:**

$$Sum = x^3 / 3! + x^5 / 5! + x^7 / 7! + ...$$

Solution 14: The program is as follows:

```
#include<stdio.h>
#include<conio.h>
void main( )
{
    float sum = 0.0;
    int t1, t2, x, i, n;
```

```
      clrscr ( );
      printf (\n Enter the number of terms:");
      scanf ("%d", &n);
      printf ("\n Enter the value of x:");
      scanf ("%d", &x);
      for ( i = 3; i <= n; i += 2)
        {
          t1 = power (x, i);
          t2 = fact (i);
          sum = sum + (float) t1/t2;
        }
      printf ("\n The sum of the series = %f", sum);
      getch ( );
  }
  power (int x, int y)
  {
      int i, pow = 1;
      for (i=1; i <=y; i++)
         pow = pow * x;
      return (pow);
  }
  fact (int n)
  {
      int j, fact = 1;
      for (j=1; j<=n; j++)
         fact = fact * j;
         return (fact);
  }
```

Please run this program yourself.

***Example* 15: Write a C program to compute a^b using recursion:**

$$\text{power } (a, b) = 1 \quad \text{if } b = 0$$

$$a * \text{power } (a, b\text{-}1) \quad \text{if } b > 0$$

Solution 15: We use the fact that a^b is simply the product of a and $a^{b\text{-}1}$.
The program is as follows:

```
#include<stdio.h>
#include<conio.h>
void main ( )
{
```

```
      float power (float, int);
      int b;
      float a, p;
      clrscr ( );
      printf ("\n Enter two numbers:");
      scanf ("%f %d", &a, &b);
      p = power (a, b);
      printf ("\n%f raise to %d = %f", a, b, p);
      getch ( );
}
float power (float x, int y)
{
    if ( y = =0)
        return 1;
    else
        return (x * power (x, y-1));
}
```

OUTPUT (after running):

Enter two numbers: 2   3

2 raised to 3 = 8.000000

***Example* 16:** Consider the very popular **Tower of Hanoi problem. It involves moving a specified number of disks from one tower to another using a third, auxiliary tower. Suppose that there are three towers A, B, and C. The game starts with the disks stacked on tower A in order of decreasing size (i.e., the largest on the bottom and the smallest on top). The aim is to transfer the disks from tower A to tower C with the following constraints:**

(a) **Only one disk can be moved at a time and that is the top disk.**

(b) **A Larger disk cannot be placed on top of a smaller disk.**

Write a C program to simulate this Tower of Hanoi problem.

Solution 16: Let us write its algorithm first:

if (n = = 1) then

                move disk 1 from tower A to C

    else

move (n-1) smaller disks from tower A to B.

move the largest disk from tower A to C.

move the (n-1) smaller disks from tower B to C.

end if

The program is as follows:

```
#include<stdio.h>
#include<conio.h>
#include<process.h>
void main( )
{
    int n;
    void tower(char from, char to, char using, int n);
    clrscr( );
    printf("\n Enter the number of disks:");
    scanf("%d", &n);
    if (n < 1)
      {
        printf("\n It is not possible");
        exit (1);
      }
    else
        tower('A, 'C', 'B', n);
}
void tower (char from, char to, char using, int n)
{
    if (n = = 1)
        printf ("\n Move disk from %c to %c", from, to);
    else
      {
        tower (from, using, to, n-1);
        tower (from, to, using, 1);
        tower (using, to, from, n-1);
      }
}
```

Example 17: **It is desired to add a user-defined function to a C library. How can this be done. Explain giving an example.**

Solution 17: The function that is to be added to the library is first compiled. Then it is added to the library using a TLIB utility named tlib.exe (a facility in turbo c). After adding the function, the linker will automatically link it with your program code as it does with inbuilt functions of C. Consider an example of a factorial function as follows:

```
int fact(int n)
  {
    int i, f = 1;
    for (i=1; i<=n; i++)
       f = f *i;
    return (f);
  }
```

Save this program in some file—say, facto.c

Now compile this file using the ctrl+F9 key. This creates a "facto.obj" file having object code.

From the DOS prompt, add the function to the library by using the command:

C:\>TLIB\TC\LIB\math.lib + \TC\facto.obj

Please note here that math.lib is the library name, + is used to add a new function to the library, and facto.obj is the file to be added. Also note that minus (-) is used to delete existing functions.

Now declare the prototype of the fact( ) in the header file—say, fact.h. This file should be included while calling the function. To use the function create a program as follows:

```
#include "c:\\fact.h"
main( )
  {
    int f;
    f = fact (5);
    printf("%d", f);
  }
```

Now compile and execute the program using ctrl+F9.

Example 18: **Distinguish between formal and actual parameters.**

Solution 18: The following are the differences:

Formal Parameter	Actual Parameter
(1) Formal parameters are the variables which are defined within the function. They are used in expressions within the body of the function.	(1) Actual parameters are the variables specified in a call to the function. When the function is accessed, actual parameters replace the formal parameters.
(2) A function header is always formal.	(2) A function call has actual parameters.
(3) They are written in the first line of the function definition.	(3) They are written in the function declaration.

For example,
 	
int facto (int n)
 	
{
 	
....
 	
}
 	
Here 'n' is a formal parameter that is declared in the function header.
	For example,
	
	int facto (5);
	
	Here, 5 is the actual parameter being passed.

Example 19: Distinguish between call by value and call by reference.

Solution 19: The following are the points of difference between the two:

Call by Value	Call by Reference
(1) In this method, the value of the variables is passed to the called function.	(1) In this method, the address of the variables is passed to the called function.
(2) In the called function, the values are received in a similar type of variable.	(2) As the address of the variable is received in the called function, it is also received in a pointer variable.
(3) Only one value can be returned by these functions.	(3) More than one value can be returned to the function.
(4) The syntax is: t = gcd(u, v);	(4) The syntax is: gcd (&u, &v);

Example 20: **Name two different styles of writing prototypes.**

Solution 20: There are two styles of writing prototypes:

> float sum (float x, float y);

Or   float sum (float, float);

Example 21: **Distinguish between library functions and user-defined functions in C.**

Solution 21: The following chart shows the points of difference:

Library Functions	User-Defined Functions
(1) Predefined in the compiler itself	(1) Not predefined in the compiler itself
(2) No user-created library functions	(2) User-defined functions created by the programmers
(3) Stored in special library files	(3) User-defined functions not stored in library files
(4) Inclusion of corresponding header file for each inbuilt function used in any program (else you will get an error)	(4) No header file for user-defined functions
(5) No execution of program beginning from library function	(5) Execution of program always beginning with user-defined function— that is, main( )
For example, log( ), cos( ), sqrt( ), printf( ), scanf( )	For example, main( ), sum( ), sort( )

Example 22: **Write an example program to show functions with no arguments and no return values.**

Solution 22: The program is as follows:

/*Functions with no arguments and no return values*/

```
#include<stdio.h>
main ( )
{
    void hello ( );   /* function declaration */
     hello( );  /* invoking function */
}
/*function definition */
```

```
void hello( )
{
    char name[20];
    printf("Enter your name");
    scanf("%s", name);
    printf("%s\n\n", name);
    printf("Hello %s, good morning", name);
}
```

OUTPUT (after running):

Enter your name: Dr. Rajiv

Hello Dr. Rajiv good morning

Example 23: **Write a C program to implement a simple calculator that can add, subtract, multiply, and divide two numbers read from the keyboard.**

Solution 23: The program is as follows:

```
#include<stdio.h>
main( )
{
    float num1, num2, result;
    char opn;
    void arithop( );
    printf("Enter any two numbers and the \n");
    printf("operation symbol (+, -, * or /) \n");
    scanf("%f %f %c", &num1, &num2, &opn);
    printf("\n %8.2f %c %8.2f = ", num1, opn, num2);
    arithop(num1, num2, opn);
}
void arithop (a, b, op)      /*arithop function */
float a, b;
char op;
{
    switch (op) {
    case '+' :
            printf("%10.2f\n", a+b);
            break;
    case '-' :
            printf("%8.2f\n", a-b);
            break;
    case '*' :
```

```
            printf("%8.2f\n", a*b);
            break;
    case '/' :
            printf("%8.2f\n", a/b);
            break;
    default:
            printf("Invalid operation");
            break;
    }
}
```

OUTPUT (after running):

Enter any two numbers and the

Operation symbol (+, -, *, or /)

44.00 / 11.00 = 4.00

Example 24: **Write a C program to compute the mean and standard deviation of n numbers that are read from the keyboard.**

Solution 24: The program is as follows:

```
#include<stdio.h>
#include<math.h>
main( )
{
    int i, n;
    float deviation, list[20];
    float sd( );        /* function declaration */
    printf("Calculating standard deviation of a…… ");
    printf("list of numbers:");
    printf("\n Enter the size of the list:");
    scanf ("%d", &n);
    printf("%d\n", n);
    printf("\n Enter the %d elements\n", n);
    for(i=0; i<n; i++)
      scanf("%f", &list[i]);
    for(i=0; i<n; i++)
      printf("%8.2f", list[i]);
    deviation = sd(list, n);
    printf("\n Standard Deviation is: %10.5f\n", devia-
tion);
}
/* function to compute standard deviation */
```

```
float sd(x, m)
float x[20];
int m;
{
    int i;
    float mean, dev, sum = 0.0;
    float avg ( );      /* function declaration */
    mean = avg(x, m);
    printf("\n\n Mean of %3d elements is:%10.2f\n", m,
mean);
    for(i=0; i<m; i++)
        sum = sum + (mean - x[i]) * (mean - x[i]);
    dev = sqrt(sum/(float) m);
    return (dev);
}
/* function to compute mean */
float avg(a, n)
float a[20];
int n;
{
    int i;
    float sum = 0.0;
    for (i=0; i<n ; i++)
        sum += a[i];
    return (sum / (float) n);
}
```

OUTPUT (after running):

Calculating standard deviation of a … list of numbers.

Enter size of the list: 5

Enter 5 elements: 12.34   56.00   78.90   34.00   78.45

Mean of 5 elements is: 51.94

Standard deviation is: 25.83064

Example **25: Write a C program to reverse n characters using recursion.**

Solution 25: The program is as follows:

```
#include<stdio.h>
#include<math.h>
main ( )
{
```

```
    int n;
    void rev ( );
    printf("Enter  the  number  of  characters  to  be  re-
versed:");
    scanf("%d", &n);
    printf("%d", n);
    printf("\n");
    rev (n);
    printf("\n");
}
void rev(n)
int n;
{
    char c;
    if (n = = 1)
      {
        c= getchar( );
        c= getchar( );
        putchar ( c );
      }
    else
      {
      c= getchar( );
      c = getchar( );
      rev ( - - n);
      putchar ( c );
      }
    return;
}
```

OUTPUT (after running):

Enter the number of characters to be reversed: 5

rajiv

vijar

Example 26: Write a C program to implement a binary search using recursion.

Solution 26: The program is as follows:

```
#include<stdio.h>
int key; /* global variable */
main( )
```

```
{
    int a[50], I, n, loc;
    int bin( );
    printf("\n\t Enter the array size:");
    scanf("%d", &n);
    printf("%d\n", n);
    printf("\n\t Please enter the array elements in ascending
    order:");
    for (i=0; i<n; i++)
        scanf("%d", &a[i]);
    for (i=0; i<n; i++)
        printf("%d", a[i]);
    printf("\n");
    printf("Enter the element to be searched:");
    scanf("%d", &key);
    printf("%d", key);
    loc = bin (a, 0, n);
    printf("\n\n");
    if (loc = = 0)
        printf("Unsuccessful  search.  %d  not  found  \n",
key);
    else
      {
        printf("Successful search\n");
        printf("%d found at position %d. \n", key, loc);
      }
}
/* recursive binary search method */
int bin (b, low, high)
int b[5], low, high;
{
    static int mid;
    int i;
    if (low <= high)
      {
        mid = (low + high)/2;
        if (key < b[mid]) {
        /* element in the lower half */
        high = mid - 1;
        bin (b, low, high);
        }
        else if (key > b[mid]) {
```

```
            /* element in the upper half */
            low = mid + 1;
            bin (b, low, high);
        }
    else if (key = = b[mid])
    /* element found */
        return (mid + 1);
}
else
    return (0 );        /* element not found */
}
```

OUTPUT (after running):

Enter the array size: 10

Please enter the array elements in ascending order: 2 4 6 8 10 12 14 16 18 20

Enter the element to be searched: 16

Successful search

16 found at position 8

Example 27: Write a C program to find the smallest element in an array of size n, using pointers only.

Solution 27: The following is the code:

```
#include<stdio.h>
main( )
{
    int i, n, small, *ptr, a[50];
    printf("\n\t Enter the array size:");
    scanf("%d", &n);
    printf("%d", n);
    printf("\n\t Enter the array elements:");
    for (i=0; i< n; i++)
        scanf("%d", &a[i]);
    printf("\n\t Echoing the array elements:");
    for (i=0; i< n; i++)
        printf("%d", a[i]);
    printf("\n");
    ptr = a;    /* assign address of a[0] to pointer 'ptr'
and it                          can be done in two ways-
either ptr = &a[0] or ptr = a */
    small = *ptr;    /* contents of a[0] assigned to
small */
```

```
      ptr ++;   /* increment pointer to next element */
     /* iterate n-1 times to search for smallest element in the
     ar ray */
     for (i=1; i<n; i++)
     {
        if ( small > *ptr)
           small = *ptr;
        ptr++; /* increment pointer to a[i+1] */
     }
     printf("\n Smallest element is %d", small);
     }
```

OUTPUT (after running):

Enter the array size: 5

Enter the array elements: -5 4 3 2 7

Smallest element is -5

Example 28: Write a C program to bubble-sort an array of size n, using pointers only.

Solution 28: The program is as follows:

```
#include<stdio.h>
#include<malloc.h>
main( )
{
   int i, n, *vector;
   void bubble( );
   printf(" Enter the array size:");
   scanf("%d", &n);
   printf("%d", n);
   /* dynamic memory allocation is done using malloc ( )
of C */
   vector = (int *) malloc (n * sizeof(int)); /* sizeof
gives size of data type in bytes */
   printf("\nEnter the array elements :");
   for (i=0; i<n ; i++)
    scanf("%d", vector + i);
   for (i=0; i<n ; i++)
    printf("%d", *(vector + i)); /* echoing */
   printf("\n");
bubble(vector, n);    /* invoke function */
printf("\n Sorted array is:");
for (i =0; i <n; i++)
```

```
        printf("%d", *(vector + i));
  printf ("\n");
  }
      void bubble (x, m)
      int *x, m;
        {
          int pass, i, temp;
          for (pass = 0; pass < m-1; pass++)
            {
              for (i=0; i < m-pass; i++)
                {
                    if (*(x + i) > *(x+i+1))
                      {
                            temp = *(x+i);
                            *(x+i) = *(x + i +1);
                            *(x+i+1) = temp;
                      }
                }
            }
        }
```

OUTPUT (after running):

Enter the array size: 5

Enter the array elements: -5 4 3 2 7

Sorted array is: -5 2 3 4 7

Example **29: Write a C program to find the length of given string.**

Solution 29: The program is as follows:

```
#include<stdio.h>
main( )
{
    char string[80], *ptr;
    ptr = string;
    printf("\n\tEnter the string whose length you want:");
    while ((*ptr++ = getchar( )) != '\n')      /* read the
string */
        *- - ptr = '\0';
    printf("\nString is %s", string);
    printf(\n Its length is %d", (ptr - string));
}
```

OUTPUT (after running):

Enter the string whose length you want: Dr. RAJIV

String is Dr. RAJIV

Its length is 9

***Example* 30: Are the following expressions the same: *ptr++ and ++*ptr?**

Solution 30: No, they are not the same. *ptr++ increments the pointer and not the value pointed by it, whereas ++*ptr increments the value being pointed to by ptr.

***Example* 31: We know that a[i] = *(a+i). What will a[i][j] be?**

Solution 31: a[i][j] will be internally converted to *(*(a+i) + j) by the C compiler.

***Example* 32: Give some applications of pointers.**

Solution 32: Applications:

1. To access array elements

2. For dynamic memory allocations

3. Use of pointer concept in call by reference

4. To implement linked lists, trees, graphs, etc.

***Example* 33: Define a null pointer.**

Solution 33: For any type of pointer, C defines a **null pointer** as a special type of pointer that is guaranteed not to point to any object or function of that type. **Note that the null pointer constant used for representing a null pointer is the integer 0.**

***Example* 34: Define a null pointer, a NULL macro, the ASCII NULL character, and a null string.**

Solution 34: A null pointer is a pointer that doesn't point anywhere.

A NULL macro is used to represent the null pointer in the source code. It has a value 0 associated with it.

The ASCII NULL character has all its bits as 0 but doesn't have any relationship with the null pointer.

The null string is just another name for an empty string—"".

Example 35: **What causes the null pointer assignment error?**

Solution 35: This error occurs when we declare a pointer and then use it before allocating memory for it. This error may also occur when we use a wild pointer. The wild pointer references the base area of the data segment. Memory or stack corruption may cause this error.

Example 36: **Can main( ) be called recursively?**

Solution 36: Yes, main( ) can be called recursively.

Example 37: **A stack is a data structure in which only the topmost element can be accessed. You can push an element and delete an element from a stack, named push and pop, respectively. Stacks work on the LIFO principle (Last-In-First-Out). Implement a stack in C. Write two functions push( ) and pop( ).**

Solution 37: The following are the two functions:

```
/*push operation on stack */
/* stack [ ] is a stack array, item is the data being
pushed onto the stack, *top is pointer */
/* to top of stack and max_size is the maximum size of
stack */
void push (char stack [ ], char item, int *top, int max_
size)
{
    if (*top < max_size - 1)
      {
        ++(*top);
        stack[*top] = item;
      }
}
/*pop operation on stack */
/* stack [ ] is a stack array, *top is pointer to top of
stack and item is the value popped off the stack */
char pop(char stack, int *top)
{
    char item;
    if (*top >= 0) {
        item = stack[*top];
        - (*top);
    }
else {
```

```
        item = STACK_EMPTY;
    }
return (item);
}
```

Summary

Arrays and pointers are related to each other. In this chapter, we have studied 1D, 2D, and 3D arrays. We have also seen the purpose of writing functions for modular programming. Different techniques of parameter passing have been dealt with. Pointers have been examined in depth using a simpler approach.

Exercises

Q1. Write a C program to find the roots of a given quadratic equation.

Q2. Write a C function to find the GCD and LCM of two numbers.

Q3. Write a function prime that returns 1 if its argument is a prime and returns 0 otherwise.

Q4. Write a C program to check whether the given year is a leap year.

[**Hint:**

```
/* testing for leap years using a 'boolean' function */
main( )
{
    int year;
    printf("Please enter a year:");
    scanf("%d", &year);
    if (is_leap(year))
        printf("%d is a leap year.\n", year);
    else
        printf("%d is not a leap year. \n", year);
}
/* 'Boolean' function is_leap returns true if year is a
leap year */
is_leap(year)
int year;
{
    return (year % 4 = = 0 && year % 100 !=0 || year % 400
= = 0);
}
```

Q5. Write a C function to read the three sides of a triangle and to determine whether they form a triangle. Also determine the type of triangle they form. You should return true if the triangle is formed and false otherwise.

Q6. The area of a triangle can be computed using Heron's formula, which defines the semi-perimeter 's' as half of the sum of the sides of the triangle. The area of the triangle is given by the formula:

Area = the square root of (s(s-a)(s-b)(s-c))

where a, b, and c are the sides of the triangle. Write a function which, when passed the sides of a triangle, returns the area using Heron's formula. The function should first make sure that the triangle is valid; if it is not, the function can return zero or a negative value as an error indicator. Use the sqrt( ) function that is inbuilt in the math library.

Q7. Write a C program to reverse an array using a single array 'a' only.

[Hint:

```
for(I = ARRAY_SIZE - 1; i>=0; i- - )
    printf("%d", array[i]);
printf("\n");
]
```

Q8. Write a simple bubble sort function.

[Hint:

```
void sort (int a[ ] , int n)
  {
    int i, j, temp;
    for (i =0; i < n -1; ++i)
      for (j = i +1; j <n; ++j)
        if ( a[i] > a[j])
          {
              temp = a[i];
              a[i] = a[j];
              a[j] = temp;

          }

  }
```

In the main( ) function, you can just call sort(array, 10);].

Q9. Write a simple function to find the GCD of two numbers, u and v.

[Hint:

```
int gcd (int , int v)
  {
```

```
      int temp;
      while ( v!= 0) {
         temp = u % v;
         u = v;
         v = temp;
      }
   return u;
   }
```
].

Q10. Now modify the module in Q9 above to find the LCM of these two numbers, u and v.

[Hint:

Use formula: lcm (u, v) = uv / gcd (u, v) where u, v >= 0.   ]

Q11. Write a function called substring( ) to extract a portion of a character string. The function should be called as follows:

substring (source, start, count, result);

where *source* is the character string from which you are extracting the substring, *start* is an index number into *source* indicating the first character of the substring, count is the number of characters to be extracted from the source string, and *result* is an array of characters that is to contain the extracted substring. For example,

substring("character", 4, 3, result);

extracts the substring "act" (3 characters starting with character number 4) from the string "character" and places the result in *result*.

Q12. Write a C program to insert an element into an existing array.

[Hint:

```
#include<stdio.h>
#include<conio.h>
void main( )
  {
     int i, element, loc, n, a[10];
     clrscr( );
     printf("\n Enter number of elements:");
     scanf("%d", &n);
     printf("\t Enter elements:");
     for (i=0; i<n; i++)
        scanf("%d", &a[i]);
     printf("\n Enter element to insert:");
     scanf("%d", &element);
```

```
      printf("\n Enter location to insert:");
      scanf("%d", &loc);
      for (i = n-1; i >= loc; i - - )
         a[i+1] = a[i];
      a[loc] = element;
      for (i=0; i <= n; i++)
         printf("\n %d", a[i]);
      getch( );
   }                                                    ]
```

Q13. Distinguish between static and dynamic memory allocation.

Q14. Write a suitable array definition to define a 1D 4-element character array called letters. Assign the characters 'N', 'S', 'E' and 'W' to the array elements.

Q15. Write a suitable declaration to declare a pointer to a function that accepts 3 pointers to integer quantities as arguments and returns a pointer to a floating point quantity.

Q16. Give the output of the following program:

```
main( )
  {
     int a[ ] = {0, 1, 2, 3, 4};
     int *P[ ] = {a, a+1, a+2, a+3, a+4 };
     printf("%u %u %d", P, *P, *(*P) );
  }
```

Q17. Explain the following declarations in C:

(a) int °P[10];

(b) int (°P) [10];

(c) int °P (void);

(d) int °P(char° a);

(e) int (°P) (char° a).

Q18. Write a C program to compute simple interest given by the following formula:

$$SI = (p * t * r) / 100.$$ Use pointers.

Q19. Write a C program to compute temperature in centigrade by the following formula:

$$C = 5/9 \ (F - 32).$$ Use pointers and functions.

Q20. Write a function that receives 5 integers and returns their sum, average, and standard deviation. Call this function from the main( ) and print the results in main.

Q21. Write a program to generate prime numbers from 1 to 1000 using arrays.

Q22. Demonstrate call by value and call by reference with suitable example programs.

Q23. Discuss all string functions and explain with example programs.

Q24. Demonstrate the relationship between arrays and pointers with suitable programs.

Q25. Which is generally more efficient—recursion or iteration? Why?

Q26. Write a C program to find if a square matrix is symmetric. Note that a square matrix is symmetric if it is equal to its transpose.

Q27. Under what conditions can one pointer to a variable be subtracted from another? How will this difference be interpreted?

Q28. Give the output:

int a=10, b=8, c;

c = a++ + b + a++;

printf("%d", c);

c = ++a + b + ++c;

printf("%d", c);

[**Hint:** 30   50].

Q29. Write a C program to input an array of 10 characters and find the number of duplicate characters, if any.

[**Hint:**

```
#include<stdio.h>
int x, c=0;
printf("\n\n Enter characters…");
for (x=0; x<10; x++)
  {
    scanf("%c", &ch[x]);
  }
```

```
for (x=0; x < 10; x++)
  {
    if (ch[x] = = ch[x - 1])
      {
        c = c+ 1;
      }
  }
  printf("\n\n No. of duplicate characters %d", c);
  return 0;
}                                                   ].
```

Q30. Explain how pointers are used to access array elements with an example of adding two single-dimensional arrays of order 10.

Q31. Explain with an example how pointers are passed to a function.

Q32. Write a C function that calculates the cross-product of 2 vectors, $(x_1, x_2, \ldots x_n)$ and $(y_1, y_2, \ldots y_n)$ as $\Sigma (x_i \ ^\circ y_i)$, t = 1 to n. Use it in the main program to input 3 vectors x, y, z and calculate the vector equation: (xy + yz).

Q33. Write down a C program that inputs 20 integers and calculates the sum of the factorials of all numbers that are possible.

Q34. Write a C program to access a string of 100 characters using pointers and output it by replacing two or blank by a single blank.

Q35. (a) Mention the return types in functions. By default, a function returns which type of a value? Give an example.

(b) Describe formal argument, actual argument, function declaration, and function definition.

(c) Differentiate between a pointer to a constant and a constant pointer.

(d) Write a C program to sort a list of strings in alphabetical order.

Q36. (a) Write a C program to print the individual digits of a 6-digit number in words.

(b) Write a C program to find the second largest and second smallest element in a vector.

(c) Write a C program to sort a given list of numbers in ascending order, using pointers.

(d) Write a C program using recursion to reverse n characters.

CHAPTER 4

STRUCTURES AND UNIONS

4.0 INTRODUCTION

We have seen that an array is a collection of similar (homogeneous) data items. But C also provides two more user-defined data types—structures and unions. They are called user-defined data types as users define them as per their needs. **We define structure as a collection of heterogeneous (dissimilar) elements that are stored contiguously in memory. Understand that a structure is a collection of a fixed number of elements that are accessed by name, not by index (as arrays are done).** The elements of a structure may be of different data types.

Say we want to store a current date—let's call it March 24, 2016—in a program. We take three different variables to store 24 (day), 03 (month), and 2016 (year). Now say again we want to store a date of purchase; again we need three variables—say, date_of_purchase, month_of_purchase, and year_of_purchase. This means we now need another set of three variables. This consumes a lot of memory. Structures are helpful here. Thus, we can declare a structure of date as follows:

```
struct date
{
    int month;
    int day;
    int year;
};
```

Here, **date** is a structure (user-defined) that has three **members,** called **month, day, and year.** The definition of **date** here defines a new data type in the language in the sense that the variables may subsequently be declared to be of type **struct date** as follows:

struct date today;

However, unlike variables of type int, float, or char, a special syntax is needed when dealing with structure variables. **A member function is accessed by specifying the variable name, followed by a period (.) or dot operator, and then the member name.**

For example,

today.day = 24;

Note that there are no spaces allowed between the variable name, the period, and the member name. So to set the year of the date, the expression is:

today.year = 2016;

And to test the value of month to see if it equals to 3, a statement is written as follows:

if(today.month = = 03)

    next_month = 01;

The **syntax of declaration of a structure** is:

```
struct stname
    {
        datatype1 list_of_variables;
        datatype1 list_of_variables;
        .......
        .......
        datatype-n list_of_variables;
    };
```

where **struct** is a keyword in C, followed by a **structure name, stname, or a tag.** The structure ends with a closing brace and a semicolon. The data items in the structure are defined by a type, followed by one or more identifiers, separated by commas.

For example,

struct Emp
```
{
    char fname[40], lname[40];
    int age;
    float basic_salary;
    char address[80];
};
```
Here, Emp is a new user-defined structure data type.

Please note that a structure declaration does not reserve any space for memory because a structure declaration is just a data type, like an int, a float, or a char. Memory is allocated only when a variable of the corresponding structure type is declared. A structure variable is declared as follows:

Syntax

struct stname stvar;

Here, *stvar* is a structure variable of the type *struct stname.*

For example,

struct date today;

We now write a complete program for the date problem:

```
#include<conio.h>
main( )
 {
    struct date
     {
        int month;
        int day;
        int year;
};
    struct date today;
    today.month = 03;
    today.day = 24;
    today.year = 2016;
    printf("Todays date is %d/%d/%d. \n", today.month, to-
day.day, today.year % 100);
 }
```

OUTPUT (after running):

Today's date is 03/24/2016

The date initializations that are done in this program are stored as shown in Figure 4.1.

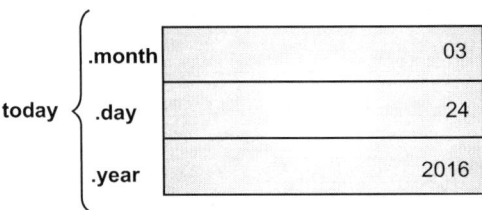

Figure 4.1: Assigning Values to a Structure Variable

When it comes to the evaluation of expressions, structure members follow the same rules as do ordinary variables in C. *So division of an integer structure member by another integer would be performed as an integer division.*

Let us again consider the Emp structure (defined earlier):

```
struct Emp
{
    char fname[40], lname[40];
    int age;
    float basic_salary;
    char address[80];
};
```

Here, 40 bytes are reserved for fname, 40 bytes for lname, 2 bytes for age, 4 bytes for basic_salary, and 80 bytes for the character array. Thus, *the size of the structure is given by the sum of the sizes of its individual elements/data items.*

It is also to be noted that the structure name may be omitted if a structure variable of a particular structure type has been declared when the structure is defined. For example,

```
struct
  {
    char fname[40];
    int age;
    float bas_salary;
  } emp;
```

But the problem here is that in such a declaration you cannot subsequently declare another variable whose type is the same as that of emp, in this case.

So we will access these members as:

emp.fname;

emp.age;

emp.bas_salary;

And once we know this, we can initialize the values of these member variables as follows:

strcpy(emp.fname, "DR. RAJIV");

strcpy(emp.lname, "CHOPRA");

emp.age = 41;

emp.salary = 82000.00;

strcpy(emp.address, "GTB NAGAR");

Before we discuss structures further, let us write some programs now.

Example **1: Write a simple program that reads the employee's name, his age, and his salary from the keyboard and displays the information.**

Solution 1: The following is the program:

```
#include<stdio.h>
main( )
  {
    struct Employee
     {
       char name[20];
       int age;
       float salary;
     };
    struct Employee emp1, emp2;
    printf("\n Enter name, age and salary of the 1st em-
ployee:");
    scanf("%s %d %f", &emp1.name, &emp1.age, &emp1.sal-
ary);
    printf("\n Enter name, age and salary of the 2nd em-
ployee:");
```

```
    scanf("%s %d %f", &emp2.name, &emp2.age, &emp2.salary);
    printf("\n First Employee details...");
    printf("\n Name: %s", emp1.name);
    printf("\n Age: %d", emp1.age);
    printf("\n Salary: %f", emp1.salary);
    printf("\n Second Employee details...");
    printf("\n Name: %s", emp2.name);
    printf("\n Age: %d", emp2.age);
    printf("\n Salary: %f", emp2.salary);
}
```

OUTPUT (after running):

Enter name, age and salary of the 1st employee: Dr. Rajiv 40   82000.00

Enter name, age and salary of the 2nd employee: Mr. Sushant 30 50000.00

First Employee details ...

Name: Dr. Rajiv

Age: 40

Salary: 82000.00

Second Employee details ...

Name: Mr. Sushant

Age: 30

Salary: 50000.00

Initializations of Structures

Just as you initialize ints, floats, chars, and arrays, you can also initialize structure variables.

For example, in the previous structure Emp:

```
struct Emp
  {
    char fname[40], lname[40];
    int age;
    float salary;
    char address[30], dept[30];
  };
```

Then a variable of this structure—say, emp1—can be initialized during its declaration as follows:

struct Emp emp1 = {"Rajiv", Chopra", 40, 82000.00, "GTB Nagar", "Computer Science"};

Or you can also write as follows:

```
struct Emp
  {
    char fname[40], lname[40];
    int age;
    float salary;
    char address[30], dept[30];
  }emp1 = {"Rajiv", Chopra", 40, 82000.00, "GTB Nagar",
  "Computer Science"};
```

Here,

emp1.fname = "Rajiv"

emp1.lname = "Chopra"

emp1.age =40

emp1.salary = 82000.00

emp1.address = "GTB Nagar"

emp.dept = "Computer Science"

As we can assign one basic data type to another basic data type variable, similarly we can assign a structure variable to another structure variable of the same type.

For example,

```
struct Emp
  {
    char fname[40], lname[40];
    int age;
    float salary;
    char address[30], dept[30];
  };
```

struct Emp emp1 = {"Rajiv", Chopra", 40, 82000.00, "GTB Nagar", "Computer Science"};

struct Emp emp2;

emp2 = emp1; /* is valid */

So now emp2 will have the same data as emp1 had.

But please note that the following initializations are invalid:

struct Emp
```
    {
        char fname[10] = "Rajiv";     /* invalid */
        int lname[10] = "Chopra"; /* invalid */
        int age= 40;    /* is invalid */
        ......
    };
```

This means that individual members cannot be initialized inside the structure declaration. If you do this, you will get a compilation error.

Array of Structures

When we want to store a large number of similar records—say, of 100 employees—then an array of structures is defined as follows:

```
struct Emp
  {
    char fname[40], lname[40];
    int age;
    float salary;
    char address[30], dept[30];
  };
```
struct Emp emp1[100];   /* declaring array of structures */

This means that emp1 is an array having 100 elements of type struct Employee. *It is after this statement only that the C compiler reserves memory space for 100 structures; the same rule applies for array of structures as for array of primary data types like ints, floats, or chars.*

Figure 4.2 shows the array graphically.

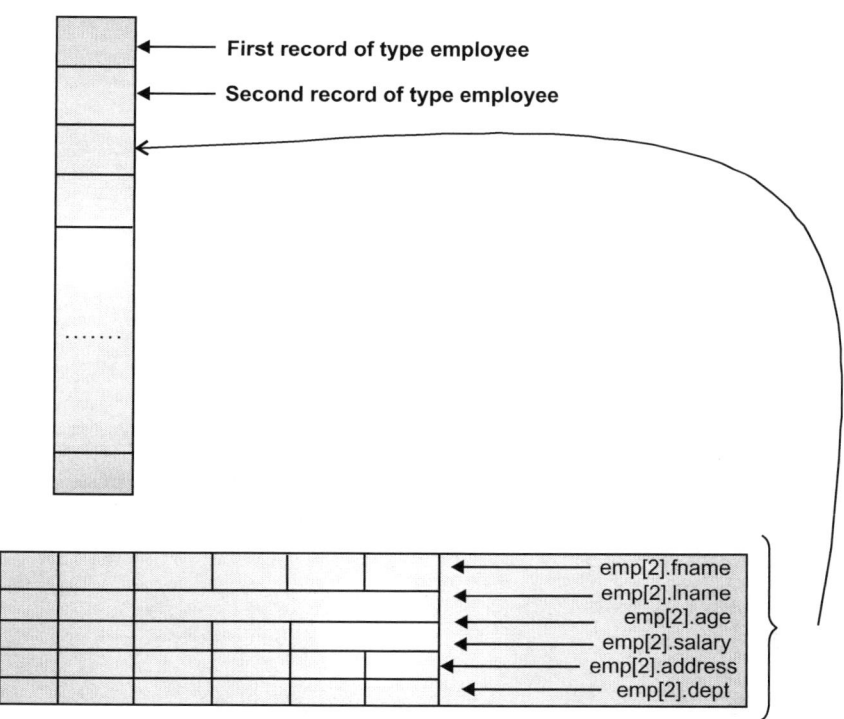

Figure 4.2: Array of Structure Being Stored

Please note here that an employee of struct Emp is selected by an index only.

For example, emp1[0] is the first element in the array of structures emp1. Each element of an array emp1 is a structure of type struct Emp.

Also note that in order to access the *fname* of the 1st employee, we use the following expression:

emp1[0].fname;

Thus, the **1 employee record** is referred to as:

emp1[0].fname;

emp1[0].lname;

emp1[0].age;

emp1[0].salary;

emp1[0].address;

emp1[0].dept;

Similarly, **the 2nd employee record** is referred to as:

emp1[1].fname;

emp1[1].lname;

emp1[1].age;

emp1[1].salary;

emp1[1].address;

emp1[1].dept;

And **the 100th employee record** is referred to as:

emp1[99].fname;

emp1[99].lname;

emp1[99].age;

emp1[99].salary;

emp1[99].address;

emp1[99].dept;

There is another way of showing this structure:

```
struct Emp
  {
    char fname[40], lname[40];
    int age;
    float salary;
    char address[30], dept[30];
  };
struct Emp emp1[100];        /* declaring array of struc-
tures */
```

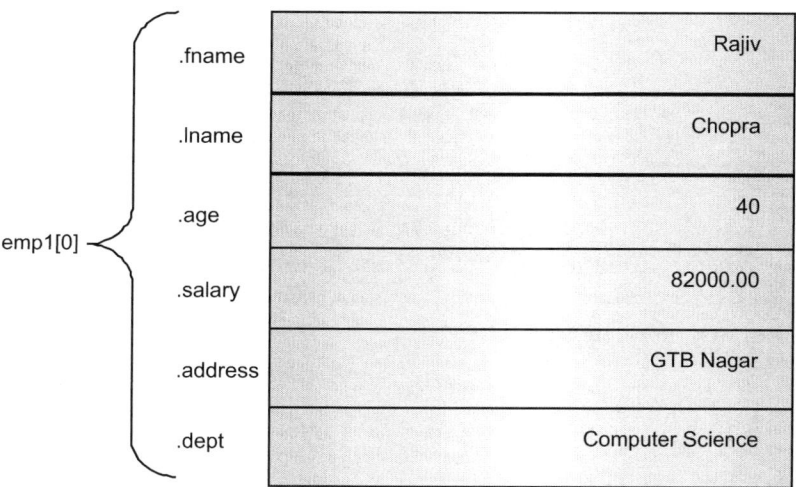

Thus, the **1st employee record** is referred to as:

emp1[0].fname;

emp1[0].lname;

emp1[0].age;

emp1[0].salary;

emp1[0].address;

emp1[0].dept;

The same procedure is followed for emp1[1] … till emp1[99] for a record of 100 employees.

How to Initialize an Array of Structures

We can initialize an array of structures in the same way as a single structure.

For example,

```
struct Emp
{
    char name[30];
    int age;
    float salary;
};
struct Emp emp1[5] = {
```

{**"Rajiv", 41, 83000.00**},
{**"Ajay", 31, 73000.00**},
{**"Sushant", 32, 17000.00**},
{**"Yash", 29, 33000.00**},
{**"Ankur", 38, 55000.00**},

};

This declaration creates an array of 5 Employee structures. The 1st set of values is assigned to emp1[0], the 2nd set to emp1[1], and so on. The initial values are separated by commas and enclosed within braces. The ending brace is followed by a semicolon.

We are in a position to write a program now.

/* to show the concept of array of structures */

```
#include<stdio.h>
void main( )
  {
    struct Employee
      {
        char name[20];
        int age;
        float salary;
    };
    struct Employee emp[5];
    int i;
```

float x, *y = &x, x= *y; /* why? */
```
    printf("\n\t Enter your 5 employees name, age and sal-
ary:          \n\n');
    for(i=0; i<5; i++)
      scanf("%s %d %f", emp[i].name, &emp[i].age, &emp[i].
salary);
    printf("\n You have entered these records\n");
    for(i=0; i<5; i++)
      printf("\n %s\t\t: %d\t\t: %f", emp[i].name, emp[i].
age,              emp[i].salary);
  }
```

OUTPUT (after running):

Enter your 5 employees name, age and salary:

Rajiv 40 82000.00

Ajay 30 67000.00

Amit 30 70000.00

Mayur 20 6700.00

Adi 30 50000.00

You have entered these records

Rajiv: 40: 82000.00

Ajay: 30: 67000.00

Amit: 30: 70000.00

Mayur: 20: 6700.00

Adi: 30: 50000.00

Note the following statement in this program:

   float x, *y = &x, x= *y;

If this statement is not present, you will get an error message:

        scanf: floating point formats not linked.

      Abnormal program termination.

Explanation: This error is due to the floating point emulator. **A floating point emulator is used to manipulate floating point numbers in runtime library functions like scanf( ) and atof( ).** There are some cases, such as arrays of structures, where float is a structure member and the reference to the float is a bit obscure; that's why the compiler does not detect the need for the emulator. To overcome this limitation, a reference to the address of a float is made. When the compiler encounters an address of a float, it automatically sets a flag to have linker link in the floating point emulator. That is why these statements force the linking of the floating point emulator into a program. Thus, to prevent this error, include the statement in the beginning of your programs.

Nesting Structures

It is possible to nest one structure within another. Such structures are known as **nested structures.**

For example,

   struct date
   {

```
        int day;
        int month;
        int year;
    };
struct Emp

    {
        char fname[40], lname[40];
        int age;
        float salary;
        struct date dob;
        struct date dobj;
        char address[30], dept[30];
    };
```

Note the restriction in a nested structure shown by the next example:

struct Emp

```
    {
        char name[40];
        int age;
        float salary;
        struct Emp e; /* is illegal */
    };
```

Thus, a member of a structure can also be another structure. That is, you can say that the individual structure members of a structure can be other structures as well. **Structures whose members are themselves structures are called nested or hierarchical structures.**

For example, say we want to nest a structure named **address** inside another structure **Employee;** there are two ways of declaring such a nested structure:

I. First method:
```
        struct date
        {
            int day;
            int month;
            int year;
        };
        struct Emp
```

```
        {
            char fname[40], lname[40];
            int age;
            float salary;
            struct date dob;
            struct date dobj;
            char address[30], dept[30];
        };
```

While using this notation, remember that the embedded structure type (date) should be declared before its use within the containing structure; otherwise, the compiler will not recognize it.

II. Second method:

```
struct Emp
    {
        char fname[30], lname[30];
        int age;
        float salary;

        struct date
        {
            int day;
            int month;
            int year;
        } dob, doj;
        char address[30], dept[30];
    };
```

In this method, you cannot use the structure date directly in other places as an ordinary structure. On the other hand, if you use the former one where the address structure is declared outside the structure **Emp**, then you can directly use the address structure in other places also.

A nested structure can also be initialized as follows:

struct Emp emp1 = {"Rajiv", "Chopra", 40, 82000.00, 24, 03, 2016, "GTB NAGAR",

"Computer Science" };

Now let us see how to access members of a nested structure.

In this example, the structure **date** is used in the structure **Emp. A particular member inside the structure can be accessed by repeatedly applying the dot (.) operator.**

For example, in this statement,

emp.dob.day = 5;

we set the day variable in the **dob** structure within **emp** to 5. Similarly, other members of a nested structure are accessed as follows:

emp.dob.month = 3;

emp.dob.year = 2016;

Also we can display the members of a nested structure as follows:

printf("%d", emp.dob.day);

printf("%d", emp.dob.month);

printf("%d", emp.dob.year);

Note that this level of nesting can go up to any level. There is no limit. Also note that a structure cannot be nested within itself.

For example,

struct Emp

```
{
    char name[40];
    int age;
    float salary;
    struct Emp e; /* is illegal */
};
```

But it is possible to have a structure pointer of its own type as its structure member.

For example,

struct Emp

```
{
    char name[40];
    int age;
    float salary;
    struct Emp*e;/* is illegal */
};
```

Such structures are known as self-referential structures.

Structures and Functions

Just as we can pass basic data types, it is also possible **to pass structure variables to functions and receive structure data types from functions.** Two techniques are used: structures as function arguments and returning structures from functions.

I. Structures as Function Arguments

C provides a means of passing an entire structure to functions as arguments in the function call. A structure variable is passed like any basic data type.

For example,

```
#include<stdio.h>
display(struct Employee);
struct Employee
{
char name[10];
int age;
float salary;
};
main( )
{
    struct Employee emp = {"Rajiv", 40, 82000.00};
    display(emp); /*passing entire structure to dis-
play( )                      function */
}
display(struct Employee e)
{
    printf("\n Employee Record:");
    printf("\n Name: %s", e.name);
    printf("\n Age: %d", e.age);
    printf("\n Salary: %f", e.salary);
}
```

OUTPUT (after running):

Employee Record:

Name: Rajiv

Age: 40

Salary: 82000.00

Explanation: Here, the struct Employee is declared outside the main( ) because we have passed an entire structure variable emp to the function display( ). If you declare the struct Employee inside the function main( ) then the function display( ) does not know the identity of the data type, structure variable emp, because in main( ) it is treated as a local declaration. To make it global, it is compulsory to declare the structure struct Employee outside the main( ) function. As you pass an array of basic data types, you can pass an array of structures to functions. In this you will use the same notation as you have used in passing an array of basic data types. **Please note that when a structure variable is passed as an argument to the functions, it is passed as call by value like any other data type. Thus, if you make any change in the calling function, it is not visible in the caller.**

II. Returning Structures from Functions

Like basic data types, you can also return structures from functions using a return statement.

For example,

```
#include<stdio.h>
struct Employee readRecord( );
display (struct Employee);
struct Employee
  {
    char name[10];
    int age;
    float salary;
  };
main( )
  {
    struct Employee emp1, emp2;
    emp1 = readRecord( );
    emp2 = readRecord( );
    printf("\n Displaying first record…");
    display(emp1);
    printf("\n\n Displaying second record..");
    display(emp2);
  }
    struct Employee readRecord( )
    {
      struct Employee e;
      printf("\n Enter name, age and salary of an employee.
      \n");
```

```
      scanf("%s %d %f", e.name, &e.age, &e.salary);
      return e; /* returning a structure */
}
```

OUTPUT (after running):

Enter name, age and salary of an employee.

Rajiv 40 82000.00

Enter name, age and salary of an employee.

Mayur 30 40000.00

Displaying first record.

Name: Rajiv   Age: 40   Salary: 80000.00

Displaying second record.

Name: Mayur   Age: 30   Salary: 40000.00

Structures and Arrays

It is also possible to define structures that contain arrays as members. One of the most common applications of this type is in setting up an array of characters inside a structure.

For example, say we want to define a structure called **month** that contained as its members the number of days in the month as well as a 3-character abbreviation for the name of the month. This is done as follows:

```
struct month
  {
    int number_of_days;
    char name[3];
  };
```

This creates a *month* structure that contains an integer member called number_of_days and a character member called *name*. The member *name* is actually an array of 3 characters. We can now define a variable to be of type **struct month** in normal fashion:

struct month a_month;

We can set the proper fields inside a_month for January with the following sequence of statements:

a_month.number_of_days = 31;

a_month.name[0] = 'J';

a_month.name[1] = 'a';

a_month.name[2] = 'n';

Or we can initialize this variable to the same values with the following statement:

static struct month a_month = {31, { 'J', 'a', 'n' } };

And we can set up 12-month structures inside an array to represent each month of the year:

struct month months[12];

Let us now write a program to show the concept of structures and arrays:

```c
/* Program to set up initial values inside the array and display them */

/* It illustrates the structures and arrays concept */

struct month
  {
    int number_of_days;
    char name[3];
  };
main( )
  {
    int i;
    static struct month months[12] =
        { { 31, {'J', 'A', 'N' } }, {28, {'F', 'E', 'B' } },
        { { 31, {'M', 'A', 'R' } }, {30, {'A', 'P', 'R' } },
        { { 31, {'M', 'A', 'Y' } }, {30, {'J', 'U', 'N' } },
        { { 31, {'J', 'U', 'L' } }, {31, {'A', 'U', 'G' } },
        { { 30, {'S', 'E', 'P' } }, {31, {'O', 'C', 'T' } },
        { { 30, {'N', 'O', 'V' } }, {31, {'D', 'E', 'C' } }
        };
    printf("Month              Number of Days\n");
    printf("--------           --------------------\n");
    for(i=0; i<12; ++i)
        printf(" %c%c%c                %d\n",
            months[i].name[0], months[i].name[1],
            months[i].name[2], months[i].number_of_days);
  }
```

OUTPUT (after running):

Month	Number of Days
---------	----------------------
JAN	31
FEB	28
MAR	31
APR	30
MAY	31
JUN	30
JUL	31
AUG	31
SEP	30
OCT	31
NOV	30
DEC	31

The following graphic shows how storage in memory is done.

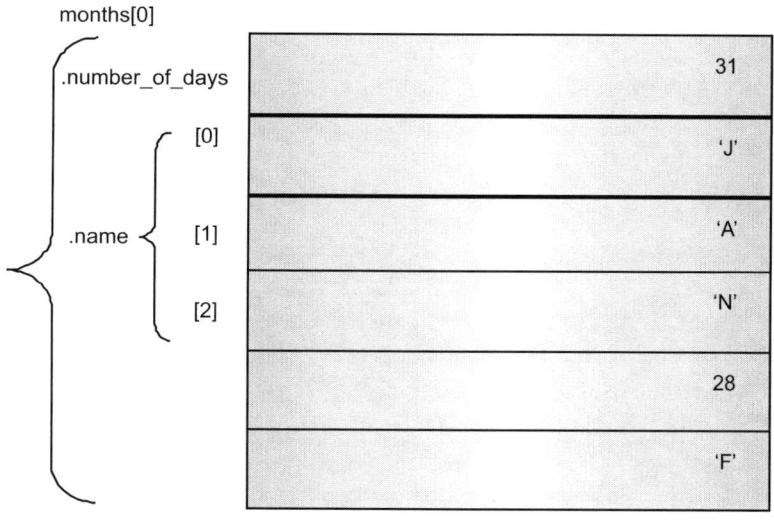

It is crystal clear from the figure that months[0] refers to the entire *month structure* **contained in the first location of the** *months* **array.** This expression is of type **struct month.** So, when passing months[0] to a function as an argument, the corresponding formal parameter inside the function must be declared to be of type **struct month.** Then the expression:

months[0].number_of_days

refers to the **number_of_days** member of the **month** structure contained in **months[0].** The type of this expression is **int.** The expression:

months[0].name

references the 3-character array called **name** inside the **month** structure of **months[0].** If passing this expression as an argument to a function, then the corresponding formal parameter would be declared to be an array of type **char.**

Finally, the expression

months[0].name[0]

references the first character of the name array contained in **months[0]** (the character 'J').

4.1 STRUCTURES VERSUS UNIONS

Like structures, unions are user-defined data types. **A union is a data type that allows different types of variables to share the same space in memory.** Unlike structures where each member has its own memory space, unions allow sharing of space among its members in memory.

Syntax

```
union unname
{
    datatype-1 ListOfVariables;
    datatype-2 ListOfVariables;
    .................
    datatype-n ListOfVariables;
};
```

Here, **union** is a keyword and **uname** is the name of the union data type. A union variable is declared as a structure variable is declared. When a union variable is created, the C compiler automatically allocates sufficient space to hold the largest data member of the union. Since all data members of the union use the same space, whenever a data member changes, all other data members will be changed automatically.

For example,

```
union Sample
{
    float x;
    int a;
    char ch;
};
```

Now you can create a union variable of type union **Sample** as follows:

Union Sample **one**;

Here, **one** is a union variable. Yet another way of achieving this is the following:

```
union Sample
{
    float x;
    int a;
    char ch;
}one;
```

Like structures, union members are accessed exactly the same way that structure members are accessed, using a dot (.) operator. The individual union members are accessed as follows:

one.x = 3.1417;

one.a = 80;

one.ch = 'R';

Please note that a union variable may contain only one meaningful value at a time and it is incorrect to store something as one type and then extract it as another. It means that union permits a part of memory to be treated as a variable of one type on one occasion and as a different variable of a different type on another occasion.

Also note that structures and unions have some differences:

1. *The size of a structure is given by the sum of the sizes of its individual elements whereas the size of the union is the maximum of the sizes of its elements.*

2. *All structure members can be accessed at any point in time whereas in unions only one of the union members can be accessed at any given time, because only one of the union members will have a meaningful value.*

Unions may occur within arrays and structures just as structures do. C also allows using a union in a structure or a structure in a union. And the method of accessing a member of a structure in a union or a union in a structure is similar to the method of accessing a member of a structure in a structure.

4.2 STRUCTURES AND POINTERS

In general, the **syntax for declaring a structure pointer** is:

struct stname *eptr;

where **struct** is the keyword, **stname** is the name of a structure data type, and **eptr** is the name of a structure pointer to a structure of type **stname. A structure pointer holds the address of a structure variable of the same data type.**

For example,

```
struct Emp
  {
    char name[30];
    int age;
    float salary;
  };
```

We can declare a **structure variable and structure pointer** as follows:

struct Emp emp;   /* declaring a structure variable */

struct Emp *eptr;   /* declaring a structure pointer */

eptr = &emp;

Here, **eptr is a structure pointer variable that points to emp.** However, you can also declare **eptr** with the declaration of the structure variable as follows:

struct Emp emp1, *eptr;

eptr = &emp1;

Please note that you can even initialize the structure pointer eptr to the address of emp as follows:

struct Emp emp1, *eptr = &emp1;

Also note that C provides a special arrow operator (->) for accessing structure members through a structure pointer. Its syntax is:

eptr -> member;

Now if **eptr** is a structure pointer of type struct Emp then you can access the structure member's name, age, and salary as follows:

eptr-> name;

eptr-> age;

eptr->salary;

Alternatively, you can also access the structure members through a structure pointer variable using the dot operator. For this you have to first dereference the structure pointer using the '*' pointer and then use the dot operator.

For example, if **eptr is a structure pointer** of type structure Emp, you can access the structure member's name, age, and salary as follows:

(*eptr).name;

(*eptr).age;

(*eptr).salary;

It is mandatory to use parentheses here because the dot operator (.) has a higher precedence than that of the dereferencing operator (*). If you omit the parentheses, these expressions are interpreted as follows:

*(eptr.name);

*(eptr.age);

*(eptr.salary);

Since **eptr is a structure pointer**, the C compiler will certainly flag an error message.

Before we continue the discussion, let us write a program to show the use of structure pointers and then show our understanding of the difference between structures and enumerators.

Example 1: Create a structure Employee and store his or her name, age, and salary. Read and display the employee's details.

Solution 1: The program is as follows:

```c
#include<stdio.h>
main( )
 {
   struct Employee
    {
      char name[30];
      int age;
      float salary;
    };
   struct Employee emp1, emp2;        /*       structure
variables */
   struct Employee *eptr1, *eptr2;    /*       structure
pointers */
   eptr1 = &emp1;
   eptr2 = &emp2;
/* Use dot (.) operator with structure vars. But pointer
with structure pointers */
   printf("\n\tEnter  name,  age  and  salary  of  first
employee:\n");
   scanf("%s %d %f", emp1.name, &emp1.age, &emp1.salary);
   printf("\n\tEnter  name,  age  and  salary  of  second
employee:\n");
   scanf("%s %d %f", eptr2->name, &eptr2->age, &eptr2-
>salary);
   printf("\n First Employee:");
   printf("\nName: %s", eptr1->name);
   printf("\nAge: %d", eptr1->age);
   printf("\nSalary: %f", eptr1->salary);
   printf("\n Second Employee:");
   printf("\nName: %s", emp2.name);
   printf("\nAge: %d", emp2.age);
   printf("\nSalary: %f", emp2.salary);
 }
```

OUTPUT (after running):

Enter name, age and salary of first employee:

Rajiv 40 82000.00

Enter name, age and salary of second employee:

Amit 30 55000.00

First Employee:

Name: Rajiv

Age: 40

Salary: 82000.00

Second Employee:

Name: Amit

Age: 30

Salary: 55000.00

A structure can also contain pointers as its member variables. **For example,**

```
struct Emp
{
    char *name;
    int age;
    float salary;
};
```

Here the structure Emp has a pointer *name* associated with it. The structure members can now be defined and used as follows:

```
struct Emp emp1 ={"Rajiv", 40, 82000.00};

struct Emp emp2;

emp2.name = "Rajiv";

emp2.age = 40;

emp2.salary = 82000.00
```

Example **2: Distinguish between structures and enumerators.**

Solution 2: Structures are a powerful and flexible way of grouping several distinct data items together under one name. On the other hand, an **enumerated**

data type can be defined for a finite set of values in the type specifier. Also remember that C does not provide facilities for reading and displaying values of enumeration types. They may only be read or displayed as integer values.

We are in a position to write some programs now.

Example 1: Write a C program to read a student's record and find his grade percentage. It should also assign the grade according to the rules given below:

Percentage marks	Grade
>=80	A
>=60 < 80	B
>=50 < 60	C
< 50	D

Solution 1: The program is as follows:

```c
#include<stdio.h>
#include<conio.h>
void main( )
  {
    struct student
      {
        char name[30];
        int roll;
        int sub1, sub2, sub3, sub4;
        float per;
      }s1;
    clrscr( );
    printf("\n \t Enter the record of the student");
    printf("\n\t Name:");
    gets(s1.name);
    printf("\n\t Roll No. :");
    scanf("%d", &s1.roll);
    printf("\n\t Subject 1:");
    scanf("%d", &s1.sub1);
    printf("\n\t Subject 2:");
    scanf("%d", &s1.sub2);
    printf("\n\t Subject 3:");
    scanf("%d", &s1.sub3);
    printf("\n\t Subject 4:");
```

```
    scanf("%d", &s1.sub4);
    s1.per = (s1.sub1 + s1.sub2 + s1.sub3 + s1.sub4) / 4.0;
    if (s1.per >= 80)
       printf("\n A grade with %f per", s1.per);
    else
       if(s1.per >= 60)
          printf("\n B Grade with %f per", s1.per);
       else
          if(s1.per >=50)
                printf("\nC Grade with %f per", s1.per);
          else
                printf("\n D Grade with %f per", s1.per);
  getch( );
}
```

Example 2: **Modify the preceding C program to read n number of students and calculate their percentages using an array of structures.**

Solution 2: The program is as follows:

```
#include<stdio.h>
#include<conio.h>
void main( )
 {
   struct student
    {
      char name[30];
      int roll;
      int sub1, sub2, sub3, sub4;
      float per;
    }list[20];
   int i, n;
   clrscr( );
   printf("\n \t Enter the value of n (total students):
");
   scanf(%d", &n);
   printf("\n Enter data of %d students", n);
   for(i=0; i<n; i++)
    {
      printf(\n Enter name, roll no, marks in 4 subjects
of %d student \n", i+1);
      fflush(stdin);
      gets(list[i].name);
    scanf("%d%d%d%d%d",   &list[i].roll,   &list[i].sub1,
```

```
&list[i].sub2, &list[i].sub3,
   &list[i].sub4);
    list[i].per = (list[i].sub1 + list[i].sub2 + list[i].
sub3 + list[i].sub4) / 4.0;
   }
   printf("\n Print the data of %d students", n);
   for (i=0;i<n; i++)
   printf("\n%s\t%d\t%f\n", list[i].name, list[i].roll,
list[i].per);
   getch( );
}
```

***Example* 3: Write the steps to implement a self-referential structure—a linked structure.**

Solution 3: When a member of a structure is declared as a pointer to the structure itself, then the structure is called a self-referential structure.

For example,

```
struct link
  {
    int data;
    struct link *p;
  };
```

This means that the structure **link** consists of two members: data and p. The member **data** is a variable of type int whereas the member **p is a pointer to a structure of type link**. Thus, the structure **link** has a member that can point to a structure of type link. This type of self-referential structure can be shown as follows:

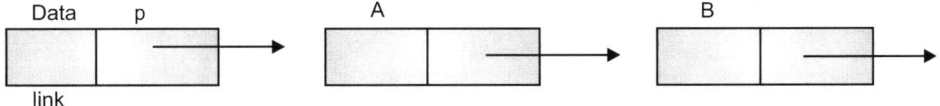

Since the pointer p can point to a structure variable of type link, we can connect two such structure variables, A and B, to obtain a linked structure as shown above. This linked structure can be obtained by the following procedure:

S1: Declare structure-link.

S2: Declare variable A and B of type link.

S3: Assign the address of structure B to member p of structure A.

These steps are coded in C as follows:

```
struct link   /* declare structure link */
 {
   int data;
   struct link *p;
 };
 struct link A, B;  /* declare structure variables A and
B */
   A.p = &B;            /* connect A to B */
```

From the diagram and code, it is clear that the pointer p of structure variable B is **dangling (i.e., pointing nowhere).** Such a pointer can be assigned to NULL, a constant indicating there is no valid address in this pointer, using the following statement:

B.p = NULL;

The data elements in this linked structure can be assigned by the following statements:

A.data = 70;

B.data = 80;

The linked structure now looks as follows:

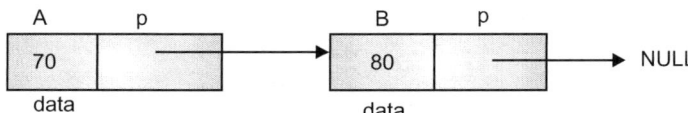

Note that the members of structure B can be reached by two methods:

(a) **From its variable name B through the dot operator**

(b) **From the pointer p of variable A, because it is also pointing to structure B; in this case an arrow operator is used.**

That is,

printf("\n The contents of member data of B= %d", B.data);

printf("\n The contents of member data of B= %d", A.p->data);

Thus, both of these statements will give the same output as follows:

The contents of member data of B= 80.

Example 4: **Give some applications of structures.**

Solution 4: Applications of structures include the following:

1. Implement database management systems
2. Change cursor size
3. Clear screen contents
4. Draw any shape using graphics on the screen
5. Receive a key from the keyboard
6. Check the memory size of the computer
7. Send output to printer
8. Mouse interaction
9. Hide/display files in a directory
10. Format CDs, etc.

Example 5: **How are an array and a structure alike; how are they different?**

Solution 5: The major points are tabulated in the following:

Array	Structure
An array is a secondary data type.	A structure is also a secondary data type.
All elements of an array are stored at contiguous memory locations.	All elements of a structure are also stored at contiguous memory locations.
An array is a collection of data items of the same data type.	A structure is a collection of data items of different data types.
An array only has a declaration.	A structure has a declaration and definition part.
No keyword is attached with an array.	The **struct** keyword is attached with a structure.
An array cannot have bit fields.	A structure may contain bit fields.

Example 6: **Differentiate between a structure and a union.**

Solution 6: The differences are tabulated as follows:

Structure	Union
1. Structures are used to store different members at different places in memory.	1. A union is used to store different members at the same memory location.
2. They are not used to conserve memory.	2. They are used to conserve memory.
3. Total memory used is equal to the sum of the sizes of its individual elements/members.	3. Total memory assigned is equal to the maximum/largest of all of the sizes of its members.
4. The keyword struct is used.	4. The keyword union is used.

5. Syntax:
 	
struct <name>
    {
member-1;
member-2;
....
member-n;
      };
	5. Syntax:
	
	union <name>
	    {
	member-1;
	member-2;
	....
	member-n;
	      };

Example 7: **Write a C program to multiply two complex numbers. Create a structure *complex* that represents a complex number and write a function that performs complex multiplication. Given that:**

$$(a + ib) * (c + id) = (ac - bd) + i(ad + bc)$$

Solution 7: The program is as follows:

```
#include<stdio.h>
#include<conio.h>
struct complex
 {
   int r;
   int i;
};
void main( )
 {
   struct complex a, b, c;
   clrscr( );

   printf("\n Enter first complex number");
```

```
   printf("\n Enter real part:");
   scanf("%d", &(a.r));
   printf("\n Enter imaginary part:");
   scanf("%d", &(a.i));
   printf("\n Enter second complex number");
   printf("\n Enter real part:");
   scanf("%d", &(b.r));
   printf("\n Enter imaginary part:");
   scanf("%d", &(b.i));
   c= multiply(a, b);
   printf("\n The resultant number is %d + %di", c.r, c.i);
   getch( );
 }
struct complex multiply(struct complex x, struct complex y)
 {
   struct complex z;
   z.r = (x.r + y.r) - (x.i * y.i);
   z.i = (x.r + y.i) - (x.i * y.r);
   return (z);
 }
```

NOTE   *Students are advised to run this program on their own.*

Example 8: Write a C program to process student records using structures.

Solution 8: The program is as follows:

```
#include<stdio.h>
main( )
 {
   struct record
    {
      char name[30];
      char regno[12];
      float avg;
      int rank;
    } student[50], temp;

   int i, j, n;
   printf("\n Processing student %d record...\n", i+1);
   printf("Student name? (type END to terminate) ");
   scanf("%s", student[i].name);
   printf("%s\n", student[i].name);
```

```
while (strcmp(student[i].name, "END") > 0)
 {
   printf("Register number? ");
   scanf("%s", student[i].regno);
   printf("%s\n", student[i].regno);
   printf("Average marks? ");
   scanf("%f", &student[i].avg);
   printf("%f\n", student[i].avg);
   i++;
   printf("\n Processing student %d record...\n", i+1);
   printf("Student name? (type END to terminate) ");
   scanf("%s", student[i].name);
   printf("%s\n", student[i].name);
 }
n = i;
/* arranging student marks */
for (i=0;i<n-1; i++)
   for (j = i+1; j<n; j++)
    {
      if (student[i].avg < student[j].avg)
       {
           temp = student[i];
           student[i] = student[j];
           student[j] = temp;
       }
    }
/* Storing ranks */
for (i=0;i<n; i++)
   student[i].rank = i+1;

/* Displaying records of students */
printf("\n\n Student   records   after   giving   them
ranks:\n");
printf("\n");
printf(" NAME      REGISTER_NUMBER   AVERAGE RANK\n");
prin tf("-------------------------------------------
--------------------------------\n");
for (i=0; i<n; i++)
 {
   printf("%  -20s   5   -10s",   student[i].name,
   student[i].                    regno);
```

```
        printf(:%10.2f %d \n", student[i].avg, student[i].
        rank);
    }
}
```

Please run this program yourself.

Example 9: **What are parallel arrays? Give an example to explain.**

Solution 9: Consider the following example:

int id[100];

double gpa[80];

double x[NUM_PTS], y[NUM_PTS];

Here, id and gpa are known as **parallel arrays** because the data items with the same subscript, like i, pertain to the same student, the *i*th student. Similarly, the *i*th element of arrays x and y are the coordinates of one point.

Example 10: **What are bit fields in structures? Give examples.**

Solution 10: Bit fields allow the packing of data in a structure. This is especially useful when memory or data storage is at a premium. An integer takes 2 bytes in memory but sometimes it happens that integer values to be stored need less than 2 bytes, wasting memory. By using these bit fields we can save a lot of memory.

Syntax (for bit-fields):

struct name

   {

      data_type var1 : bit_length;
      data_type var2 : bit_length;
      ·······
      ·······

   };

Here, data_type can be int or unsigned int; var1, var2, … are the names of the variables; and bit_length is the number of bits used for a particular variable. **Note that the maximum value of a bit-field of length n is 2^{n-1}.**

For example,

(a) Packing several objects into a machine word like 1-bit flags can be compacted—symbol tables in compilers.

(b) Reading external file formats—nonstandard file formats could be read in like 9-bit integers.

C allows us to do this in a structure definition by putting bit length after the variable:

```
struct packed_struct {
    unsigned int f1:1;
    unsigned int f2:1;
    unsigned int f3:1;
    unsigned int f4:1;
    unsigned int type:4;
    unsigned funny_int:9;
    } pack;
```

Note here that packed_struct contains 6 members: four 1-bit flags (f1 ... f3), a 4-bit type, and a 9-bit funny_int. Also note that C automatically packs these fields as compactly as possible, provided that the maximum length of the field is less than or equal to the integer word length of the computer. If this is not the case then some compilers may allow memory overlap for the fields while other would store the next field in the next word. You can access members as usual:

pack.type = 6;

But please keep the following points in mind while using bit fields:

1. **Only n lower bits will be assigned to an n-bit number.** Thus, you cannot take values larger than 15 (4 bits long).

2. Bit fields are **always converted to integer type** for computation.

3. You are allowed to **mix "normal" types with bit fields.**

4. **Bit fields save memory.**

5. **The unsigned definition is important**—ensuring that no bits are used as a flag.

6. **Bit fields lack portability between platforms.** Several reasons exist for this:

   • Integers may be signed or unsigned.

   • Many compilers limit the maximum number of bits in the bit field to the size of an integer.

- Some bit fields are stored left to right while others are stored from right to left in memory.

7. The solution to the portability problem is to use bit shifting and masking to get the same results, although this is not very easy.

Applications of Bit Fields

Several device controllers like disk drives and OS need to communicate at a low level. Device controllers contain several **registers** that may be packed together in one integer.

Example 11: Give the output of the following program:

```
#include<stdio.h>
main( )
 {
   struct a
    {
      category : 5;
      scheme : 4;
    };
   printf ("size= %d", sizeof (struct a));
 }
```

Solution 11: size = 2

Explanation: As we have used bit fields in the structure and the total number of bits turns out to be more than 8 (i.e., 9 bits) the size of the structure is being displayed as 2 bytes.

Example 12: For what kind of applications are unions useful?

Solution 12: The union is used basically to prevent the computer from breaking up its memory into many efficiently sized chunks, a condition that is called memory fragmentation. The union data type prevents fragmentation by creating a standard size for certain data.

Summary

In this chapter, we have studied about structures and unions in C. Both have their own advantages, disadvantages, and applications. We have also discussed the linked structure known as a **self-referential structure,** which is used in the creation of linked lists and tree data structures. Also, we compared arrays with structures and unions. Bit fields were also discussed. Using structures several complex problems have been solved.

Exercises

Q1. (a) Create a structure declaration for an employee of an organization consisting of the following fields:

employee code, name, department, date of birth, date of hiring, basic salary

Write a program to print details of the employee, whose basic salary is greater than $20,000.

(b) Write short notes on union data types and enumerable data types.

Q2. Write down the declarative statement that creates a structure consisting of the following information about books in the store:

Book-Id	4 characters
Book-Name	20 characters
Book-Price	real number
Num-copies	positive integer

How much memory is needed by this structure? Create two variables, b_1 and b_2, of this structure type. Write down a statement in C to calculate the sum of books processed, represented by b_1 and b_2.

[Hint:

```
struct Book
  {
    char book-id [4];
    char book-name[20];
    float book-price;
    unsigned int num_copies;
  } b1, b2;
```

Total memory required by the structure: 30 bytes (i.e., 4 + 20 + 4 + 2 bytes = 30 bytes).

The statements in C are:

struct book b1, b2;

flat sum;

sum = b1.num_copies ° b1.book-price + b2.num_copies ° b2.book-price;**].**

Q3. Explain structure and union.

Q4. (a) Explain briefly the difference between a structure and a union and provide an example.

(b) How does a structure differ from an array? Write a C program to implement an array of structures.

Q5. What is the difference between a structure and a union?

Q6. Differentiate between structure and union in C. Write a C program to store student details using union.

Q7. Explain how a structure can be passed to a function?

Q8. Write a C program to read n records with names and addresses and sort them.

[Hint:

```c
#include<stdio.h>
#include<conio.h>
struct list
  {
     char name[12];
     char add[50];
  };
void main( )
  {
     struct list1[10], t;
     int i, n;
     clrscr( );
     printf(\n Enter the number of records to arrange:");
     scanf("%d", &n);
     printf("\n Enter %d names and addresses", n);
     for (i=0; i < n; i++)
       {
          fflush(stdin);
          printf("\n Enter %d name", i+1);
          gets( l[i].name);
          printf("\n Enter %d address", i+1);
          gets( l[i].add);
       }
     for (i=0; i < n; i++)
       {
          for (j = i+1; j < n; j++)
            {
                if ((strcmp (l[i].name, l[j].name) > 0))
```

```
            {
                t = l[i];
                l[i] = l[j];
                l[j] = t;
            }
        }
    }
printf ("\n Sorted list is: \n");
for (i =0; i<n; i++)
 printf("\n %s\t %s", l[i].name, l[i].add);
getch( );
} ].
```

CHAPTER 5

FILE HANDLING IN C

5.0 INTRODUCTION

Files have long been used for storing data. Files are traditional data structures. They are useful for sequential operations like reading from or writing to a file. You need to create a file, open it, write to it, and finally close the file. You can also read from a file. When the data of a file is stored in the form of readable and printable characters, the file is called a **text file.** On the other hand, if a file contains nonreadable characters in binary code, the file is called a **binary file.** For example, *the program files that are created by an editor are stored as text files whereas executed files generated by a compiler are stored as binary files.*

5.1 FILE POINTERS

First, we have to open a file. As we open a file a link is established between the program and the OS. Thus, the OS now comes to know the name of the file, the data structure, and the mode in which the file is to be opened (reading or writing; text mode or binary mode). The filename can have any extension like .docx, .xlsx, .txt, and so on. **Note that the data structure of a file is defined as FILE, which is present in the <stdio.h> header file.**

Syntax (of declaring a file pointer)

FILE °fp;

where FILE is the data structure included in stdio.h and fp is a file pointer which points to the start of the file.

Syntax (of opening a file)

fp = fopen ("filename", "mode");

where fp is a pointer to a structure of FILE type. fopen( ) is a library function having two arguments; one is the filename and the other is the mode in which we want to open the file. It is defined in stdio.h and returns a pointer known as a file pointer to the FILE structure for the specified file, which we store in a pointer variable fp. Table 5.1 lists the different **file-opening modes:**

Table 5.1: File-Opening Modes

Mode	Purpose
r	Opens a text file for reading. If the file exists, it sets up a pointer that points to the first character in it, else it returns NULL.
w	Opens a text file for writing. If the file exists, its contents are overwritten, else a new file is created with a pointer pointing to the first position.
a	Opens a text file for adding data at the end of an already existing file. If the file does not exist, a new file is created with a pointer pointing to the first character, else data is added at end.
r+	Opens a text file for both reading and writing. Possible operations are reading existing contents, writing new contents, and modifying existing contents. Returns NULL if file does not exist.
w+	Opens a text file for both reading and writing. Possible operations are writing new content or reading and modifying existing content. If file does not exist, it will be created for update.
a+	Opens a text file for both reading and appending. Possible operations are reading existing contents and adding new contents at the end of file; it cannot modify existing contents. If file does not exist, it will be created.
rb, wb, ab, rb+, wb+, ab+	Binary file versions of the preceding modes, each with the same characteristics as its respective text file mode.

For example,

fp = fopen ("text.dat","w");

The OS will now open the file text.dat and prepare it for writing.

Problems When Opening Files

1. We try to open a file for reading which does not exist.

2. We try to open a file for writing but sufficient space is not available on the disk.

3. We try to open a file that has been corrupted.

Solution: We must check whether the file is opened successfully or not before reading or writing. The Fopen( ) function returns NULL (a sentinel value defined in stdio.h) if the file cannot be opened. Let us see how this is done.

```
fp = fopen("text.dat","w");
if (fp = =NULL)
  {
    printf("\n Cannot open file text.dat");
    exit (1);
  }
Or we can also write it in another way:
if ((fp = fopen("text.dat","w")) = = NULL)
  {
    printf("\n Cannot open file text.dat");
    exit ( 1);
  }
```

NOTE *Note here that if the file is not opened successfully, it will give the following message:*

'cannot open file text.dat'

When you have finished working with a file, it must be closed. This is done by using library function fclose( ).

Syntax (closing a file):

fclose (fp);

where fp is a file pointer associated with a file which is to be closed. Always close any file that you open. It is a good programming practice.

File input/output (I/O) operations are of different types as categorized below in Figure 5.1.

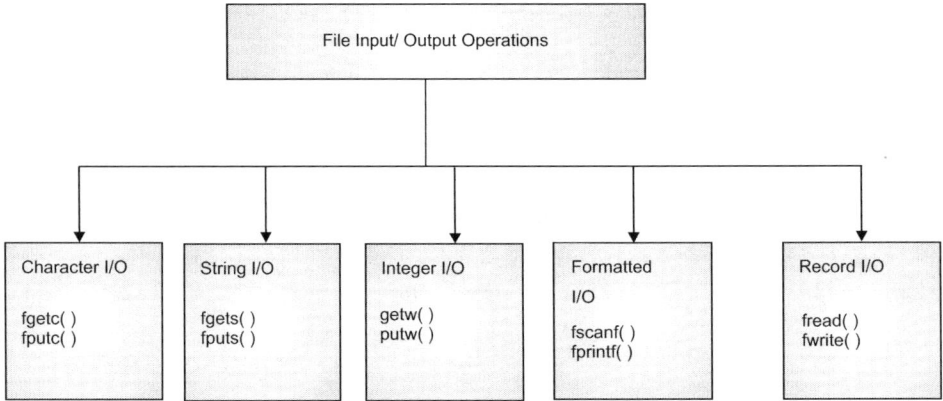

Figure 5.1: File I/O Operations

5.2 CHARACTER INPUT/OUTPUT WITH FILES

Just as we can read and write data from the keyboard using getchar( ) and putchar( ) functions, we can read or write one character at a time using character I/O functions.

Writing to a File

Before writing to a file we must open it in write mode.

Syntax

fputc (ch, fp);

where ch is a **character variable** or constant and fp is a **file pointer.**

Reading Data from a File

The data that is written into a file can also be read from the same file using the fgetc( ) function.

Syntax

ch = fgetc(fp);

where ch is a **character variable** and fp is a **file pointer**.

The fgetc( ) function is used to read one character at a time from a file to which fp is pointing. It gives either the read character or the end-of-file (EOF) character if EOF is reached. **Please note here that EOF is also present in the <stdio.h> file.**

5.3 STRING I/O FUNCTIONS

It is also possible to read or write data more easily in the form of strings.

Writing to a File

We can write data into a file in the form of strings. We use the fputs( ) function for this.

> **Syntax**
>
> **fputs (s, fp);**
>
> where s is a string constant or variable and fp is a file pointer. This function is used to put or write data into a file as compared to the puts( ) function, which is used to write data onto the screen.

Reading Data from a File

The data that is written into a file in the form of strings can also be read by using the fgets( ) function.

> **Syntax**
>
> **fgets (s, n, fp);**

where s is **string**, n is **the maximum length of the input string,** and fp is the **file pointer.**

This function reads a string at a time; if it reads the EOF character, it will return a NULL value.

5.4 INTEGER I/O FUNCTIONS

Just as we can read or write data on a character-by-character basis or string-by-string basis, we can also read and write data in the form of integer numbers.

Writing Data to a File

For writing data in form of integers, we use the putw( ) function:

Syntax

putw (n, fp);

where n is an **integer constant or variable** to be written into a file and fp is a **file pointer.**

Reading Data from a File

For reading data from file, use the getw( ) function:

Syntax

getw (fp);

This function returns an EOF character when an EOF is encountered.

5.5 FORMATTED I/O FUNCTIONS

Formatted I/O functions are used to read or write any type of data (char, int, float, string, etc.) from a file. These functions behave like console I/O functions—scanf( ) and printf( ). The only difference is that the formatted I/O functions are used for files now.

Writing Data to a File

For writing formatted output from a file, we use the fprintf( ) function:

Syntax

fprintf(fp, "format string", list);

where fp is a **file pointer**; **format strings** are %c for char, %d for int, or %f for float; and **list** is the number of variables to be written to a file.

Reading Data from a File

For reading formatted data from a file, we use the fscanf( ) function:

Syntax

fscanf(fp, "format string", list);

where **list** is the list of addresses where the values are to be stored.

5.6 BLOCK (OR RECORD) I/O FUNCTIONS

Block or Record I/O functions are used to read or write a structure or an array from a file. These functions are basically used to read or write database files—for instance, if we want to read or write a complete record of an employee from a file in the form of structure.

Writing Data to a File

To write a block of data into a file, we use the fwrite( ) function:

Syntax

fwrite (ptr, m, n, fp);

where **ptr** is an **address of a structure or an array written into a file, m is the size of structure or an array, n is the number of structures or arrays** to be written, and **fp is a file pointer.** After writing the block, this function returns the number of data items written. If less than requested, an error has occurred. In this case, the file must be opened in binary mode.

Reading Data from a File

To read a block from a file, we use the fread( ) function:

Syntax

fread(ptr, m, n, fp);

where **ptr** is the **address of a structure or array read from a file, m is the size of the structure or array, n is the number of structures or arrays** to be read, and **fp is a file pointer.**

Examples

We are in a position to write some programs based on files now.

Example 1: **Write a C program that accepts one line of text from the keyboard one character at a time and writes it into a disk file. Then read that file, test1.dat, one character at a time and print the result on the screen.**

Solution 1: The following is the program:

```
#include<stdio.h>
#include<conio.h>
void main( )
```

```
{
   FILE *fp;
   char ch;
   clrscr( );
   fp = fopen("test1.dat", "w");
   if (fp = = NULL)
      {
        printf("\n Cannot open file");
        exit(1);
      }
   printf("\n Type a line of text and press Enter key
   \n");
   while (( ch = getche( ) ) != '\r')
      fputc(ch, fp);
   fclose (fp);
}
```

OUTPUT (after running):

Type a line of text and press Enter key

I am Dr. Rajiv Chopra

/* now reading data from the file */

```
#include<stdio.h>
#include<conio.h>
void main( )
  {
     FILE *fp;
     char ch;
     clrscr( );
     if ((fp = fopen("test1.dat", "r")) = =NULL)
        {
          printf("\n Cannot open file");
          exit(1);
        }
     while ((ch = fgetc (fp)) != EOF)
        putchar(ch);
     fclose(fp);
     getch( );
  }
```

OUTPUT (after running):

I am Dr. Rajiv Chopra

If you have to read and write strings rather than characters (as shown above), we use the fputs( ) and puts( ) functions.

Example 2: Write a C program to

(a) **Write integer data into a file.**

(b) **Read the same data from the file.**

Solution 2(a):

```c
#include<stdio.h>
#include<conio.h>
void main( )
{
      FILE *fp;
      char ch;
      clrscr( );
      if ((fp = fopen("test1.dat", "r")) = =NULL)
      {
            printf("\n Cannot open file");
            exit(1);
      }
      while (ch = ='y')
        {
            printf("\n Enter any integer:");
            scanf("%d", &n);
            putw (n, fp);
            printf("\n Want to eneter another number
            (y/n)?");
            ch = tolower (getche( ));
        }
      fclose (fp);
}
```

OUTPUT (after running):

Enter any integer: 11

Want to enter another number (y/n) ? y

Enter any integer: 22

Want to enter another number (y/n) ? y

Enter any integer: -45

Want to enter another number (y/n) ? n

Solution 2(b):

```
#include<stdio.h>
#include<conio.h>
void main( )
{
 FILE *fp;
 int n;
 clrscr( );
if ((fp = fopen("test3.dat", "r")) = =NULL)
 {
        printf("\n Cannot open file");
        exit(1);
   }
   while (( n = getw (fp)) != EOF)
   {
        printf("\n %d", n);
    fclose (fp);
    getch( );
   }
```

OUTPUT (after running):

11

22

-45

Example 3: **Write a C program to**

(a) **Enter data of mixed data types in a file.**

(b) **Read formatted data from the same file.**

Solution 3(a):
#include<stdio.h>
```
#include<conio.h>
void main( )
{
    FILE *fp;
    char ch = 'y', name[30];
    int age;
    float salary;
```

```
        clrscr ( );
        if ((fp = fopen ("test4.dat", "w")) = =NULL)
        {
              printf ("\n Cannot open file");
              exit (1);
        }
        while (ch = ='y')
         {
              printf ("\n Enter name, age and salary:");
              scanf ("%s%d%f", name, &age, &salary);
              fprintf (fp,  "%s\t/%d\t%f\n",  name,  age,
              salary);
              printf ("\n More records (y/n)?");
              ch = tolower (getche ( ));
              }
         fclose (fp);
        }
```

OUTPUT *(after running)*:

Enter name, age and salary: Rajiv   41   82000.00

More records (y/n)? y

Enter name, age and salary: Ajay   52   52000.00

More records (y/n)? y

Solution 3(b):

```
        #include<stdio.h>
        #include<conio.h>
        void main ( )
        {
FILE *fp;
char name[30];
int age;
float salary;
clrscr ( );
if ((fp = fopen ("test4.dat", "r")) = =NULL)
{
              printf ("\n Cannot open file");
              exit (1);
}
while ( fscanf (fp, "%s%d%f", name, &age, &salary) !=
EOF)
```

```
                    printf("%s\t%d\t%f \n", name, age, salary);
        fclose(fp);
        getch( );
        }
```

OUTPUT (after running):

Rajiv   41   82000.00

Ajay   52   52000.00

Example 4: **Write a C program to**

   (a) **Write an array of 8 elements to a file.**

   (b) **Write a structure to a file.**

   (c) **Read a structure from a file.**

Solution 4(a):

```
        #include<stdio.h>
        #include<conio.h>
        void main( )
        {
           FILE *fp;
           int a[8], i;
           clrscr( );
        if ((fp = fopen("test.dat", "wb")) = =NULL)
         {
                   printf("\n Cannot open file");
                   exit(1);
         }
        printf("\n Enter 8 numbers:");
        for (i=0; i<8; i++)
           scanf("%d", &a[i]);
         fwrite(a, sizeof(a), 1, fp);
         fclose(fp);
         }
```

OUTPUT (after running):

Enter 8 numbers:

11

22

33

44

55

66

77

88

Solution 4(b):

```c
#include<stdio.h>
#include<conio.h>
void main( )
{
  struct
   {
        char name[30];
        int age;
        float sal;
} emp;
FILE * fp;
char ch = 'y';
if ((fp = fopen("test.dat", "wb")) = =NULL)
{
        printf("\n Cannot open file");
        exit(1);
}
while (ch = = 'y')
   {
        printf("\n Enter name, age and salary:");
scanf(" %s %d %f", emp.name, &emp.age, &emp.sal);
        fwrite(&emp, sizeof(emp), 1, fp);
        printf("\n More records (y/n)?");
        ch = tolower (getche( ));
   }
fclose(fp);
}
```

OUTPUT *(after running)*:

Enter name, age and salary: Rajiv 41 82000.00

More records (y/n)? y

Enter name, age and salary: Mayur 31 55000.00

More records (y/n)? n

Solution 4(c):

```
#include<stdio.h>
#include<conio.h>
void main( )
{
   struct
     {
       char name[30];
       int age;
       float sal;
   } emp;
   FILE * fp;
   clrscr( );
   if ((fp = fopen("test.dat", "rb")) = =NULL)
   {
        printf("\n Cannot open file");
        exit(1);
   }
   while (fread (&emp, sizeof (emp), 1, fp) = = 1)
   printf("\n %s\t%d\t%f", emp.name, emp.age, emp.
sal);
        fclose (fp);
        getch( );
}
```

OUTPUT (after running):

Rajiv   41   82000.00

Mayur 31   55000.00

Example 5: **Write a C program to read a file and to count the number of characters, spaces, tabs, and newlines in that file.**

Solution 5: The program is as follows:

```
#include<stdio.h>
#include<conio.h>
void main( )
    {
    FILE *fp;
```

```
        char ch;
        int c=0, s=0, t=0, l=0;
        if ((fp = fopen("file1.dat", "r")) = =NULL)
        {
                printf("\n Cannot open file");
                exit(1);
        }
        while (1)
          {
                ch = fgetc (fp);
                if ( ch = =EOF)
                        break;
                c++;
                if ( ch = =' ' )
                        s++;
                if ( ch = ='\t' )
                        t++;
                if ( ch = ='\n' )
                        l++;
          }
            fclose(fp);
            printf("\n Number of characters = %d", c);
            printf("\n Number of blank spaces = %d",
s);
            printf("\n Number of tabs = %d", t);
            printf("\n Number of lines = %d", l);
            getch( );
        }
```

***Example* 6: Write a C program to copy the content of one file into another file on a character-by-character basis.**

Solution 6: The following is the **file copy** program (i.e., from source file to destination file):

```
        #include<stdio.h>
        #include<conio.h>
        void main( )
          {
          FILE *fp, *ft;
          char ch;
          clrscr( );
          if ((fp = fopen("file1.dat", "r")) = =NULL)
          {
```

```
                    printf("\n Cannot open source file");
                    exit(1);
            }
            if ((fp = fopen("file2.dat", "w")) = =NULL)
            {
                    printf("\n Cannot open target file");
                    exit(1);
            }
            while (1)
              {
                    if ((ch = = fgetc (fp)) != EOF)
                            fputc (ch, ft);
                    else
                            break;
              }
            fclose (fp);
            fclose(ft);
      }
```

Example 7: Write a C program to merge two files using command line arguments.

Solution 7: Argument 1 refers to the first file. Argument 2 refers to the second file. Argument 3 refers to the resultant merged file. The following types should be used to run this program: a.out, f1, f2, f3.

/* Merging two files to get the third merged file from command line */

#include<stdio.h>

main(argc, argv);

int argc;

char *argv[ ];

```
      {
        FILE *fp1, *fp2, *fpt3;
        int i, j, k, n1, n2, c1=0, c2=0, c3, dup=0;
        if ( argc != 4)
          {
            printf("No. of arguments on command line =%d\n"
      argc);
            printf("Usage: a.out arg1 arg2 arg3 \n\n");
          }
        else
```

```
    {
        printf("\n Numbers in the 2 files should be in as-
cending                         order\n");
        printf("Terminate entry of each file ctrl-d (EOF)
\n");
        printf("\n Input numbers for file %s\n", argv[1]);
        fp1 = fopen (argv[1], "w");
        while ((scanf ("%d", &i)) != EOF)
          {
            putw (i, fp1);
            c1++;
          }
        fclose (fp1);

        /* Displaying contents of file-1 */
        printf("\n List of %d numbers in file %s \n\n", c1,
argv[1]);
        fp1 = fopen (argv[1], "r");
        while ((i = getw (fp1) != EOF)
            printf ("%5d", i);
        fclose (fp1);
        printf("\n");
        printf("\n Input numbers for file %s\n", argv[2]);
        fp2 = fopen (argv[2], "w");
        while ((scanf ("%d", &i)) != EOF)
          {
            putw (i, fp2);
            c2++;
          }
        fclose (fp2);

        /* Displaying contents of file-2 */
        printf("\n List of %d numbers in file %s \n\n", c2,
argv[2]);
        fp2 = fopen (argv[2], "r");
        while ((j = getw (fp2) != EOF)
            printf ("%5d", j);
        fclose (fp2);
        printf("\n");
        c3 = c1 + c2;
        i =0;
        j =0;
```

```
/* simple merge-sort */
fp1 = fopen (argv[1], "r");
fp2 = fopen (argv[2], "r");
fp3 = fopen (argv[3], "w");
n1 = getw (fp1);
n2 = getw (fp2);
while ((i != c1) && (j!= c2))
{
    if (n1 < n2)
      {
            putw (n1, fp3);
            n1 = getw (fp1);
            i++;
      }
else {
    if (n1 > n2)
      {
        putw (n2, fp3);
        n2 = getw (fp2);
        j++;
      }
else {
        putw (n1, fp3);
        n1 = getw (fp1);
        n2 = getw (fp2);
        i++;
        j++;
        dup++;
        }
        }
    }
    if ( i = = c1) {
     do {
        putw (n2, fp3);
        } while ((n2 = getw (fp2)) != EOF);
     }
    else {
     do {
        putw (n1, fp3);
        } while ((n1 = getw (fp1)) != EOF);
     }
    fclose(fp1);
```

```
        fclose(fp2);
        fclose(fp3);
    printf("\n\n List of %d numbers in file %s\n", c3 -
dup,                    argv[3]);
    printf("After simple merge sort: \n\n");
    fp3 = fopen (argv[3], "r");
    while ((k = getw (fp3)) != EOF)
        printf("%5d", k);
    fclose(fp3);
    printf("\n");
    }
}
```

OUTPUT (after running):

Numbers in the 2 files should be in ascending order

Terminate entry of each file with ctrl-d (EOF)

Input numbers for file f1

List of 7 numbers in file f1

1	3	5	7	9	11	13

Input numbers for file f2

List of 9 numbers in file f2

2	4	6	8	10	12	14	16	18

List of 16 numbers in file f3

After simple merge sort:

1	2	3	4	5	6	7	8	9	10
11	12	13	14	16	18				

***Example* 8: In the following code**

```
#include<stdio.h>
main( )
  {
    FILE *fp;
    fp = fopen("trial", "r");
  }
```

fp points to

(a) The first character in the file.

(b) A structure containing a char pointer which points to the first character in the file.

(c) The name of the file.

(d) None of the above.

Solution 8: The correct choice is b.

***Example* 9: Give the output of the following program:**

```
#include<stdio.h>
main( )
  {
    FILE *fp;
    fp = fopen ("c:\tc\trial", "w");
    if ( !fp)
        exit( );
    fclose (fp);
  }
```

Solution 9: In this program, the path of the filename should have been "c:\\tc\\ trial". Just writing \tc will make it \t.

***Example* 10: Between fgets( ) and gets( ), which is preferable?**

Solution 10: Since gets( ) cannot be told the size of the buffer into which the string supplied would be stored but fgets( ) can, fgets( ) is safer.

***Example* 11: Give the output:**

```
main( )
  {
    printf("\n%%%%");
  }
```

Solution 11: %%

***Example* 12: Give the output:**

```
main( )
  {
    int n=5;
    printf ("\n n=%*d", n, n);
  }
```

Solution 12: n = 5

Example **13: Write a C program that reads a text file and displays the number of vowels, consonants, words, and lines in the file.**

Solution 13: The program is as follows:

```c
#include<stdio.h>
#include<conio.h>
main( )
  {
    int vowel = 0, words =0, cons = 0, line = 0;
    FILE *F1;
    char a, *name;
    printf("\n enter the name of file");
    scanf("%s", name);
    f1 = fopen (name, "r");
    while (( a = fgetc(F1)) != EOF)
      {
        if (toupper(a)  = ='A'  ||  toupper(a)  = ='E'  ||
toupper(a)                          = ='I'  || toupper(a)  =
='O'  || toupper(a)  = ='U'  )
        {
            vowel ++;
        }
        else
        {
          cons++;
          if (a = =' '  || a = = '.')
          {
                words++;
          }
          if (a = ='\n')
          {
                line++;
          }
        }
      }
    fclose(f1);
    printf("\n Number of vowels are = %d", vowels);
    printf("\n Number of consonants are = %d", cons);
    printf("\n Number of words are = %d", words);
    printf("\n Number of lines are = %d", line);
```

```
    getch( );
}
```

Example 14: **Write short notes on random access files.**

Solution 14: In random access files, it may be possible to access a particular data item from any position in the file. There is a restriction for random accessing—all data items must be of the same size or record length must be fixed. In the case of random access, the file pointer is used. By controlling the position of the file pointer, random access of a file can be made possible. Here, *random* means that data can be read from or written to any position in a file without reading or writing all of the preceding data. For random access to files of records, the following functions are used:

1. fseek( )—moves the file pointer to a new location in the file

2. ftell( )—finds the current position and sends it to a new location in the file

3. rewind( )—positions the file pointer to the beginning of the file

Summary

Despite the popularity of databases today, the concept of files still exists. This is because files perform certain tasks that are best done using that format, like sequential processing of records. Files are used for storing information that can be processed by programs. All data and programs are stored in files. Even the editor you use, like tc editor or tc++ editor, uses and works on files only. Even when you are sending attachments in an email, these are files that are attached and sent.

Exercises

Q1. Write a C program that compares the contents of two files and issues the following messages:

File 1 and file 2 are identical.

Files are the same.

File 1 and file 2 are different at line number = ...

Files are different.

Names of the files are taken to be command line arguments.

Q2. Compare text files and binary files.

[**Hint:**]

Text Files	Binary Files
Newline is converted into carriage return and linefeed combination before being written to the disk and again converted into newline when read from disk. It will count 2 characters instead of 1 in text mode (i.e., one for carriage return and the other for line feed).	No conversion takes place. Only one character is counted for newline.
End of file is indicated by the EOF signal.	No EOF signal exists. The end of file is checked by counting the number of characters present in the directory entry of the file.
In text mode, the number of characters is stored as a character-by-character format (1234 will take 4 bytes; 1234.56 will take 7 bytes on disk). Numbers with more digits require more disk space. For example, fscanf( ) and fprintf( ) use text mode.	Numbers can be stored by changing them into binary format. Each number will occupy the same number of bytes on disk as it occupies in memory. Thus, storage of numbers in binary files is more efficient. For example, fread( ) and fwrite( ) functions use binary mode.

Q3. What are command line arguments? Why do we use them? How are they passed to main? Discuss with suitable examples.

Q4. Write a C program to read and display the last few characters of a file. Read the name of the file and number of characters from the keyboard.

Q5. How do you print the contents of a file on the printer?

[**Hint:**

        fputc (ch, stdprn);

        where ch is the character we want to print and stdprn is the standard printer instead of using fp (i.e., file pointer)]

Q6. What functionality is given by files? Showcase the use of sequential files and their implementation in detail with the help of suitable C programming codes.

Q7. A file contains student records with the following data: roll number, name, and marks in four subjects. Write a C program that reads the records in the file and outputs a list showing the roll numbers of students whose marks exceed 40% in each of the four subjects.

Q8. In the context of C programming, explain the different file opening modes.

Q9. Write a C program to read records, arrange them in ascending order, and write them to a target file.

APPENDIX A: C PROGRAMMING LAB PROJECTS

1. Write a C program to find the **roots of a given quadratic equation** using:

   (a) If-then-else statements.

   (b) Switch statements.

2. Write a C program to find the **GCD and LCM** of two integers.

3. Write a C program to **reverse** a given number and check whether it is a **palindrome**. Output the given number with a suitable message.

4. Write a C program to evaluate the given polynomial $f(x) = a_4x^4 + a_3x^3 + a_2x^2 + a_1x + a_0$ for a given value of x and the coefficients using **Horner's method.**

5. Write a C program to copy its input to its output, **replacing** each string of one or **more blanks by a single blank.**

6. Write a C program to read n integer numbers in ascending order into a single-dimensional array and then to perform a **binary search** for a given key integer number and report success or failure in the form of a suitable message.

7. Write a C program to implement the **bubble sort** technique on a single-dimensional array. Display your arrays properly.

8. Write a C program to find out the **average word length** on the host machine.

9. Write a C program to compute the approximate value of exp(0.5) using the **Taylor series expansion** for the **exponential function.**

10. Write a C program to **multiply two matrices.**

11. Write a C function rightrot(x, n) and hence the main program to return the value of the integer x **rotated to the right** by n bit positions as an unsigned integer. Invoke the function from the main with different values of x and n and print the result with suitable headings.

12. Write a C function isprime(x) and hence the main program to read an integer x and return 1 if the argument is **prime** and 0 otherwise.

13. Write a C function reverse(s) and hence the main program to **reverse a string** s in place. Invoke this function from main for different strings and print the original and reversed strings.

14. Write a C program to find out whether the given **string is a palindrome.**

15. Write a C function **match-any (s1, s2)** that returns the first location in the string s1 where any character from the string s2 occurs or -1 if s1 contains no character from s2. Do not use any inbuilt standard library function. Invoke the function match-any (s1, s2) from the main for different strings and print both strings and return value from the function match-any (s1, s2).

APPENDIX B: KEYWORDS IN C

There are 32 keywords in C as follows:

auto	double	if	static
break	else	int	struct
case	enum	long	switch
char	extern	near	typedef
const	far	register	union
continue	float	return	unsigned
default	for	short	void
do	goto	signed	while

APPENDIX C: ESCAPE SEQUENCES IN C

Character	Escape Sequence	ASCII Value
Bell (alert)	\a	007
Backspace	\b	008
Horizontal tab	\t	009
Newline	\n	010
Vertical tab	\v	011
Form feed	\f	012
Carriage return	\r	013
Quotation mark (")	\"	034
Apostrophe (')	\'	039
Question mark (?)	\?	063
Backslash (\)	\\	092
Null	\0	000

Most compilers allow the apostrophe (') and the question mark (?) to appear within a string constant as either an ordinary character or an escape sequence.

APPENDIX D: OPERATOR PRECEDENCE AND ASSOCIATIVITY

Precedence Group	Operators	Associativity
Function, array, structure member, pointer to structure member	( ) [ ] ->	L → R
Unary operators	- ++ - - ! ~ * & sizeof (type)	R → L
Mul, div, and remainder	* / %	L → R
Add and subtract	+ -	L → R
Bitwise shift operators	<< >>	L → R
Relational operators	< <= > >=	L → R
Equality operators	= = !=	L → R
Bitwise *and*	&	L → R
Bitwise *exclusive or*	^	L → R
Bitwise or	|	L → R
Logical and	&&	L → R
Logical or	||	L → R
Conditional operator	? :	R → L
Assignment operators	= += -= *= /= %= &= ^= |= <<= >>=	R → L
Comma operator	,	L → R

[**Aid to memory:** UARL CA C]

APPENDIX E: STANDARD LIBRARY STRING FUNCTIONS

Functions	Use
strlen( )	finds the length of string
strlwr( )	converts a string to lowercase
strupr( )	converts a string to uppercase
strcat( )	appends one string at the end of another
strncat	appends first n characters of a string at the end of another string
strcpy( )	copies a string into another
strncpy( )	copies first n characters of one string into another
strcmp( )	compares two strings
strncmp( )	compares first n characters of two strings
strcmpi( )	compares two strings without regard to case
strnicmp( )	compares first n characters of two strings without regard to case
strdup( )	duplicates a string
strchr( )	finds first occurrence of a given character in a string
strrchr( )	finds last occurrence of a given character in a string
strstr( )	finds first occurrence of a given string in another string
strset( )	sets all characters of a string to a given character
strnset( )	sets first n characters of a string to a given character
strrev( )	reverses a string

REFERENCES

Chopra, Rajiv. 2014. *Principles of Programming Languages*. New Dehli: I.K. International Publishers.

Chopra, Rajiv. 2015. *JAVA Programming*. New Dehli: New Age International Publishers.

Chopra, Rajiv. 2016. *Object Oriented Programming Using C++*. New Dehli: New Age International Publishers.

Cooper, Herbert, and Henry Mullish. 2006. *The Spirit of C*, 28th ed. New Dehli: Jaico Publishing.

Hanly, Jeri, and Elliot Koffman. 2014. *Problem Solving and Program Design in C*, 7th ed. Boston: Pearson.

Jones, Jacqueline, and Keith Harrow. 2009. *C Programming with Problem Solving*, rpt ed. New Dehli: Dreamtech Wiley.

Kanetkar, Yashwant. 2015. *Let Us C*, 13th ed. New Dehli: BPB Publications.

Prakash, Satya. 2015. *Programming in C*. New Dehli: I.K. International Publishers.

Tondo, Clovis, and Scott Gimpel. 1989. *The C Answer Book*, 2nd ed. Upper Saddle River, NJ: Prentice Hall.

INDEX

A

Access 2d arrays in C 155
Actual parameter 257
Algorithm 12
American Standards Institute (ANSI) 1
Arithmetic assignment operator 53
Arithmetic operators 51
Arithmetic View of Pointer 237–239
Armstrong numbers 93
Arrays
    access 2d arrays 155
    character array 165–166
    declare 2d arrays 155
    definition 141
    display elements 156
    2D regular arrays 142
    initialize 156
    issue of copying arrays 146–150
    multidimensional arrays 155
    one-dimensional array 143
    read elements 155
    two-dimensional arrays 155
Ascending order 183–185
Assembler 17
Assembly language 21–22
Assignment operators 53
Associativity 53, 60–61
Auto storage class 119

B

Binary files 339
Bit fields 310–312
Bitwise operator
    bitwise AND operator 55–56
    bitwise OR operator 56
    bitwise XOR operator 57
    left shift operator shifts 58
    one (1s) complement operator 57–58
    right shift operator 58
Block comment 28
Block/record I/O functions 323–338
Block Statements 112–118
Boolean data type 45
Break Statement 109–110
Bubble sort method 179

C

Call by reference 257
Call by value 257
Called function 217
Calling function 119, 220, 230
Case statement 69
C/C++ 2
cc. 16
Character array 165–166
    read characters 165
    write characters 165–166
Character input/output 320–321
Codeblocks 30
Comma operator 58–59
Comments 28
Compilation 16
Compiler 20–21
    assembler 17
    command a.out 18
    debugging phase 18
    definition 15
    preprocessing phase 17
Compound statement 112
<conio.h> header file 43

Const 49
Const variables 49
Continue Statement 110–111
C programming language
    algorithms and pseudocodes 2–8
    assembler, linker, and loader 19–22
    auto storage class 119
    block statement 112–118
    break Statement 109–110
    compiler 15–19
    continue statement 110–111
    data input and data output 42–44
    data types 44–47
    definition 1
    do-while Loop 84–87
    enumeration 47–51
    extern 121
    file handling (*see* Files)
    flowchart 8–14
    for loop 87–108
    getchar( ) function 41
    global declaration section 39
    if statement 63–67
    ISO/IEC 9899:1990 1
    library functions 44
    main( ) Function 39–40
    operators 51–61
    preprocessor 35–38
    preprocessor directive/command 22–27
    putchar( ) function 41–42
    register 122–135
    return statement 111–112
    special constant section 38–39
    static storage class 119–121
    switch and break 68–73
    type casting (or coercion) 62
    while Loop 73–84

D
Debugging phase 18
Data types
    character 45
    double precision floating point 45–46
    floating point 45
    integer 45
    void 46
Declaration section 23
Declare 2d-arrays in C 155
#define constants 49

Delimiters 28
do-while Loop 84–87

E
Empty statement 112
Enumeration 47–51
End-of-file (EOF) 41
Extern 121
Extra bit 139

F
Fclose (fp) 319
Fgets (s, n, fp) 321
Fibonacci series 80, 91, 227
File pointers 317–320
Files
    and binary files 339
    block/record I/O functions 323–338
    character input/output 320–321
    formatted I/O function 322
    integer I/O functions 321–322
    pointers 317–320
    string I/O functions 321
Floyd triangle 106–107
Flowchart
    and algorithm 12
    definition 8
    notations 11
    parallelogram 10
    symbols 10
Fopen( ) function 319
For Loop 87–90
Formal parameters 257
Formatted I/O function 42–44, 322
fprintf( ) function 322
Fputs (s, fp) 321
Functions
    definition 215–216
    library/inbuilt functions 215
    return Statement 218
    user-called functions 218–228
    user-defined functions 215
fwrite( ) function 323

G
gcc. 16
getchar Function 41, 182
Global declaration 39
Global variables 50–51

GNU C compiler gcc 15
Golden Rule 10
Goto Statement 72–73
Greatest element 151

H

Header file 13, 23, 26
Heron's formula 270
High-level language 21–22

I

Include command 23
Integer I/O functions 321–322
Integrated Development Environment
    (IDE) 30
International Standards Organization
    (ISO) 1
Iterative method 224

J

JAVA2 2

L

Left shift operator shifts 58
Library functions 44, 258
Library/inbuilt functions 215
Linkage Editor 21
Linked program 21
Linker 21
Local variables 50
Loop
    do-while Loop 85–87
    for Loop 87–90
    while Loop 73–85

M

main( ) Function 39–40
Module
    characteristics 213
    top-down analysis 213
Multidimensional arrays 155
Multi-way selections 10

N

Nested if-else construct 65
Nested loops 84–85
Newline character 27
NULL character 166
Null statement 112

O

One (1s) complement operator 57–58
One-dimensional array 143
Operators
    arithmetic assignment operator 53
    arithmetic operators 51
    assignment operators 53
    bitwise operator 54–58
    comma operator 58–59
    increment/decrement operators 52–53
    logical operators 54
    relational operators 53–54
    size of operator 59
    ternary operator 60

P

Parallel array 310
Parameter transmission techniques 228–234
Pointers
    and addresses 234–235
    arguments 241–243
    arithmetic view of pointers 237–239
    array of pointers 243
    and arrays 239–241
    files 317–320
    passing arrays 244–245
    and structure 298–312
    variables 235–236
    void pointers 236–237
Preprocessor 35–38
printf( ) function 44
putchar function 41–42, 183–184

R

Recursions 223–224
Recursive method 224–225
Rectangular arrays 142
Register 122–135
Return Statement 111–112, 218
Reverse photo 91
Right shift operator 58
Ritchie, Dennis 1, 35
Run command 20

S

scanf( ) function 43
Semantic error 17
Sentinel value 111
Standard input-output functions 42–44

Statement section 23
Static storage class 119–121
String
    array of strings 175–182
    gets( ) and puts( ) Functions 168
    inbuilt string functions and "string.h"
        Header File 170
    I/O functions 321
    strcmp( ) Function 172–173
    strcpy( ) Function 171–172
    strlen( ) Function 170–171
    strlwr( ) and strupr( ) Functions 174–175
    strrev( ) Function 173–174
Structure
    applications 306
    array of structures 282–291, 306
    definition 275
    and enumerators 301–303
    function arguments 291–292
    initializations 280–282
    and pointers 298–312
    return structures from functions 292–296
    vs. unions 296–297, 307
    variable 277
Subprogramming 212–213
Syntax error 17

System flowcharts 9
Switch statement 68–69

T

Text files 317
Top-down analysis 213
Two-dimensional arrays 155
Type casting (or coercion) 62
Type qualifier 49

U

Unary operator 59
Unformatted I/O functions 43
Unions *vs.* structure 296–297, 307
Unsigned integer 45
User-called functions 218–228
User-defined functions 215

V

Variables 46–47
Visual Basic 9 2
Void pointers 236–237
Volatile modifier 49

W

While Loop 73–84